Lucy Freeman and the publishers have attributed the figure of sparks to these paragraphs thinking, perhaps, of the sparks from fanned embers, as Shelley did—or perhaps the sparks from a forge, or from a whirling grindstone. All of these showers are pretty in fact and in meaning, and I am flattered by the inference. But maybe these sparks are like the incandescent rain that falls from the children's fireworks on the 4th of July. They amuse and even delight for a few moments, and the little glowing points of light fall harmlessly and pleasingly to the ground. Nothing is burned, or hurt, but often a brief after-image remains pleasantly in the observers' eyes. The west wind may not have a burden worthy to be carried "over the universe" like the poet's, but if it only delights for a moment and leaves after images in the minds of a few contemporaries, I am content.

Karl Menninger, M.D.

KARL
MENNINGER, M.D.

SPARKS

edited by Lucy Freeman

Thomas Y. Crowell Company
New York   Established 1834

Acknowledgment is made to Brunner/Mazel, Inc., for permission to quote from *Hope: Psychiatry's Commitment* on page 76; to *The Nation* for permission to quote from the October 7, 1939, issue on page 104; and to *The Psychoanalytic Review,* Vol. 21, 1934, through the courtesy of the Editors and the Publisher, National Psychological Association for Psychoanalysis, New York, N.Y., for the quotation on page 146.

Manufactured in the United States of America

ISBN 0-690-75825-1

1 2 3 4 5 6 7 8 9 10

Library of Congress Cataloging in Publication Data

Menninger, Karl.
   Sparks.

   Includes bibliographical references.
   1. Psychiatrists—Correspondence, reminiscences, etc. 2. Menninger, Karl.
I. Freeman, Lucy, ed. II. Title.
RC339.52.M45A33 1973   616.8′9′008   73–4698
ISBN 0-690-75825-1

BY KARL MENNINGER, M. D.

The Human Mind

Man Against Himself

Love Against Hate (with Jeanetta Lyle Menninger)

Theory of Psychoanalytic Technique

A Psychiatrist's World, The Selected Papers of Karl Menninger, M.D.

A Manual for Psychiatric Case Study

A Guide to Psychiatric Books (with George Devereux)

The Vital Balance, The Life Process in Mental Health and Illness (with Martin Mayman and Paul Pruyser)

The Crime of Punishment

Acknowledgments

First and foremost, to Dr. Karl Menninger and to Jeanetta Lyle Menninger, who gave invaluable help in the conception and execution of this book. To Lewis F. Wheelock, executive assistant to Dr. Menninger, and Edward Weiss, noted artist and advertising executive of Chicago, for important suggestions. To Virginia Eicholtz, managing editor of the *Bulletin of the Menninger Clinic*; Verne B. Horne, archivist of The Menninger Foundation; Marilyn J. Kollath, of Dr. Menninger's Chicago office, and Berenice Brinker, of his Topeka office; and to Scott Bartlett, our agent, and my niece, Dale Schroedel, for her help in typing.

Contents

Preface

. . . Be thou, Spirit fierce,
My spirit! Be thou me, impetuous one!

Drive my dead thoughts over the universe
Like withered leaves to quicken a new birth!
And, by the incantation of this verse,

Scatter, as from an unextinguished hearth
Ashes and sparks, my words among mankind!

Ode to the West Wind
Percy Bysshe Shelley

At a reception for writers given by the American Psychiatric
Association in Washington, D.C. in May 1971, Dr. Karl Menninger and
I enjoyed a reunion when our paths crossed once again at a convention.
While catching each other up on the latest news, I told him how much
I enjoyed his *Reading Notes*.

The *Notes* consist of reviews and comments on current books and
articles, plus observations and opinions about any subject that appeals
to Dr. Menninger's fancy, from earthworms to superegos. They have
appeared regularly since 1945 in the bi-monthly *Bulletin of the Menninger Clinic* and also, since 1970, in the weekly *Psychiatric News*,
the latter as a result of a suggestion made by Alexander Sareyan,
director of Mental Health Materials Center, to Robert L. Robinson,
editor of *Psychiatric News* and director of public affairs of the American Psychiatric Association.

With Dr. Menninger at the reception was his wife, Jeanetta Lyle
Menninger, editor of the *Bulletin of the Menninger Clinic* for thirty-
five years until she retired in 1971. She and her husband represent a
full partnership of participation in each other's work in the tradition
of Charles and Mary Beard, Sidney and Beatrice Webb, and Will and
Ariel Durant.

I said to Dr. Menninger, "The *Notes* should have even more

readers. Have you ever thought of letting someone make a book out of them?"

Reading my mind, he gallantly replied, "You're welcome to try."

A publisher found and a contract signed, I flew to Topeka. One of the first things I learned was that Dr. Menninger did not prepare the *Reading Notes* as a special weekly or monthly assignment. Rather, the columns stemmed from a lifelong custom of jotting down brief, random notes reporting odd or interesting facts and stimulating or controversial ideas from books and articles he had read. Some of the notes were not so much considered reflections as quick insights or reactions to events, people, books, and ideas. They were in large part fired off to stimulate the minds of the young psychiatrists he had taught.

Dr. Menninger's habit of making notes on books dates back to 1921 when he began attending informal meetings of friends who called themselves the "Naked But Unashamed Club." They met at the University Club of Topeka every Saturday afternoon, sometimes talking all afternoon and far into the night. They included, in addition to Dr. Menninger, a banker, a newspaper publisher, an editor, a surgeon, and professors from Washburn University. Occasionally one of them brought a special guest—Carl Sandburg, Sherwood Anderson, Edgar Lee Masters, Bertrand Russell, Albert Byfield, Nelson Antrim Crawford.

"We would discuss current books we thought interesting," Dr. Menninger recalls. "I remember the impact James Harvey Robinson's *The Mind in the Making* had on us. And Wilfred Trotter's *Instincts of the Herd on War and Peace*. Also new books or articles by Freud. Then there was *Moon Calf* by Floyd Dell, one of the earliest psychoanalytic novels. In those days, literary people were much more interested than doctors in psychoanalysis. Frequently, one or two of us wrote up and read our thoughts about a book or a point we wanted to spring on the others."

In addition to the *Reading Notes*, Dr. Menninger permitted me to go through many of his files, including those of published and unpublished articles, speeches, and formal letters to and from colleagues. The material relating to psychiatric history particularly intrigued me —a glimpse behind the scenes of the profession in which he was a pioneer.

The files overflowed his office and library, even into closets. As I read on, I felt as though I were encased by a shower of sparks. And through it all, I thought that for the first time I actually was coming to know the mind of The Man from Topeka.

Today Dr. Menninger is chairman of the board of trustees of the Menninger Foundation and of The Villages, Inc., a nonprofit organization that provides homes for children. He and his father, the late Dr. Charles F. Menninger, founded the Menninger Clinic in 1919, after he had received his medical degree (*cum laude*) from Harvard in 1917. He worked and taught at the Boston Psychopathic Hospital, as it was then called, with Dr. Elmer Ernest Southard, Dr. Harry Solomon, Dr. Abraham Myerson, Dr. Marion Kenworthy, Dr. Lawson Lowrey and others.

The Menninger Foundation, an outgrowth of the Menninger Clinic, was founded in 1945. It is a nonprofit center for psychiatric diagnosis, education, research, treatment, and prevention. It includes the C. F. Menninger Memorial Hospital which has 150 beds, a day hospital, a children's hospital, the Southard School, a department of neurology, neurosurgery and internal medicine, adult outpatient diagnostic and psychotherapy services, and the Menninger School of Psychiatry founded by Dr. Menninger in 1946, with assistance from the Veterans Administration, and now, from the Kansas State Hospital, the Santa Fe Hospital, the Forbes Air Base Hospital, and the Boys State Industrial School.

As I went through Dr. Menninger's files, first in Topeka and then in Chicago where the Menninger Foundation has an office often occupied by him, the concept of this book grew like Topsy, changing from a collection of the *Reading Notes* to an inclusion of other important material: landmark speeches and unpublished writings, such as his memoir of meetings with Freud and Schweitzer; his justly famed appreciations of his home town and home state; his tributes to his father and his teachers; his testimony before Congressional committees on war and crime; his reviews of works by Havelock Ellis and Alfred Kinsey; and letters he had written to colleagues on diverse matters, from the treatment of homosexuals to the nature of prejudice.

The material in the completed book spans half a century—1922 to 1972. I have tried to show what kind of man could, with one book, *The Human Mind,* published in 1930, change the thinking of a nation. Written in clear, non-technical language, it created an atmosphere that led to an acceptance of Freud's theories—an acceptance that enabled psychiatry and psychoanalysis to flourish in the United States as in no other country. *The Human Mind,* together with his later books, especially *Man Against Himself* and *Love Against Hate*, opened the way to a new form of help for literally millions of troubled people. *The Crime of Punishment* was also very influential, calling as it did for a re-examination of our punitive penal system.

From Dr. Menninger's writings, I selected items and passages that I thought most arresting as well as most representative of his thinking. He went over everything, occasionally editing his original wording and updating his views, either in new notes or in conversation, so that this work includes his thoughts, present as well as past. His conversational style, like his writing, is direct, succinct, and imaginative. His mind is of the sort that quickly pares a problem to its essentials or delights in finding the common element in two seemingly unrelated propositions. More sparks!

The same themes about which he has written in his books—*Love Against Hate, Man Against Himself, The Crime of Punishment, The Vital Balance*—appear in his speeches, articles, letters and throughout the *Reading Notes* where he further develops his thoughts. Thus these themes make up a good part of this book. But added to them are other themes, such as his interests in Americana, his love of nature, his enjoyment of puzzles, games, and interesting trivia. These are minor but no less fascinating aspects in the life of a man who, though he writes prolifically, does not withdraw from the arena of human activity to do so. Even as he writes, he is busy making psychiatric history —testifying before Congress; serving on the board of the National Council of Crime and Delinquency; inspecting the Tombs, New York City's house of detention for male prisoners, to report on its conditions in Federal court. He is a man of action as well as philosopher, teacher, humorist, crusader, and friend.

Working in Kansas proved a novel experience for me, accustomed as I am to a cell in the concrete canyons of Manhattan. Dr. Menninger has two offices in Topeka, one on the West Campus of the Menninger Foundation and one at the Veterans Administration Hospital which he helped design and bring to Topeka. The office on the West Campus, which contains his vast files, is located in the Tower Building, looking out on flower gardens, fountains, forests of walnut, oak, pine and pecan trees, and grazing horses. The decor of the office tells who and what Dr. Menninger loves. Photographs of his family, including his daughters and his son, Dr. Robert Menninger, a psychoanalyst at the Menninger Clinic, adorn walls, desk and bookcase shelves. Hanging on the wall that faces his desk are photographs of his father, his two brothers, the late Dr. William C. Menninger, and Edwin Menninger, who lives in Stuart, Florida; Dr. Southard; Freud; Helen Keller, and the late President Kennedy. Shelves hold, besides books, a mass of artistic shapes and colors—Indian and prehistoric artifacts, and polished stones. A mobile of graceful shells dangles from the ceiling and a colored glass butterfly dances from one window.

The people with whom Dr. Menninger works, all of whom hold deep affection for him, are used to occasional abruptness in act or word. But though he may sound brusque at times, the brusqueness is underlaid with compassion and a sense of the human comedy.

He once approached Mrs. Verne B. Horne, archivist at The Menninger Foundation, who preserves and catalogues his speeches, and handed her a paper napkin. On it were scribbled four or five words in his forceful handwriting, a handwriting as individualistic as he.

"Here's a speech I gave last night," he said.

She gasped, asked, "Is this all?"

"Didn't say much." And he was gone from the room, all six feet of him, a giant of a man physically as well as intellectually. Actually he had spoken for an hour to a university convocation of several thousand students and faculty.

Dr. Menninger is a man of many interests with a mind that never seems to rest. Seward Hiltner describes him as having "the most richly and constructively complex mind it has ever been my privilege to know." One minute Dr. Menninger is describing half-ironically, half-seriously, his reactions to *Lucia di Lammermoor,* which he had just heard once again at the Metropolitan Opera House in New York. The next moment he is playing a complicated bridge hand, successfully making the contract of six no trump, or planning a picture to paint in the improvised studio of his Chicago office.

He spends about one third of his time in Topeka, one third in Chicago and one third giving lectures, or attending meetings and conventions. Last year he traveled forty-five thousand miles to present speeches, sit on the boards of the many organizations to which he belongs, or serve as consultant on matters of prison reform or psychiatry. His unflagging energy makes the whirling dervish seem like slow motion, in spite of having celebrated his seventy-ninth birthday.

He is fascinated by changing colors, from those in autumn leaves and the flowers in formal gardens to kaleidoscopes which he has collected for sixty years. He has a favorite that he takes out every Christmas and hangs on the tree. "It's the very essence of exciting change," he says of its colors and shapes. In a sense, his life could be compared to a kaleidoscope, so shining and vivid its facets and complexities.

One afternoon in Chicago Dr. Lewis Wheelock, a historian, who is Dr. Menninger's executive assistant, and I were chatting with Dr. Menninger. I asked him about the place of love in this world of war and hate. He thought for a moment, then mused, "Oh, love struggles along in spite of the war and hate. Love just struggles along. Something good happens every now and then and love somehow prevails—for a while."

No doubt someone else would have chosen other of Dr. Menninger's writings and arranged the selection in different style. But whatever the choice or the form, the same sense of dedications and commitments would undoubtedly emerge, as I hope they do in this labor of love.

January 15, 1973
New York, New York

Lucy Freeman

CHAPTER ONE

The Man from Topeka

*The Man from Topeka—Dr. Karl, as everyone who works with him
calls him—has fought long and hard to help those in need—economi-
cally, physically, and psychologically. He has tilted, often with success,
at the dragons of prejudice, greed, cruelty, and hatred. He has not
deferred to stupidity or cupidity, whether of politician, policeman, or
pedant.*

*He has had an important impact upon the thinking of America,
which is well known; not as well recognized is the influence he has
had upon his hometown, Topeka—and the influence that Topeka, in
turn, has had upon him. And this is one of the keys to the man. For
Karl Menninger is a Kansan—and proud of it; a child of the nineteenth century who matured with the twentieth; a man who, in a dis-
oriented age, has not lost his sense of time and place.*

*He spoke of what Topeka has meant to him in a talk titled "My
Town," which he gave on December 5, 1953, over the radio network
of the National Broadcasting Company; a talk which later was printed
in the* Menninger Quarterly, Winter, 1954. *His wife inspired him to
select this particular subject. "Jean pointed out that I had never paid
tribute to the people of Topeka," Dr. Karl recalls. "Of course, not
everyone had liked the idea of a hospital for the mentally ill being
located in town. Some people accused me of bringing in dangerous
foreigners and even an alleged Communist! But in spite of such opposition, the citizens of Topeka always came through to help us with*

1

flying colors, and I was very glad to have this opportunity to tell them Thank you."

Listeners of the radio audience: My name is Karl Menninger. I'm here in New York attending a medical meeting. I live in Kansas, but I have also lived in Wisconsin, in Boston, in New York, and in Chicago. For a long time now I have lived in the Kansas town in which I was born. It's my town. I would like to tell you about it.

My town is Topeka. It's the capital of a great state. Topeka was founded ninety-nine years ago this very day by a shivering group of ten idealistic young men who had spent the night in a crude log cabin on prairie-grass beds. After they had viewed, as they recorded, "The beautiful conformation of the land spread out before us," their chairman sat down upon a sack of flour and they drew up the Articles of Association. That night their cabin caught fire and burned to the ground.

The young Pennsylvania engineer who sat on the sack of flour had previously surveyed Minnesota and Missouri before deciding that Topeka was the most beautiful and promising area for the development of his dreams. He planned the city of Topeka, and he planned a railroad to run north to Atchison, and west across Kansas, *maybe* as far as Santa Fe, New Mexico. His friends laughed at this and considered him a visionary fool. But Cyrus K. Holliday was a genius, and his railroad and his city have outgrown even his vision.

Topeka isn't a very big town. When I was a boy, we used to watch the census figures and look forward to the time when we would pass thirty thousand population and be a big city! It is more than triple that now, but it is still not a big city! I hope it never will be. Sometimes I wish it were only thirty thousand again.

My parents were pioneers in Kansas, and in Topeka. They came west because of certain ideals. This part of the country was really developed by idealists, you may remember. It was tough going then . . . pretty primitive. Lots of hard work. Not many amusements. But lots of hope.

Not many streets were paved in my town when I was born. I can remember the mud. My father was a real horse-and-buggy doctor, and I often rode along with him on his calls. I can remember the horse cars, too . . . and the buggies and gigs and phaetons and carriages. The pioneers planned wide streets for Topeka, and planted lots of trees along them. They seemed big to me, even when I was a boy playing under them or climbing them. And lots of trouble to trim around when we mowed the lawn.

In those days, our town was a publishing center. The state capitol was here and the headquarters of a great railroad. But printing and publishing and education—they were our local pride. I have forgotten how many millions of copies of our papers and magazines go out all over the world every month.

We still publish and we still have the Santa Fe and the Rock Island and Union Pacific and Missouri Pacific, too. We have an airport and some factories and a county lake and a big air base and a supply depot and a municipal university. Several insurance companies head up in Topeka. It is surrounded by beautiful countryside of fertile farms and ranches. (And, by the way, we do *not* raise wheat or pump oil—that's farther west and south. We grow alfafa and apples and beef and chickens.) Pretty country. Hillier than you think. Out of my office windows I see trees and meadows and hills in the distance; summer and winter, there are birds flitting about near the window. I like that kind of an office.

When I was a boy, my brothers Edwin and Will and I used to dream of organizing a sight-seeing bus for Topeka such as we had seen in San Francisco and Salt Lake City. We thought we could meet people at the railroad stations and give them quite an interesting tour. We knew about some sights that most visitors never saw. Interesting too. We could show them where they trained Dan Patch, the great race-horse. We could show them an oak tree all twisted around with a hackberry. We could show them an elm tree that reached out nearly three hundred feet in all directions. Biggest elm in the world, we thought.

We could show them a haunted house and several Indian graves and The Mound, where old Jim Burnett used to live; he was an Indian that weighed four hundred pounds and had a pony that pulled him in a cart without reins. We could show them the old Underground Railway stations—two of them. We might even take them by the "insane asylum." That was a mysterious place where most people never ventured. It had a big wooded park around it, and some of us fellows had been in there, hunting walnuts or just peeking at the wild men. We had seen the great stone castles with the barred windows. Occasionally we actually saw some of the "crazy people," marching along in groups with guards beside them who motioned to us to stay back. It was scary. But quite a sight!

That was a long time ago.

I sometimes feel as if my boyhood dream about running a sightseeing bus had almost come true. Hundreds of visitors come to Topeka today—I guess I should say thousands. People come to consult our great Historical Library and Museum and they come to speak at our university and they come on business and conventions. But perhaps most of them come to visit our hospitals, especially our psychiatric hospitals. Several of our people do little else but show visitors around, every day. We might go with them for a few minutes tonight, if you like.

I am sure that they would show you all the things I have mentioned; and our beautiful high school and churches and pretty homes and lawns and our municipal rose garden that my father started, and the new library and the Kaw River. They would show you a lot of things.

But finally, they would get around to showing you our hospital.

It is funny how this little publishing town, this railroad town, this state capitol town, should have turned into such a hospital city. There is the big Santa Fe Hospital and the tuberculosis hospital and the fine Catholic hospital. We have one of the finest medium-sized general hospitals in the world, really owned by the city although it is a private hospital. The farsightedness of the Episcopalian pioneers who set aside the ground, plus the generosity of one of the early doctors and the vision of Dr. Merrill Mills, our senior surgeon, were supported by the contributions of every citizen of the community. Then there is a private psychiatric hospital, too, which began twenty-five years ago and is just completing a new building that has all the modern features that could be discovered anywhere in the world. We are proud of it, too, because it was contributed to us, contributed by people all over the United States.

Then I am sure that your guides would show you the Winter Veterans Administration Hospital because it is kind of special. General Omar Bradley and General Paul Hawley started a training program for young psychiatrists at this hospital right after the close of World War II, and more of those young doctors have been trained here than in any place in the world. This training is still going on, too, in spite of the fact that the old Army-hospital pavilions are just about to fall down. With nearly a section of land to build on, however, and an appropriation from Congress last year, there will be a magnificent new psychiatric hospital there to replace the old one, and it will still be the

Veterans Administration's chief training hospital. Lots of people come to see it.

Your guides would probably tell you how thousands of people moved to Topeka to help operate this hospital, to take care of other thousands of people who came to Topeka to be cared for in it, or to study or attend lectures. They will probably tell you how many thousands of Topekans—businessmen, housewives, college students, store clerks, lawyers, and plumbers—come out on Saturday afternoon and Sunday and evenings and mornings and holidays to do volunteer service. Some have given over seven thousand hours service to it, and twenty-seven organizations have regular working representatives. One of our volunteers, who has come for seven years, is blind, and one comes out in a wheelchair.

It's the same at the State Hospital. And I'm sure our guides would take you over to see that. Because it is a part of the system. Topeka is the only city in the world, I guess, where the federal government and the state and the county and the city and private organizations all work together cooperatively and harmoniously in one integrated unit.

You will be surprised when you see our state hospital. Its buildings are pretty old but its beautiful grounds look like a college campus. You'll be welcomed and you won't see any wild men walking around with guards. You will see lots of people out on the grounds, playing baseball, sketching on easels, sitting under trees talking, mowing the lawns, making bouquets from the garden, or picking strawberries, and nurses in white here and there. You would even see children playing around on the grounds, too, because there is a Children's Department. You won't believe these are patients—but most of them are.

You will have a hard time parking because there are lots of cars there now. Didn't used to be *any*. There is an Out-patient Department where people from all over Kansas come for psychiatric advice, without any implication of their being called "insane" or some other damning word. And relatives of patients who were once frightened away and discouraged from coming are now encouraged to come, and often. The patients give parties for their relatives right on the wards, and a good time is had by all. This makes for a good deal of popular education, too. There is a big canteen on the hospital grounds; people lunch in it and have Cokes and coffee, and the Junior League girls of Topeka are the cooks and waitresses. Good food, too. There are tree clubs and bird clubs and sewing classes and art classes among the patients. A professor of music from the university comes down every weekend and supervises a staff of musicians and musical programs which have been organized in various parts of the hospital with an orchestra and a band and various choruses and quartets. Oh, it is a lively place, the State Hospital! And it is a part of the community. That's the important thing.

For example, you know how at Christmastime some towns have a municipal Christmas tree. Well, in Topeka our municipal Christmas tree is located on the State Hospital grounds! It has a big Santa Claus on top, and the patients help decorate it. At the foot there is a big box and the people of the town drive through the grounds to see the lights and the Santa Claus, and they drop gifts in the box, thousands of them. Every patient gets presents at Christmas.

Some of our patients at the State Hospital only sleep there; in the daytime they work in various stores and factories and hospital kitchens and other places. This is often the first step in their moving out of the hospital and returning to normal life. For from that institution, formerly called the insane asylum, now the great majority of our new patients leave within twelve months to return to their homes or to useful work. And the people of Topeka know this, now. They know that most mentally ill patients get well if they are treated right—treated with kindness and patience and love and skill, not only by doctors and nurses and aides and therapists but by the whole community. The people in my town are no longer afraid of patients. They know too many of them. And they feel responsible for them.

Some of our patients have been in the hospital for quite a while, so long that they have almost forgotten how to live outside. So, when they do get well, they are a little shy about various social amenities. A group of women in our town started a club for patients who were soon to leave the hospital, to help retrain them in social living. The club meets at the homes of various women about town for teas and luncheons and little parties. They have lots of fun relearning how to be with people in the outside world. Its originator, Mrs. George Bishop, was written up in the *Ladies Home Journal*.

But she is only one of many citizens who have discovered that it is not only the sick people who are benefited when a town becomes interested in psychiatric illness. There is something about work with sick minds and hearts that makes ordinary people more sensitive to suffering, more tolerant, more human—even to each other. They discover that love cures people, the ones who receive love and the ones who give it, too.

I don't mean to say that the people in my town are better than

6

the people in your town, but I think we are better than we used to be, partly because of living so close to our sick people and seeing them get well, with such a little help from us.

The thing I am trying to emphasize here is that it is a two-way process. There is a woman in our town who for years led the life of an invalid, although she wasn't any one's *patient*. She never went out socially but stayed at home, lonely, frightened, and depressed. She heard about the club I was describing and somehow they managed to get her to invite them to her home. She was so amazed that these nice people were actually mental patients that she became one of the regular sponsors of the club and went everywhere with it. Well, in the course of things, she regained her own mental health completely and has a real zest for life now and takes part in lots of other things. The patients themselves catch on to this phenomenon, and feel proud to think that the ones that are helping them are also being helped by it.

At Winter Hospital we have a nationally known artist who gave up her personal career in favor of teaching painting to our patients. The chef of one of our hotels was badly burned one day through the clumsiness of one of our patients who was working as his helper, but before he was taken to the doctor for treatment, he took time to comfort the patient and assure her that he knew it was only an accident and could happen to anyone and for her not to feel bad.

I was buying a suit recently and noticed one of our patients sitting in the corner of the store, doing nothing. I asked the manager about him, and he said, "Oh, yes, I hired him; most of the time he is a pretty good clerk, but the last few days he has been a little depressed and hasn't done much. But we'll carry him along, and he'll be back on the job shortly."

There is a leading banker in our town who is now one of the officers of The Menninger Foundation. I have often heard him confess, in his earnest appeals to audiences in other cities, how he used to scoff at the whole psychiatric business. He tells his listeners that they will wake up someday, as he did, and realize that the stone rejected by the builders has become the head of the corner.

Just before I came here I was walking through the State Hospital and I saw one of our local store owners helping a group of patients make Christmas decorations. His downtown store was jammed with shoppers, I am sure, right then, but that didn't interfere with his regular weekly visit to his group at the State Hospital.

I can't prove it, but I am pretty sure that when people overcome their fear and prejudice against mental illness, they become healthier-minded, and hence more tolerant in other ways. None of our hospitals makes any differentiation with respect to race or sex or color among patients or employees or volunteers. This came about very naturally. It rubbed some people the wrong way at first, but no one stopped coming and I think everyone likes it better now. They are even proud of themselves.

I am proud of them, too. I am proud of all this, and grateful, too. Because, as you see, the people in my town have been very good to me. I mean they listened to what we told them a long time ago, and there is nothing so nice as to have people listen to you! Oh, there were some skeptics and scoffers; it was kind of tough sometimes in the early days. And, to tell the truth, we didn't think of ourselves as missionaries. It was a good town and my brother and I wanted to come back here to it, after living in the East a while. We have been as surprised as anyone else at the result. We didn't start out to convert anyone.

We just started out with an ideal. It was mostly my father's. He celebrated his ninety-first birthday last summer, and everyone loves him. They've named a street after him in Topeka, and talk of naming other things for him. Long ago he had the ideal of doctors working together. He said if we would work together and strive for the highest standards, people would be grateful and come here from everywhere. He used to be a general practitioner, but way back before 1918 he had been specially interested in psychiatry. He greatly admired the wonderful Ernest Southard of Harvard. Southard believed that people who recognized their own mental problems and tried to do something about them were often the finest and wisest people in the world. Something can be done for *them*.

The ones to worry about are those who don't ever suspect *themselves* of any mental infirmity but are always sure that it is all the *other* people in the world who are crazy or wicked or disloyal. Some of these people whom no one calls crazy might well be locked up somewhere for life; it might prevent a few kidnapings and other crimes. But a long way from Topeka, if you please; because our conception of psychiatric hospitals here is not confinement; we think they are places to get well in, places in which to be treated, places in which to learn to understand one's self, to learn how to live.

It may strike you as odd for me to call psychiatry learning how to live, but all you have to do to realize how many people don't know how to live is to look about you. And a good many of them do come to us. One out of every twelve children born in this country goes to a mental hospital some time during his life. That's about two hundred and fifty thousand people a year somewhere in our country. One out of every two patients going to a doctor or to a general hospital for what he calls a physical illness is suffering from a condition which is at least partly mental. It costs us more than a billion dollars a year in tax funds just to take care of these patients as inadequately as we do now. All this is to say nothing about crime and vandalism and juvenile delinquency and industrial sabotage and absenteeism and drunkenness and divorce, all of which we psychiatrists regard as evidence of not knowing how to live very well.

It is an awareness of these problems that has sustained the members, governors, and trustees of The Menninger Foundation in their efforts to develop in Topeka a center of psychiatric work—treatment, education, and research in the field of mental illness. I have said a good deal about the help my fellow townsmen have given me. I haven't said much about how the people of Milwaukee and Chicago and Los Angeles and San Francisco and Dallas and Houston and Minneapolis and Wilmington and New York and Washington have helped us. I haven't described how our governors and trustees come to Topeka regularly for our meetings, sending their money ahead of them and after them. And I haven't said much about the visitors from Canada and Peru and Baghdad and Siam and Calcutta and Copenhagen that keep coming all the time to see what we are doing or to join us for a time in Topeka. I haven't said much about my father, who inspired all this, or about my brother Will, who has always been my partner. He has devoted himself for the last few years to the *national* community, trying to show perceptive men and women in business, industry, medicine, and the home that psychiatry is *their* business—not the esoteric specialty of a few doctors, but the proper study of all of us by all of us.

I haven't mentioned our American psychiatric colleagues who have given us so much help by visits and lectures and counsel. Nearly five hundred of them are members of The Menninger Foundation. I haven't said much about the professional men and women on the staffs of our clinics and hospitals in Topeka, who carry on all this work. When they are not working, they are playing in our Civic Orchestra or acting in our Civic Theater or teaching in our Sunday schools or working in our Art Institute and our Audubon Club and our Parent-Teacher Associations, and all the rest.

What I have been talking about has been the joint and united effort of all these people. There are over ten thousand of us in Topeka directly connected with psychiatry, either as patients or relatives or as doctors or nurses or aides or secretaries or gardeners or something! There are ten thousand more who are indirectly connected with us in helping people to learn to live and *indirectly* learning to live themselves.

So you see Topeka has changed since I was a boy. It has become rather psychiatric. But I don't believe even our worst enemies would call it a "crazy" town. No, it is a pretty nice town. It is a friendly town. It is a busy town. It is an intelligent town. I love it. When I finish with this broadcast, I'll get on the train and go back to it. It's where I belong, there with those "dear hearts and gentle people, the folks in my hometown."

My father had an idea and an ideal; my brother and I worked at it, but *everybody* helped develop it. We're all proud, together. I couldn't begin to tell you how many people helped. Still do. I'd like to call out some of their names over the radio right now, and say, "Hello, Dave! Hello, Laird! Are you listening to this? Have I told the story right? This is the way we did it, isn't it?"

But I can't call all the names; there are so many. Some of them are asleep now; some of them are lying in our Mount Hope Cemetery. That includes my mother; she helped, too; still does.

And, since last Monday, it includes my wonderful father.

It includes some of the fellows with whom I picked up walnuts out there on the grounds of the "insane asylum" a long, long time ago.

Well—that's our town. I am proud of it. This is my tribute to it. We grew up together. It has changed in half a century—so have I. Psychiatry has changed Topeka, and perhaps Topeka has helped to change psychiatry.

An article about Kansas written in December, 1939, for Kansas Magazine, *was one that "my brother Will always liked so much," comments Dr. Karl. It was titled "Bleeding Kansas."*

Sometimes, when I have just returned from the mountains or the seashore, friends who meet me on the street exclaim sympathetically but enviously about my trip, "Were you not sorry to leave?" They ask, "Isn't it hard to come back from such beautiful places into the drab monotony of our Kansas scenery?"

When they say such things I cannot answer them; I cannot even look at them for fear of betraying my thoughts. I look at the ground or I look past them to the horizon. Inwardly I recall the words of a

THE MAN FROM TOPEKA

famous Kansan who wrote to his wife on December 10, 1854: ". . . Our food is mush, molasses, and bacon, mixed plentifully with dirt three times a day. Thus we live in Kansas. *A more lovely country I certainly never saw*—and yet it looks worse now than at any other season. I am told by those who know that in the spring and early summer when the grass and shrubbery and flowers appear it is beautiful beyond conception. So I think it must be. And in a few years when civilization by its magic influence shall have transformed this glorious country from what it now is to the brilliant destiny awaiting it, the sun in all his course will visit *no land more truly lovely and desirable than this. . . .*" [KM] [See "Letters of Cyrus Kurtz Holliday, 1854–1859" (Edited by Lela Barnes), *Kansas Historical Quarterly,* 6:246, 1937.]

This man was one of the truly great Kansans because he had vision, a vision not only for the future, but for the present realities. And he had come to Kansas from one of the most beautiful states in the union, Pennsylvania.

I am well aware that the other side of the road looks smoother and the grass in the opposite field greener, but I believe this inability of some Kansans to appreciate their own state has a far deeper psychological origin. It is observable in so many different ways. I have sometimes called it, in our professional jargon, a characteristic feeling of inferiority. We seem to share it with Arkansas, which is also a beautiful and creditable state, but whose citizens are often ashamed of having originated there. I see the self-depreciation of Kansans exhibiting itself in the form of a sense of uneasiness, an apologetic manner when in the association of representatives of older and wealthier states, and in a tendency to join with them in a bantering ridicule of our state instead of recognizing how much this represents a defense of their own ignorant provincialism. But more serious, I think, is a kind of asceticism, a willingness to accept as our fate and lot a far less comfortable and joyous existence than could be ours almost for the asking. This, too, springs from our self-depreciation.

No one could ask for a better illustration of this than the prohibition sentiment of the state. I know, as everyone else knows, that there are relatively few total abstainers in Kansas, but to keep up appearances we must not buy or sell liquor publicly. We must smuggle it in from Missouri to the cynical but gratified amusement of our less hypocritical eastern neighbors. We comfort ourselves with the logic that because some men are fools, others must be martyrs. And because some are martyrs, others must go along with them. The fact that there may be joy in wine is forgotten in the face of the fact that there may be tears in rum. Kansans have no sense of superiority about their prohibition. Some console themselves with a puritanical sense of self-righteousness, but it is cold comfort. For the same energies that have prohibited the open sale of liquor would have gone much farther had they been invested in the promotion of beauty, the improvement of highways, the enlargement of parks, the fostering of music and art.

Not but what we have done fairly well with music and art. I am proud of what we have done. But I am afraid that most of my fellow Kansans are not. They are not proud of it because they realize that it is so much less than we could have done had we not had an ascetic disapproval of joy or anything that would make it appear that we were a happy, progressive, successful state. We want to be "bleeding Kansas." When someone calls us a typical prairie state we get angry, not because we think we have been misunderstood but because we fear we have been understood too well and our shame publicly exposed.

I would be happy to believe that our feelings of inferiority are only the expression of an innate modesty, a feeling of revulsion against the flamboyant, bombastic egotism of California and the similar arrogance of a few other states. Unfortunately I cannot believe this. Kansas does not refrain from announcing that it has the best of this or the best of that because of our essential good taste; Kansas does not announce it because Kansas does not believe it. When I tell friends that I think our scenery is beautiful and that our climate is delightful (Cyrus Holliday said that it was better than that of sunny Italy) my friends think I am ironic or a little "touched." They would much rather read in the paper that we had broken a heat record so that they could use it to prove their martyrdom than to reflect that hot weather is the healthiest weather of all and that fewer people die from the effects of climate in Kansas than in almost any other state. Yesterday it was 97 in Los Angeles; it was 70 in Topeka. But I am sure this fact was not headlined by any Kansas newspapers, and I am more certain that it was not headlined by any California papers. Last week New England was ravaged by a terrific windstorm which did more damage in one hour than all the tornadoes have done in Kansas since the dawn of civilized history, but I am sure that this was not noted by any Kansas newspapers nor by any of the eastern newspapers which still play up "Kansas cyclones."

Not long ago the son of a colleague came to me for advice in regard to entering my Alma Mater, the Harvard Medical School. He was afraid that he would not be admitted. I remarked that the fact that he was a Kansan would probably be to his advantage in his con-

sideration by the committee. "Well," he exclaimed, "that will be the
first time that coming from Kansas ever did me any good!" I could not
think of any reply to this. He was a handsome young fellow, a member of the third generation since the pioneers. His family has prospered
(in Kansas!) and he was as nattily dressed, as sophisticated in manner
as the boys I have known from Harvard and Hopkins, and Pennsylvania. But the poor fellow does not know it. He labors under a sense
of inferiority which is pitiful. He goes to college with a sensitiveness
which will probably make him either a recluse or a noisy eccentric.

I am fairly familiar with physicians across America, and I can
honestly say that I believe that we have within the confines of our
state medical men quite as capable as those in most other comparable
localities. Ambitiously we endeavor to maintain a medical school, but
we do not trust it to be staffed by Kansas doctors. The students of the
medical school of the University of Kansas, are instructed by men
borrowed from Missouri, Missouri doctors from Kansas City.

The phenomenon of the city of "Kansas City, Missouri," is perhaps the most brilliant illustration of my thesis. Poor Kansas City is an
orphan town; it has no parent state. Missouri disowns it as a metropolis;
St. Louis is the Missouri city, and Kansas City should be the Kansas
city, but it isn't. Rather, it is and it isn't. It is located largely in
Missouri, populated largely with ex-Kansans, depends upon Kansas for
its economic existence, supplies Kansas with traveling salesmen, truck
drivers, and racketeers, instructs Kansans how to vote, and considers
Kansas its great backyard. Kansans, nonetheless, think it is a great
metropolis and speak of it reverently as "the city."

Think of a state smart enough to issue a magazine like this one!
Think of a state with people wise enough to abolish capital punishment fifty years ago. Think of a state with people in it capable of
erecting a structure like the Santa Fe Railroad or an organization like
the Capper press. Think of a state with a Historical Society such as
ours. We have heard a lot about wheat, but consider the trees; we are
the only state in the union without a national forest, and yet we are
also the only state in the union with more trees in it than at the
time it was settled. Think of a state with people in it like William
Allen White and Ed Howe and Nelson Antrim Crawford, William
Herbert Carruth and Esther Clark, John James Ingalls, Charles M.
Sheldon, Kirke Mechem, and W. G. Clugston, Birger Sandzén, and
many others. You know this is not a state of mediocrities. The same
humility of spirit is to be observed in the Kansas intellectuals, in the
Kansas voters, and in the Kansas press. In their eagerness to be broad-

minded, tolerant, democratic, they have listened receptively to many prophets, some false, some true, and have followed them fervently. This fervent response—a response sometimes bordering on fanaticism—is regarded by many Easterners as characteristic of the people of Kansas. In abolition, prohibition, Populism, antitobacco legislation, Brinkley worship, Winrodism, etc., they have gone off the deep end with desperate seriousness, and in so doing earned for themselves the name of being a humorless, puritanical people, incapable of joy and grudging in their attitude toward those happier than themselves.

This is not a pretty reputation and naturally one shrinks from accepting this description of oneself and his friends and neighbors. Oddly enough, however, we do accept it almost unanimously and meekly endure the opprobrium and ridicule of other states. This I believe to be due to a humility and self-distrust so great as to be crippling to our energies.

For the fanaticism of Kansans is due, I believe, not so much to puritanical self-righteousness, the desire to reform and inhibit, as to a wish to identify themselves with the best, the most idealistic and fruitful ways of life. And because they feel pathetically unequal to maintaining these ideals and to living at the high pitch at which they conceive other more gifted people to be living, they fence themselves about and reinforce their tense strivings with laws and prohibitions.

In discussing Kansans it is usually assumed that their strictness is aimed at coercing other people to their beliefs, to reform the wicked. The reformer's psychology is often described as being a desire to keep others from the sinful pleasures he secretly indulges in or at least burns to indulge in. This unsympathetic portrayal of the reformer as a hypocrite and a dog in the manger has some truth in it; but this very intolerance of the intolerant betrays an unconscious hypocrisy in the hypocrite-hater. To put away the temptation to indulge in more paradoxical but perhaps confusing expressions, let us state it more plainly by saying that at heart everyone is a reformer in the sense that he must curb certain antisocial tendencies in himself which he openly deprecates but yearns to indulge. We say that his attitudes are unconscious because he is not aware of such yearnings and would probably develop all kinds of defensive symptoms if he began to be aware of the strength of unlawful desires in himself. The activities of the zealot who rushes about making life miserable for other people may be considered as one form of defensive symptom of this type. His activity therefore is chiefly directed against himself, in spite of its apparent direction toward the world in general. The world may avoid him, trip him up, laugh at him, and find many ways of overcoming the discomfort he causes, but he has no way of circumventing his own unrelenting harshness toward himself which drives him to take desperate measures to reinforce his failing defense against antisocial urges.

I began by saying that we live in a beautiful state, a state settled by brave, intelligent, and far-visioned people; then I had to add that our intelligence and our vision do not seem to have prevented us from developing a vast inferiority, not a real inferiority but a feeling of inferiority. I related this inferiority to feelings of over-conscientiousness which in turn I think may be an echo of the pioneer struggles of our immediate ancestors. We need writers and artists to proclaim the beauty of Kansas and to demonstrate the intelligence of the majority and not the eccentricity of the lunatic fringe.

The members of the press have a special responsibility in this matter. I have long felt that the newspapers could modify the unfavorable opinions of the outsiders if they would modify the feelings of Kansans about themselves. For the men of the press reflect this attitude of inferiority; indeed they encourage it; they exploit it. They like to brag about breaking heat records and raising freaks. They feel a little shamefaced in writing about our cultural attainments. The newspaper reporters seem to feel impelled to pull a wisecrack if possible, and the deskman would rather think up a funny headline than an accurate one. They deceive themselves into thinking the people like this. The truth of the matter is that too many of the newspapermen do not take their own work seriously. They do not take their state seriously. If the Wichita newspapers, for example, would give more space to the glories of Kansas and less to the iniquities of Topeka; if the Topeka newspapers would give more space to the cultural activities of the city and less to the political goings-on in the State House, and if all the editors of all the papers would read *Kansas Magazine* and print excerpts from it instead of lifting paragraphs from the *Kansas City Star*, we would have an even better state than we have now, and we would have more fun living in it or visiting outside of it.

Many years later (1962) Dr. Karl rose to the defense of Kansas again as he refuted an editorial in Harper's Magazine, *September, 1962, in one of his* Reading Notes:

One of the wise, thoughtful writers of the country has stumbled. In his September issue, friend John Fischer, editor-in-chief of *Harper's*, wrote an excellent editorial regarding certain changes in American industrial development and discussed the intangible assets of certain inspiring sites. He named North Carolina, New England, Puerto Rico, the Northwest, Wisconsin, Michigan—curiously omitting Colorado—and then it happens. Rhetorically he exclaims, "How could anybody create either a great university or an enticing environment in Kansas or North Dakota?"

"This," comments James A. McCain, a former North Carolinian, now president of the State University in the *Journal of the Kansas Industrial Development Commission*, "reflects a widespread image of this state, although . . . a grossly distorted image." It probably is the image held by the man in the street of Philadelphia, the factory worker in Rhode Island, the lobster fisherman in Maine, and the sharecropper in Alabama. But by one of the most intelligent, educated, and sophisticated men in one of the most metropolitan and broad-minded cities in the world?

I think we ought to do something about this. We ought to invite Mr. Fischer and some of his friends to visit us. We should show them our several state universities, our many excellent colleges, our Lindsborg Festival and art center, the Eisenhower Library at Abilene and the William Rockhill Nelson Museum and the incomparable Linda Hall Library on our "front porch."

We would like to take Mr. Fischer and his party up a beautiful hill west of Topeka, past lakes and lawns through groves of trees and meadows of wild flowers to our Clock Tower building, a replica of Philadelphia's Independence Hall. They might take a moment to look at the historical museum or the exhibits of medical art and medical history or the psychiatric archives or the offices of the Education Department of The Menninger Foundation. Emerging from the building they might take a quick look at the sunset reflected on the river to the northwest or at the city stretching out below to the south and east.

Then they might follow some of the invisible threads leading from this center to the state hospitals of Kansas and the state hospitals of twenty other states. They might skip four miles south to the handsome VA Hospital, long the pilot and leader in this great chain; and on six miles to the Forbes Air Force Base hospital and psychiatric center. Or they might follow threads in other directions to a score of clinics and hospitals where psychiatry in a new key is taught, practiced, and utilized and where various research projects inspire hope for a better use of the manpower in these other states which Mr. Fischer found so much more inspiring.

THE MAN FROM TOPEKA

Or we could take Mr. Fischer east on the turnpike through the hills of Shawnee and Douglas to the Mount Oread heights and there give him a look at the most beautiful university campus in the world, with a panorama of buildings set in a panorama of scenery and nurturing an expanding panorama of ideas and cultural development.

We are not through with Mr. Fischer yet. We would want to turn him around and take him west to another range of hills edging the beautiful Blue Valley, perhaps soon to be a national park. Here we'd show him the first and the finest agricultural school in the land, now a State University, well deserving that name in spite of Mr. Fischer's derogations about our uninspiring milieu. No skyscrapers, no slums, no dirty streets, no tower bridges . . . none of the attributes of the Manhattan in which Mr. Fischer lives and from which he sits in judgment. But serenity and dignity, earnestness and dedication, beauty and aspiration—these he would find in Manhattan, Kansas.

Then he might drive south to Matfield Green where even Mr. Fischer might catch his breath in awe at the 100,000-acre stretches of beauty in the famous Flint Hills before going east to Neodesha and winding through the lovely and famous Sycamore Valley, where more kinds of plant life grow than anywhere else in the U.S. (over 1,500 species). From there Mr. Fischer and his party could drive slowly through various kinds of mining to the metropolitanism of Kansas City (Kansas!) or head farther east into the Boston and Ozark mountains. But wherever he went I don't think he would forget us.

It may be our fault that people like Mr. Fischer remain as ignorant of Kansas in 1962 as our ancestors and his were in 1862. "Bleeding Kansas" they called it—poor bleeding, boiling, beaten Kansas. "Other states boast of their advantages," wrote Kenneth Davis in *The New York Times* some years ago. "Kansas [with a kind of amused chuckle] boasts of her ills. Other states speak loudly of their blessings and softly (or not at all) of their misfortunes; Kansas does [or did] the reverse. She spread abroad tall tales of her anguish: the worst droughts, the dreariest landscapes, the biggest winds, the smallest potatoes, the most voracious grasshoppers. She displays a masochist's delight in suffering or a tough guy's pride in being able to 'take it.' Consciously or unconsciously, Kansans have encouraged the popular view of their state as 82,000 square miles of monotony so boring and dull as to be in itself a sufficient cause of religious and moral excesses."

We ought to remember more often—and spread more widely— the words of the great Cyrus K. Holliday written 100 years ago: *"A more lovely country I certainly never saw—and yet it looks worse now*

[*December*] *than at any other season.* [Dr. Karl's italics] I am told by those who know that in the spring and early summer when the grass and shrubbery and flowers appear it is beautiful beyond conception. So I think it must be. And in a few years when civilization by its magic influence shall have transformed this glorious country from what it now is to the brilliant destiny awaiting it, the sun in all his course will visit *no land more truly lovely and desirable than this."*

I submit in answer to Mr. Fischer that *someone* might indeed think of this neighborly, industrious, productive, beautiful, uncrowded state as capable of being a center of learning and of inspiration for the youth and for the cultivation of scholarship and appreciation of beauty and the promotion as a mentally healthy vision of the good life.

Dr. Karl's strong idealistic streak was instilled by his parents. He has talked and written of his family on a number of occasions. Undoubtedly the most important of these was the celebration on July 11, 1952, of the ninetieth birthday of his father, Dr. C. F. Menninger, who was the founder of the family in Topeka and a central figure in the Menninger developments. For the birthday dinner, which was attended by relatives and close friends, Dr. Karl prepared a special tribute, formally yet joyfully acknowledging his many debts to his father.

"I was always attached very strongly—consciously and warmly—to my father," Dr. Karl says. "In writing this speech, the only question was whether I would be able to give him enough tribute for all the things he had done. I didn't want to be too fulsome; he wouldn't have liked that. But as the piece turned out, he did like it.

"I remember clearly the day I read it. Shortly before this, I had had to write comments on several colleagues who had died. I thought that if my father were not so strong and sturdy, I'd be writing one on him instead."

Dr. Karl's tribute to his father was published in A Psychiatrist's World: The Selected Papers of Karl Menninger, M.D., *edited by Dr. Bernard H. Hall and others.*

It falls to my lot with a sadly increasing frequency these days to write some words of appraisal in connection with the passing of a colleague or a friend. At such times I attempt to review in my mind the chief contributions to their fellow men and the pervading spirit of their lives, and set them down on paper. We do this partly to comfort ourselves for our lost friend, and partly to convey to the family a confirmation of our affection and our sympathy.

It is a very different matter to undertake an appraisal of one who is still with us after many years of living and working, and whom we hope to have with us many years yet, without blinking the inevitability of our ultimate separation. This is a far more joyous task and a more grateful one, through the knowledge that what we have to say will come to his living ears as a part of that always unfulfilled debt that we all owe to one another in the way of acknowledgment and testimonial. We cannot live without each other; there is in life a constant giving and taking, and perhaps we too seldom reflect upon the balance of debits and credits until it is too late.

And so it is my special honor and my pleasurable duty to formulate what is in the hearts of my brother and my sister, my wife and myself—and no doubt of many others. But I am the eldest son of the man we are talking about. I have known him intimately longer than anyone else. I am more in his debt than anyone else. So I am grateful for the opportunity to acknowledge this for myself and for my brothers.

I have read in the papers and I have heard from the lips of friends and I have seen in telegrams and letters of appreciation, the many fine things my father has done. But we who have lived close to him know so many fine things that no one knows that he has done. The infinitely many little occasions of simple kindnesses, personal thoughtfulness, gentle encouragement, generous giving,* and the courage of bearing infirmity with dignity and patience. Not only do I know of all this through observation and through infinitely many contacts and experiences, but I know it deep in the core of my personality. Whatever good my brothers and I may have accomplished, for which we get so many kind words of praise, my father and the two women who have been his wives made possible.

My earliest memory of Father is of his leaving a Sunday afternoon outing, just as we were starting, to take care of a patient who had been hurt in an accident, and who was brought to our cottage. I have many more memories, on the one hand of his taking us on outings into the country and on the other hand of his sacrificing his personal pleasure to his professional duty. Still another early memory is that of my father sitting at his desk at night studying medical books. To study,

---

* January 27, 1973: A letter was received today from a friend in London, telling of meeting a man whose father chanced to be passing through Topeka, found himself penniless, sought out my father, explained his plight, and left with fifty dollars.

to be with his family, and to be faithful to his professional obligations were three of the principles that my brothers and I grew up with.

You have read sketches of his life. You know how he first came to Kansas to help found a college and teach, and how, when he returned again to Kansas, he straight off organized a medical study group. You know how he soon became a civic leader, spearheaded the Board of Health in its concern for better public-school hygiene, helped to reorganize the Chamber of Commerce, proposed and developed a nationally famous rose garden, helped in the teaching at our local medical school, and participated in the medical activities of Christ's and St. Francis hospitals, and in the county and state societies.

You know, too, how he preached the gospel of cooperation by doctors. You have heard that it was the inspiration he derived from the Mayo Clinic that led to the development of the Menninger Clinic. Sometimes I hear him say that it was I and not he who developed the Clinic and the Sanitarium and the psychiatric center. Let me explain to this group of intimate friends why this is not so; it is the essential part of this tribute I want to pay him. When Ernest Southard died in Boston and I returned to Topeka, Father had been in practice thirty years. Most men who had had this much experience and so well-established a career would not have taken kindly to the bumptious, eccentric, and impulsive gyrations executed by a youngster scarcely out of his internship, particularly this youngster. Most men would have said "Do this," "Do that," "Take this case, take that case," "Use this treatment and use that treatment." Not Father. All he said to me was, "Let's work together. I will help you in any way I can. Feel free to leave town as often as you can and see what other doctors are doing; I'll carry on for us here. Attend medical meetings. Take all the journals and read them, and if you write for some of them send reprints to doctors who may not take the journals."

I proposed a new laboratory. He was delighted. He had always managed to maintain one and did the laboratory work himself, but we got the wonderful Mildred Law! She was a highly competent young woman, then a laboratory technician, but subsequently and for many years an executive planner and official in the Menninger operations. I proposed a secretary, and later an office nurse and a psychologist. With every proposal I made he agreed with enthusiasm.

It happened that, because of my interest in a new specialty at a particularly prosperous time in the world's history, I almost immediately got quite a few patients of my own, and sometimes my income during those early months was almost as great as his. With the magnanimity and maturity and dignity and the real love that characterized him, he reacted not with envy or discomfiture of any kind, but only with pride and pleasure.

Having seen many young doctors since then, I can visualize now how arrogant and presumptuous and cocksure and self-centered and really ignorant I was. When I think of some of the mistakes I made, I marvel at the patience and gentle forbearance of the most wonderful partner a man ever had. I remember some times when, through some error of mine or some decision of the Almighty, things looked very dark. I remember that at those times he gave me from his wisdom and experience the greatest comfort that could be received. I have quoted some of the things he told me in those early days to many successive waves of students, who will, I am sure, pass them on to their students and their children so that, without his knowing it, Father's words are probably already immortal.

I have often wondered in recent years how Father could have put up with me. But he did more than put up with me. He encouraged me and counseled me and helped me. "We must work together," he always said. "Let us do it thoroughly, honestly, and the best we can. Let it be said that anything the Menningers undertake to do, they do well." Having made these points, my father crystallized the spirit of working together in a group by the most magnificent and eloquent self-effacement. He stepped quietly into the background. He surrendered everything he had done, every personal ambition, to the goal of having a group of doctors working together with one purpose.

It is this capacity for living in the present with an eye to the future but never a glance to the past that has made him actually, really, truly, the founder and spirit of the Menninger Clinic. More than anyone else I know, he is described by the passage so difficult to understand, but so true, "Let him who would be the greatest among you be the servant of all."

I do not believe my father thinks of himself as "the servant of all." I do not think he thinks about himself at all. He is just interested in the infinite phenomena of life, in learning all he can about it, and he loves to examine it piece by piece. He is the perennial student, and the greatest naturalist I have ever known, but this preoccupation with the details of nature has never kept him from having a warm personal interest in every human being he meets. He is as gentle and kindly and gracious in talking with a stranger or a friend as he is in his gentle, warm, personal handling of a chip of rock or a rose or a shell.

Recent studies by scientists into the processes of aging have reversed some popular notions about the progressive loss of our natural powers. It has been observed that some individuals continue to grow as long as they live, and that after sixty years some powers are actually greater than in earlier years. I think my father illustrates this phenomenon. Physically, of course, he is not quite as strong as he once was, but his memory remains resonant. His interest in everything in the world continues unabated. His reverence for the mystery of the universe and its Creator deepens.

I want him to know from my lips what my brothers and I trust he has long since realized from our actions, that he is the great inspiration of our lives—ours and many others'. Each of us could say that our highest ambition can be only to reach the age of ninety with our vision as undimmed as his, our purposes as unchanged, our affection for God and his creatures as unswerving. And I hope that then— or even now—my children and grandchildren and foster children can feel half as fervently and tenderly toward me as we, today, feel toward our father, Charles Frederick Menninger.

Dr. C. F. Menninger lived to be ninety-one. Thinking back about his father, Dr. Karl reminisces:

Deafness has been a great black cloud in my life because my father was so deaf. It determined many aspects of our lives—where we sat at concerts, how we spoke at the table, who heard the telephone ringing, and who didn't hear it!

My father's deafness looms in my memory of his image as though it were a great impalpable dark tumor around his ear. I remember my mother frequently speaking of "Dear Daddy and his poor, bad ear." I recall painfully the irritations I sometimes felt because he didn't understand me, when he really didn't hear me.

Once I got furious at him for not stopping to pick me up as he rode by in his horse and buggy and I called out to him. Actually he hadn't heard me. When I got home, I was very disagreeable. I denounced him. I hurt his feelings so badly he said, "I really didn't hear you at all, son." Then I think he spanked me.

As he grew older, he wore a hearing aid most of the time. He was very patient about it. Now that I have had a little experience with one, I marvel at his patience. He spent thousands of dollars trying to find a good hearing aid.

I also had trouble with my ear as a child, and people would say

THE MAN FROM TOPEKA

I was just like father. Mother arranged for me to sit in the first row of classes so I could hear. But my ear wasn't bad enough to keep me out of the army or navy even though it caused me a lot of trouble as an adolescent because of ear infections from swimming. I didn't actually wear a hearing aid until I was about seventy-five, but no doubt I needed one earlier.

Dr. Karl's Reading Notes *often mention his father. For example:*

The Menningers get the credit and the blame for a good many things in Topeka. One credit line which is sometimes omitted is to Dr. C. F. Menninger for having helped establish the splendid Reinisch Rose Garden in Gage Park. I don't know whether my father or that very able horticulturist Fred Reinisch actually suggested the rose garden, but they both worked on the idea and got Tom Doran, a lawyer, interested and he gave some money toward it. They persuaded the city commission to make an appropriation to support it and the garden was started in 1919. Very few roses were grown in Topeka at that time —the gardens of Professor Harshbarger, Fred Anton, and my father and a few others were exceptions and people did not realize what ideal rose climate we have.

Dr. Karl has not written much about his mother. Asked if he felt he really knew her, he replies vehemently:

Know her? I should say I did. I almost felt I was her. I knew how she felt about almost everything.

She was even more energetic and perhaps more formidable than my father. She wanted no chicanery. No deceit. No hocus-pocus. No hypocrisy. She disapproved of any kind of affectation. When she thought someone was affected, she wouldn't say it to their face, but she would tell us later of her feelings of disapproval. Affectation in people also makes me very uncomfortable.

My mother had many people dependent on her for all sorts of things. She seemed to enjoy their dependence. At Christmas she made hundreds of cookies, and hand-dipped chocolate creams and dates, working like a Turk for days. My brothers and I would get in our little pony cart and ride out and distribute them, following a route planned by her. She always remembered anybody she had had any relationship with and anybody she had heard of who was poor and needy. For in-

23

stance, the old Negro janitor who did all the work at the church. Nobody gave him much at Christmas, but Mother would go all-out for him and his family.

She started teaching art in Topeka about 1895 but there were more people interested in learning about the Bible than art. They may have read the Bible a little, but they had heard a few stories from it and wanted to know more. I wouldn't say she was a very religious woman, though. Her Bible classes were non-sectarian. They became so popular that instead of teaching once a week she found herself teaching three classes a week. At first the class was held in the Presbyterian Church but then she thought that was unfair to women of other religions—Catholics might have had indigestion if they went inside a Presbyterian Church then—so she moved it to the YWCA. She had a few Negro women in the class though at first the others did not like it. Later she had an all-black class.

I remember how upset Mother was for days after one graduation exercise. She had invited as speaker a man from a neighboring town, a religious education authority. In his address, he referred three or four times to the "niggers." Murmuring and booing, some of them left the room. To her this was an example of hypocrisy by a professional Christian.

Of his two brothers, Dr. Karl says:

Will, who was six years younger, was attached to me like a son. He was always quiet. We called or wrote each other every day of our lives. Edwin, two and a half years younger, is more like me. We still speak on the phone once a week. He lives in Stuart, Florida, and his deepest interest today is horticulture, especially flowering trees.

Edwin has suffered great sorrows and setbacks. He had a terrible accident in college. He was always one to joke and horse around. One day he mixed up some explosives in the chemistry lab to take over to the fraternity house. On the way he fell. The mixture exploded and blew off his left hand and blew out his right eye. He almost died from the infection that set in. Father saved him by a very ingenious medical treatment. This ended Edwin's medical and musical aspirations.

Edwin and I had quarreled frequently as boys, although not seriously, but never again after this accident. He has since done so much that it is practically unbelievable. He was a reporter, then cable editor of the New York *Herald Tribune* for a while. He was editor of his own newspaper in Florida for many years, but his hobby of horticulture, which has led him to write and illustrate with photographs six unique books, has gradually absorbed him completely.

In Reading Notes *Dr. Karl tells about another grave accident that Edwin suffered nearly fifty years later, and about his continuing accomplishments in the face of adversity.*

Just before Christmas in 1966, my brother Edwin, well past his seventieth birthday, suffered a severe automobile accident in which many bones were broken and the vision in his one good eye seriously impaired. It didn't seem possible that he would pull through. But pull through he did with excellent surgical attention and wonderful encouragement and support from his wife and many friends. He has slowly recovered much of his former vigor. During 1967 he completed the manuscript of his forthcoming book on *Flowering Vines of the World,* even though he had to do much of his reading of source material and letters from foreign countries vicariously.

For his work with trees, my brother has received awards from the American Horticultural Society, the Fairchild Tropical Garden, and the Botanical Garden of Rio de Janeiro. He was given an honorary Doctor of Science degree by Florida State University in 1965. His book *Fantastic Trees* has been chosen for a listing as one of fifty outstanding trade books of 1967. His own Alma Mater (Washburn University) may not know it, but he is one of their most illustrious graduates, one "who has built a name for himself throughout the world equal to that of his illustrious brothers" as a recent press clipping stated.

I receive a letter from him nearly every week. "My vision improves slowly but definitely," he said. "I am still walking a mile daily and the 'severe' charley horse in my left thigh is nearly all gone away. My book is coming okay. I sent my color slides to New York this week —150 of them."

You can put this in your file of miracles, but I don't know whether I mean most the miracle of a double recovery from terrible accidental injuries, or the miracle of the man who has persistently wanted others to enjoy more fully the flowers and trees and vines of the world.

CHAPTER TWO

Of Sycamore Trees
and Six No-Trump

One way to get to know a man is to know the many books that he has read. Asked which books had influenced him the most, Dr. Karl replied:

When I was a child my mother read to me aloud. There was *Black Beauty* and *Alice's Adventures in Wonderland*. And *The Swiss Family Robinson,* which I liked better than *Robinson Crusoe.* Then, all the books by Ernest Thompson Seton influenced me greatly. But especially *The Biography of a Grizzly.* It made an indelible impression upon me, gave me the deepest interest in this great North American mammal, even a sympathy with his alleged bad disposition. I liked Lobo the Wolf, too, mentioned in Seton's *Wild Animals I Have Known.* These books didn't cause my love of animals but were associated with it. I also remember, with special nostalgia, *At the Back of the North Wind.*

In my pre-Freud days, of the books that influenced me most, I recall *The Brothers Karamazov, Of Human Bondage,* and *The Way of All Flesh,* the latter particularly because of its psychological understanding. Also *Jude the Obscure, Quo Vadis,* and *Ben Hur.* The latter influenced my thinking greatly—the theme of the justification of the establishment of Christianity.

OF SYCAMORE TREES AND SIX NO-TRUMP

I liked all of Charles Dickens—I want to reread him and get his picture of prisons more clearly in my mind. I only read a few books by Thackeray and Scott, authors I didn't enjoy too much. I liked Sherwood Anderson, John Galsworthy, John Masefield. I did not care for James Branch Cabell or Faulkner, who it seemed to me was just trying to talk dirty before the use of four-letter words. Nor did I like Dreiser.

I always read everything H. L. Mencken wrote. I knew him, as I did Carl Sandburg, whom I enjoyed. I liked *John Brown's Body* by Stephen Vincent Benét. And Eugene O'Neill's plays influenced me greatly. I also read *The American Mercury, The Nation, The Freeman, The Dial,* and *The New Republic* always.

Though the bulk of the reviews in his regular column are of works in the psychiatric field, Dr. Karl's interests range far beyond the boundaries of his profession and he often pauses to comment on books and articles that reflect them.

Some time ago my sister-in-law Cay [Mrs. William Menninger] gave me a little book which she had found appealing. It got covered up on my bedside table, and I didn't read it until last night. *Heaven in My Hand* (1957) by Alice Lee Humphreys is a collection of vignettes written in Quaker or Biblical language. Of all the things I have seen about teaching, it is the most effective, because it is so simple and so beautiful. Wise, too. It's about the child who brought the teacher an icicle for a present, unidentified until it melted, and the little boy who delighted in blowing air up her sleeve, and about the little girl who laid her head on her desk and fell asleep, and the little boy who finally provoked the teacher into giving him two spanks after which he sidled up to her and said irresistibly, "You are still my sweetheart," and the mother who came to thank her for teaching her boy to spell I C E, a word which seemed to comfort him in his deathbed fever. If I were a millionaire I would buy 1000 copies of this book and give one to every teacher in town and in some other towns; not being a millionaire, I am only going to get half a dozen and send them to some of the teachers I know who are like this teacher and will read this little volume like a prayer book. (I re-ordered.)

One of my Christmas presents was a book entitled *Wonderful Old Lawrence* (Kansas) by Elfriede Fischer Rowe, published in 1971. I don't know exactly how to describe this book. I can say that it is a series of short essays of a few hundred words each about such things as "The Old Fire Bell," "The First City Directory," "The Only and Oldest Lawrence Whist Club," and "Changing Times and Customs."

It has two extraordinary merits. It is written in a charming style —simple, clear, somewhat colloquial, and quite unpretentious. And secondly, it is so—I am tempted to say—*accurate*. What I really mean is that it describes things in precisely the same way that I too remember them. (That's one kind of accuracy.) For example, in mentioning some of the home remedies prevalent 50 years ago, it mentions the rock candy–rye whiskey mixture on the sideboard; the hot toddy of lemon juice and sugar; the juice of a baked onion made into a syrup; the sticks of horehound candy for sore throat; poultices of goose grease and turpentine rubbed on your throat and chest; and a soft flannel wool cloth called a compress, on a wet washing, wrapped around your throat; vegetable soup in a tall black iron kettle for convalescence, etc.

There is a whole chapter on telephone numbers which brought back to my mind quite clearly many things which would seem strange now. There used to be black, blue, red, and white party lines with corresponding color-code numbers. There used to be many numbers with letters after them, especially J and R. There were two telephone companies in most Kansas towns, including Lawrence, Topeka, and Kansas City—the Home and the Bell. I can only remember one telephone number at our house in Topeka; it was 85. My father's office telephone number was 19. A little later these were enlarged to four-figure numbers and usually the old number was incorporated.

Well, anyway this Lawrence book will make you nostalgic if you are past 60—no matter where you lived.

. . . Through the courtesy of Nyle Miller, I was able to find a rare copy of the *Kansas Historical Collections,* Volume 5, 1891–1896. Why is it that some people are interested in transmitting records for the next generation, and some don't give a hang?

Dr. Karl rarely throws bouquets—unless he thinks they have been earned, of course:

This reviewer of *Existential Psychoanalysis* by Jean-Paul Sartre (1953) can only record his dismay at discovering that although he was hitherto interested in and somewhat acquainted with existentialism, and although this book is written in English (translated) and although there are few unfamiliar words, he has no idea what the author is trying to say. It certainly has nothing to do with psychoanalysis as officially defined and customarily used. Sample: "The obscenity of the feminine sex is that of everything which 'gapes open.' It is a summons to being as all holes." Provocative obscurantism of this sort (also modern poetry) may be *art*, but it's not science, in *my* opinion, nor art to *my* taste.

The blurb on my copy of this book, *Deer Park*, by Norman Mailer (1955), says that it is mature (No!), disturbing (No!), entertaining (No!), too strong for some readers' taste (Yes), downright shocking (No!). In my opinion, add "very dull, very phallic, quite pointless."

Not surprisingly for the boy who was entranced by The Biography of a Grizzly *and* Lobo the Wolf, *Dr. Karl is an enthusiastic naturalist.*

Frequently I run across information which seemingly has nothing whatever to do with psychiatry but which serves to remind me of what a small part of the world we see and what a small part of the total accumulation of knowledge any one man can acquire. I had not realized, for example, that an accidental discovery made by an observing scientist, Lorenzo L. Langstroth, in 1851 was the beginning of scientific bee culture, which still lags so much that certain phases of American agriculture are seriously handicapped. This discovery was that space less than 3/8″ was always sealed by the bees with bee glue, and spaces wider than 3/8″ are filled with honeycomb. Exactly 3/8″ is therefore a magic number with bees, without which none of our modern beehive construction could have been possible.

Animal Wonder World by Frank W. Lane (1951) is an extremely interesting collection of trivia and the unusual in nature. For example, the quickest reaction time of human beings using large muscles is about 1/2 second, and for small muscles, about 1/10 of a second. Some animals, birds, and insects are very much quicker; numerous animals seem to be able to actually dodge a rifle bullet. A cheetah can accelerate to 45 miles an hour in two seconds from a standing start. Did you know that for many birds, ants are a stimulant something like catnip for a cat? And that "tucking ants under their wings" is still an unexplained mystery habit of birds?

Nothing is so curious to me as the wide prevalence of snake phobia. All the literature stressing the rarity of poisonous snakes and the prevalence of beneficial snakes seems to do no good. When you try to convince even intelligent people that some varieties of snakes make charming, affectionate, and intelligent pets, they become either hysterical, ribald, or uneasily suspicious of your sanity. The *Audubon Magazine* for May–June [1954] attributes this less to unconscious factors, as many have always done, than to ignorance and false education. The Bedford Audubon Society in Upper Westchester County has combated similar prejudice by a systematic educational program involving some 1200 children. The snake matter is only a detail; the education deals with conservation, wildlife preservation, and all sorts of things.

In a recent visit to Dr. James Folsom at Tuscaloosa, I was served a most delicious fish which I insisted was the best panfish I had ever eaten. I was told it was catfish, which I did not think possible since I had supposed I disliked catfish. But I learned that these were very special; they are raised on a "fish farm" and prepared for the market fresh each day. I thought this was most ingenious of the Alabamans —only to learn later that there is a fish farm a few miles from my home in Topeka.

Be that as it may, there is no lobster farm in either Alabama or Kansas. As one quite fond of lobster and quite sad at its rapid destruction and near elimination from the restaurant market, I was glad to learn that John Hughes, an authority on the lobster, working with John Sullivan, a practical lobster culturist, have raised and released millions of young lobsters into the ocean since developing a hatchery on Martha's Vineyard some 20 years ago.

Furthermore they have discovered how to detect pregnant lobsters caught in commercial traps before killing them and they have discovered how to make lobster eggs hatch three months earlier than normal and they have found a way to preserve more of the catch between the emptying of the traps and the arrival of the lobsters at the docks. These researchers have been financed by the Massachusetts Legislature, another big credit to it, in my opinion. And the point of it all is that plans are being made to develop lobster farms—on land, of course—in which the commercially feasible number of eatable-size lobsters can be grown and marketed at a cost less than the present market price for "wild" lobsters.

At the colloquium for the alumni reunion in April, 1966, there were several references to a presentation I had made at a colloquium long ago on the relation of the earthworm to man's destiny.

OF SYCAMORE TREES AND SIX NO-TRUMP

I ran across my notes for that commentary recently. It was in 1947. I had taken the information from an article by a man in London published in *Natural History* for April of that year. It began: "Eyeless, legless, faceless, and voiceless, the earthworm is not much to look at —a mere squirming piece of flesh. Yet, with its powerful muscles, its two stomachs (one inside and one outside), and its false teeth, it is able to carry out remarkable works. Its task is to eat the earth."

The article goes on then to explain that the earthworm eats dirt, extracts what it needs and casts the rest out in "delicate little towers." These castings add up in weight to half a pound or more in a year. Using Charles Darwin's estimate of 50,000 worms per acre (this has been found to be too *low*), the weight of the excreted soil in a year comes to 20–40 tons per acre! Stones on an uncultivated field will sink at the rate of two inches a year, and a concentration of worms can make them sink much more rapidly, as has been the case, for example, with some of the great slabs of Stonehenge. It is the worms which bury and preserve archeological ruins and artifacts. Whole Roman villas have been lowered into the ground and covered over by the patient work of millions of worms.

Worms also lower hills and widen valleys. And, of course, they assist in creating soil by mixing little rock particles with vegetable ash and furthering their decomposition. They plow the earth, they harrow it, they drain it, they push it around. On our Veterans Administration Hospital campus of about 160 acres, the earthworms move *over ten tons* of this earth, one way or the other, each and every twenty-four hours, while *we* work and sleep.

The *National Geographic* is an American phenomenon. However dull some of the text on occasions, every now and then an issue comes out which is a gem, for example, the March, 1966, issue . . . the star articles are the one on squids by Professor Gilbert L. Voss of the Institute of Marine Science, University of Miami, and the one on an albino gorilla photographed in the wild.

Squids, as you may or may not know, vary from a matter of inches to as much as 60 feet in length. They have reverse jet nozzles so they move backward or forward swiftly without turning around. Many are capable of self-illumination and color change. Most of them can squirt ink. Some of them supply the sperm whale with its chief nutriment; but some are large enough to give even a whale a hard time. The famous episode in Victor Hugo's *Toilers of the Sea,* is not an impossibility; apparently boats have been upset by the larger squids and men dragged to their doom. The mandibles of one squid are powerful enough to cut heavy wire.

There is an extraordinary picture of the gorgeous flower arrangement of egg strands being carefully arranged one by one by a mamma squid. Other ladies then come along and add their contributions to the "bouquet" until they make a great mop.

And then comes an incredible picture showing that Aristotle was right when he wrote (about 330 B.C.) that squids in copulation "unite at the mouth by an interlacing of their tentacles." This is how it is, *sometimes*. But not always; there are *two* Pompeian fresco-type of illustrations of how else it can be done (by squids), taken at Woods Hole, Massachusetts.

You may have seen the article in the July, 1967, issue of *National Geographic* about the gigantic toads of East Africa, as big as a bucket. They are edible and nonpoisonous. But coming closer home, there is another toad that you should learn about because (1) it is getting common in southern Florida and (2) it is very dangerous! Glands back of the eyes emit an extremely poisonous substance which need only touch one's skin to cause virulent effects. People have a morbid dread of snakes—so few of which are dangerous—and now this poisonous toad turns up. This was reported in *Science News* for July 8, 1967.

But we consulted Professor Edward H. Taylor of Kansas University about this news item and he writes: "The toad in Florida has been an endemic resident along the Rio Grande for a great many years; I have caught them at several points in Texas as much as 30 years ago. The Japanese distributed the species in many of the Pacific Islands where they have increased greatly. I am told that the Japanese used them for food. With the skin removed, I would imagine there was little or no poison left.

"It is true that these large toads sometimes when attacked by a dog can throw out venom—squeeze it out with muscles—and, if a dog gets it in its mouth and gut, he may be killed. The venom does not normally affect the skin in any way if kept from mucous membranes or the eye."

While in Chicago early in April, I was struck by the merry hubbub going on about the Purple Martin. When it was about time for the martins to arrive from the South, there were articles in all the papers about it. A "Purple Martin Day" was declared and many people appeared on the streets with large purple buttons bearing a picture of the bird. A drink called a "purple martini" was advertised. A book appeared in the store windows (actually published last year) by J. L. Wade of Griggsville, Illinois, the Purple Martin capital of the country: *What You Should Know About the Purple Martin: America's Most Wanted Bird.*

The book tells a lot of interesting things about the multiple values of Purple Martins because of their energetic insectivorousness, the popular appeal of their graceful flight, and their cheerful chirping. The thousands of martin houses erected in Griggsville came about because of a pest of mosquitoes which the Purple Martins were successful in dispelling. Special aluminum martin boxes were invented and widely distributed by Mr. Wade, through our friend, Paul Cory of the Moorman Company, and many others. I have a couple of these myself. The chief enemy of the Purple Martin is, of course, DDT spraying.

Asked about his favorite tree by the magazine American Forests, *Dr. Karl wrote the following essay for the June, 1950, issue:*

Like many of the previous contributors to this series I feel uncomfortable about naming one favorite from among the many trees I know. I shall feel guilty of a certain disloyalty and unfairness which my friends, the trees, might resent. Trees seem very human to me, not in some fanciful way but in a deeply emotional way. I speak with some diffidence of this emotion because I perceive that there is a wide variance among people with regard to such a feeling. To see a tree chopped down for utilitarian purposes, valuable as these may be, pains me sharply, to the astonishment of some of my friends. The sight of the felling of great trees, which seems to thrill the average movie audience, arouses in me only the most unpleasant sensations, similar to those more conventionally experienced when the hero of a story finally loses his life. Journeys I took some years ago through parts of the states of Oregon, Washington, and the upper peninsula of Michigan left me depressed for weeks: inconsiderate destructiveness as a trait of human beings seemed too nakedly revealed.

As a psychiatrist I am interested in the way people (including myself) feel about things. Reactions such as I have described can be called by different names—sentimentalism, neuroticism, pantheism, totemism, identification. They are bound to be ridiculed by the practical man who regards trees only as so much lumber from which so many useful things can be made. But when I think of the destruction of the topsoil and the devastation of floods which have followed so regularly the application of this "practical" principle, I wonder if it isn't in part an illusion and in part an excuse for cupidity. Recently one of my neighbors—a very "practical" man—cut down a beautiful walnut tree and transformed it into boards for a corral for his horses. I asked him about it, because he is intelligent and approachable. He was astonished that I concerned myself. "A tree is a tree," he said.

Having this deeply emotional reaction toward trees, I cannot name a favorite tree. Instead I shall mention several which are especially endeared to me, but in different ways. The sycamore has always impressed me with its grandeur and its uniqueness. The massiveness of its trunk and the majestic sweep of its branches give this tree a truly grand architecture, unsurpassed by any other tree. The sycamore is also one of my oldest acquaintances among the trees, for its spectacular, dappled branches and white trunk, and the round seedpods swinging from its branches all through the winter, stamped its identity upon my mind during early school days.

Of the less common trees the yellowwood is one of my favorites, producing quite different emotional reactions of an aesthetic sort. Its smooth, clean bark, the airy grace of its foliage, and its occasional display of fragrant white flowers combine to create an effect of delicate beauty. Although it is a hardy little wild tree, it attains its richest beauty of foliage and flowers only under cultivation—a circumstance which is particularly gratifying to the cultivator of trees.

And of the common trees I love the cottonwood because, like us Kansans who have named it the official tree of our state, it withstands both adversity and prosperity. To the thousands who live on the great prairies of the Southwest, the groves of cottonwoods represent "the forests," and often provide the only natural shade for many miles for men and beasts.

I am tempted to mention other favorite trees, for it seems to me that trees, like music, have the power to evoke feelings and moods. And who can name his favorite mood? But I was invited to write a page, not a book.

I have a file for which I can find no more helpful index tab than "Extraordinary People." There are so many ways for people to be extraordinary these days that perhaps you think this file is running over, but it isn't. Here is one of the recent additions taken from the Toronto *Star* and reprinted in *Atlas*, March, 1968:

> Joachim Foikis is a chap living in Vancouver who decks himself out in the traditional garments of the court fool and sits on

the steps of the courthouse in the afternoon sun, and wanders down the streets with his cap and bauble. He calls himself the Town Fool, but he is a learned man with degrees in various subjects from various universities. While he pretends to be foolish and plays with the children he meets on the street, he enlightens all that will listen to him with a profound wisdom. He abandoned a career in librarianship and entered a life of total insecurity. The world he says is governed by folly and the acceptance of this is the beginning of wisdom. He is a mature man of 36 with two children and a loyal and supportive wife. He is very religious, but has no use for churches. He radiates joy and kindness and seeks nothing for himself but a license from the city to be the Town Fool and, as such, to receive a farthing from every fool in town as his medieval predecessors did.

Will someone really competent please volunteer to be a fool in our town?

There are 168 hours in a week. Of this total, about 67 are occupied with sleeping, washing, dressing, and toileting; meals (eating, not preparing them) occupy perhaps 14. This leaves 87 hours to be accounted for. About one-half of these are spent in earning a living. What do we do with the other forty odd?

Of course, one man's trivia often is another man's research. Take, for example, the case of spinach and the "Popeye Syndrome", reported by a London doctor:

Richard Hunter, who with his mother has made such startling revisions of our understanding of America's last King [through their discovery that George III's recurring spells of madness were caused by a genetic disease, porphyria], submitted a charming vignette to the *Lancet* for April 10, 1971, about the origin and uses of spinach and why Popeye (if you can remember that far back) was always so suddenly and greatly invigorated by this herbal medication.

Americans, writes Richard Hunter, began eating spinach in quantity about 1920 when it was shown to contain body building calcium and iron; they ate it even more when they learned it was also rich in vitamins A and C. (More recently it has been hinted that eating spinach may not be an unmixed blessing, but I won't go into that.) But, says Hunter, spinach has been used in medicine for centuries, although an 18th century medical encyclopedist wrote that for all its present popularity, it was "unmention'd and unknown to the Antients.

35

It is so called by the Moderns, from its spinous Seed . . . We are not certain where it grows spontaneously . . . but it refuses no Soil or Climate, and is in Use in almost all Parts of Europe."

Well, actually, spinach was introduced from Persia in the 15th century. It was first mentioned in the medical writings of the 16th century. William Turner said, "Spinage is an herbe lately found & not long in vse but it is so wel knowen amongst al men in al countrees that it nedeth no description . . . I knowe not wherefor it is good sauinge to fill the belly & louse it a litle. But with those profittes it hurteth the stomach and bredeth winde."

And now for Hunter's current discovery. In 1941 Mitchell and others made an extract from spinach called folic acid which was used in the treatment of anemia in 1945. "Three years later vitamin B_{12} was synthesized and a new era of research into the biological roles and functional relationships of vitamin B_{12} and folic acid began.

"Recently it has been reported that folic acid may cause nervous and gastrointestinal symptoms in susceptible subjects which resemble in mild form those caused by sympatheticomimetic agents. A possible mechanism for this effect is suggested by the fact that brain-amine synthesis requires a pteridine cofactor."

Now here comes the paragraph that is going to tax your scientific acuity; in fact, it taxes mine so much that I am not going to quote all of it. "Since excess folic acid inhibits the enzyme dihydrofolic-acid reductase, which converts dietary folate to the biologically active tetra-hydrofolate derivative, high tissue concentrations of folic acid could theoretically cause a fall in available cofactor." Well, since all that is so, the possibility exists that spinach supplies folic acid which stimulates brain metabolism and that's why Popeye pops, QED.

Well, there's a lot more to it, but that's a hint. You can borrow this issue of the *Lancet* or write the editor at 54 Porchester Gate, London, W2.3HP for a reprint.

P.S. I had completed the reference to Dr. Hunter's article above on Popeye when with the inexorability of coincidence, my eye fell upon Dale Tussing's article in *Change* magazine for October, 1971—"Education, Foreign Policy and the Popeye Syndrome." Now, what do you think the "Popeye Syndrome" is? It proves to be a pattern represented in hundreds or thousands of cartoons and movies in which this unadorned and far from prepossessing common man is going about his business, without ever initiating any conflicts, only to be attacked by an obviously evil brute against which Popeye fights back valiantly. He is nearly annihilated, what with unfair tactics and similar wickedness, but with his last ounce of energy, he opens and eats a can of spinach. Thereupon Popeye changes completely, and with no holds barred, he completely disposes of the wicked foe.

Tussing emphasizes that here we have evil and good; good does not start fights even against evil. "Good guys are never the first to use rough and dirty methods." Tussing points to the same plot in the Mike Hammer stories by Mickey Spillane, suggests that the Popeye Syndrome appears not only in certain well-known domestic problems but in our foreign policy—for example—World War I up to the moment when we had to make the world safe for democracy and after which Wilson is quoted as having said, "America is the only moral nation on the earth"; the Spanish-American War, which could not begin until a pretext had been supplied, similarly the Mexican War, the Indian wars, the Civil War between the states—well, you take it from here. The theory goes on in a most interesting way to develop attitudes toward the Vietnam mess, campus struggles, black militancy, the hard hats.

Instead of destroying all the marijuana fields, shouldn't we go to work on all the spinach patches?

The origins and meanings of words account for a large subdivision of "trivia."

Not that it is of any importance but the word *trump* in bridge is derived from the word "triumph," which is the name of the Elizabethan card game from which bridge and whist have derived. In case anyone wants to look it up, an article in *The American Scholar* (1951) by Thomas Kyd proposes that Shakespeare's *Antony and Cleopatra* is a disguised card game just as *Through the Looking Glass* is a disguised chess game.

February 21 [1956]—The first known use of the word *neuroses,* according to Dr. [Henri] Ellenberger, who says it is a fact quoted everywhere, occurs in the following reference: CULLEN, WILLIAM: *Synopsis of Nosology: Embracing the Definitions in the Original Latin of the Genera and Species of Diseases with an English translation on the opposite page. To which are added, The Classification of Diseases, by* JOHN MASON GOOD, *and The Arrangement of Diseases of the Skin, by R. Willan, intended for the use of students and young practitioners.* London. Burgess & Hill, 1828. On one side of the page the text is in

OF SYCAMORE TREES AND SIX NO-TRUMP

Latin; the opposite page is in English. On page 48, four classes of illness are listed: febrile, nervous, cachectic and local. On the Latin side, "nervous diseases" is rendered as "neuroses." Under this in the English translation is the following description: "Character: Preternatural affection of sense and emotion without ideopathic or primary pyrexia, and also without local disease."

And in a Reading Note *in 1957:*

Does anyone know where the word *psychiatry* came from? In Heinroth's *Ehrbuch der Storungen des Seelenlebens* (Leipzig 1818), page 143, credit is given to a man named Weikard, "the much praised and much abused author of *The Philosophical Physician* (Frankfort, Hanau w. Leipz. [whatever that means] 1782)." Dr. Ellenberger tells me the word *psychiatry* was not in common use at the time Heinroth wrote his textbook, and occurs in no other contemporary or earlier text that he has been able to examine. From the form of Heinroth's expression, in which he amends Weikard's term "philosophical medicine" with a word that he considers more correct, psychiatry, one wonders if it was indeed Heinroth who introduced the word psychiatry into medical terminology. Dr. Ellenberger thinks that the word *psychiatry,* which they spell *psychiatrie,* was apparently coined on the model of the word *Chimiatrie,* which was widely used in the eighteenth century. He says that Heinroth and his contemporaries didn't use the word, but spoke of *Irrenheilkunde* and sometimes of *Pneumologie.* The French used the word *alieniste* for the psychiatrist until a relatively recent date. Dr. Ellenberger says he remembers how the famous De Clerambault declared, "I am not a psychiatrist, I am an *alieniste.*"

And in 1972 he had this to report of one of his daughters:

My daughter, Julia, is achieving considerable success and repute as a teacher and a teacher of teachers in California. The *California English Journal* for October, 1971, contains an article by her on "Galumphing" —a neologism made up of gallop, triumphant, and "ing." She describes how she got junior high school students very interested in the dictionary, the meaning of words, and their proper pronunciation by the use of a device such as the one made famous by Lewis Carroll, combining words or parts of words to make new words which suggest both of the parent words. First the students figured out what frumious, galumph, chortle, slithy, mimsy, frabjous, and beamish meant, and then they had an opportunity to form some new words themselves.

As a high school freshman Dr. Karl learned to play chess and played avidly all through high school and college. As a student in Boston, he played chess with his professor, Dr. Elmer Ernest Southard, the man who influenced him most in becoming a psychiatrist. "Southard said he lacked confidence in himself until he learned to play chess in Harvard College," recalls Dr. Karl. "He became a champion player and lost his shyness. In the hospital where I worked he would play chess with us at lunch, standing up."

Dr. Karl wrote a special article about chess for the issue of the Bulletin of the Menninger Clinic devoted to hobbies.

It was hard for me to decide which of my hobbies to write about. Most of my time outside of working hours goes into my horticultural experiments and collections, and some more of it into books and music. But it seems to be necessary for some of us to have a hobby in which aggressiveness and destructiveness are given opportunity for expression, and since I long ago gave up hunting (because it is too destructive) and golf (because I was so unskillful) I have found myself returning more and more to the most ancient and, in the opinion of many, the best of all games.

Ernest Southard, who inspired my enthusiasm for psychiatry, also inspired my interest in chess. Southard, as a college freshman, had been an unpopular, asocial individual who felt lonely and somewhat rejected because he was not taken into any of the clubs, had no athletic abilities, and was not outstanding in any of his classes. He did play a little chess, however, and when a call was issued for aspirants to the Harvard Chess team to play against Yale, he responded and, to his own great surprise, won a place on the team. It was not long before he was the champion of Harvard and then the champion of Massachusetts and of New England. These chess victories constituted a turning point in his life. He had discovered that he could really do something better than most other people could do it; this gave him confidence that he might also excel in something besides chess.

At 33 he was made a full professor (of psychiatry) at Harvard. During the next very busy ten years of his life when he would work long hours at his multiple duties as physician, teacher, director, author, poet, lecturer and advisor to the war department he would frequently stop after lunch for a game of chess with us (staff members of the Boston Psychopathic Hospital). On Saturday nights he would quite often brush aside all duties and responsibilities and go to the musty rooms of the old Boston Chess Club, taking one of us with him. "Come on," he would say. "We must go and wash our minds."

Many years have passed since then, and now I play sometimes with the Topeka Chess Club, which, while not Bostonian, has a flavor of its own. It meets, as a rule, in an unpretentious private home. Each man brings his board, pieces, books and chess journals. Tables are arranged in a row which may extend into the kitchen. The members are, almost without exception, men, although women are welcome and occasionally put in an appearance. Playing proceeds assiduously and silently. Refreshments are served about eleven o'clock and consist usually of a glass of root-beer or a plate of popcorn. The games are never suspended for these refreshments, unless by accident. One snowy-haired player, an author and historian, is celebrated for his inadvertent interruptions of the game at this point. In ordinary life he is the meekest, kindest, gentlest man imaginable; over the chess board he becomes fiercely rampant and belligerent. He moves with lightning speed, crashing his moved piece to the board with a clatter that occasionally jars all of the other pieces out of their places. In anyone else this would be very bad form, but in this beloved player it is expected and understood. Occasionally, the violent sweep of his gestures extends to the glass of root-beer and a painful delay ensues while the spilled fluid is mopped up. This accomplished, however, stillness reigns again in the room except for the clicking of the old gentleman's emphatically placed men of war.

I mention this as a testimony to the aggressions released in so apparently peaceful a game as chess. Whatever else it is, chess is not a relaxing game. Playing chess is a very intense and exciting experience which only one who has gotten well into it can fully appreciate. Some people find it exhausting, others obsessively absorbing. A colleague claims to have nearly failed in his second year at medical school because he and his roommate became so absorbed playing chess with one another. I confess that occasionally I have felt as if I were wasting some time at it; then I recall Southard's tremendously busy life and his philosophy of washing one's mind, and I go and play another game and enjoy it.

An urbane friend of mine who plays very skillfully was giving me some pointers one evening after having administered several defeats. Considering his own gentle temperament, I was very much surprised to hear him say, "Perhaps you are not mean enough; you know you have to have a mean streak in you to play this game successfully." What he meant was that one has to be ruthless and vigilant as one does in all competitive contests and the fact that chess appears to be such a pacific "old man's" game in the eyes of many belies this underlying fierceness.

There are many legends of the origin of chess. According to one story, it was invented by the Buddhists in India as a substitute for war because they felt that actual war and the necessary slaying of one's fellow-men, no matter for what purpose, was immoral. And a Burmese story has it that chess was invented by a Talaing Queen who was very fond of her Lord and hoped by this distraction to keep him out of war. According to another legend, the game was invented by the wife of Raven, King of Ceylon, in order to amuse him with an image of war while his metropolis was closely besieged. There are various Chinese stories of which this is typical: A certain General, who was a genius as well as a good soldier, was attempting to conquer Shensi province. Winter came on and his soldiers, "finding the weather much colder than what they had been accustomed to, and also being deprived of their wives and families, became clamorous to return home." To keep them amused and at the same time "inflame their military ardor" the General invented the game of chess with which the soldiers became so delighted that they not only passed the winter without further discontent but in the spring conquered the rich country of Shensi.

The psychology of chess has been studied by a number of psychiatrists and psychoanalysts, particularly Ernest Jones, Isador Coriat, Ben Karpman, Alfred Binet and, very recently, Joan Fleming and Samuel Strong.[1] Fleming and Strong emphasize the successive waves of emotion from tempered composure and prudence at the beginning of the game to sharp concentration on plotting, excitement on the detection of a weak spot, alarm and anxiety on the part of the threatened player, exultation of success in crushing the opponent, admiration and envy of the opponent's technique, and a wish for revenge in

---

[1] Jones, Ernest: The Problem of Paul Morphy. *Int. J. Psa.*, 12:1, 1931.

Coriat, Isador: The Unconscious Motives of Interest in Chess. *Psa. Rev.*, 28:30, 1941.

Karpman, Ben: The Psychology of Chess. *Psa. Rev.*, 24:54, 1937.

Binet, Alfred: *Psychologie des Grands Calculations et Jouers D'Echecs.* Paris, 1894.

Fleming, Joan, and Strong, Samuel M.: Observations on the Use of Chess in the Therapy of an Adolescent Boy.

a return game. These authors insist that the game is an intimately social game since it has a meaning shared by both players, requires each player to put himself in the other player's position, and affords a progressive interpenetration of minds.

Ernest Jones states that chess playing was a favorite recreation of some of the world's military leaders, including William the Conqueror and Napoleon. He points out that the motive actuating chess players is not only the conscious one of pugnacity (which characterizes all competitive games) but also "the grimmer one of father-murder," since the goal of the game is the capture (immobilization) of the King, a familiar symbolic father figure. But I believe Jones errs in equating capture and murder. There is a legend about the origin of the game which deals with this very point: There were two brothers, a good one and a bad one; the bad brother declared war on the good brother but was routed and as he was escaping on his white elephant, the good brother ordered that he be pursued and captured without a hair of his head being harmed. This was done; the bad brother was surrounded and sat still on his white elephant; his captors went to assist him to dismount, only to find him dead from heart failure or shame or some other obscure cause, but not through any aggressive act of the victorious brother and his warriors. This incident is said to have suggested the game and certainly it expresses its refined sadism, by which the King alone of all the pieces is immune to capture or loss, and the whole object of his antagonist is to force him into helpless immobility. The aggressor has defeated him but has scrupulously refrained from injuring him.

Perhaps this subtle difference in the type of aggression has something to do with its attraction for its devotees. The chess player entraps his adversary rather than bludgeoning him. All authorities agree that chess is a miniature war in which the aggressive patterns characteristic of different personalities are clearly discernible in the nature or style of play adopted. As every chess player knows, there are the strong attackers, the strong defenders, the provocative players, the cautious players, the attack-from-behind players, the so-called classical and romantic styles of play, etc. Some individuals are particularly skillful in the use of the Queen, an individually powerful piece; others are especially fond of the Pawns (the underdogs); others like the Bishops (oblique attack); others the Knights (ingeniously indirect), etc. A recent book on chess is organized about the theme that each of the famous chess players of history had a certain psychology in his style which is examined and demonstrated by excerpts from recorded games.

Although it has been played for perhaps as long as five thousand years, and although it has a literature greater than that of any other game, chess cannot be said to be a popular form of recreation. I have wondered why this is so: the game is not difficult to learn, much less so, for example, than bridge; it is very inexpensive (in contrast to poker, golf and backgammon); it requires less time than many games and it is not, as many people think, a slow, dull game. The pictures of two individuals sitting peacefully regarding a piece-studded board before them are exceedingly misleading. Silently they are plotting (and attempting to execute) murderous campaigns of patricide, matricide, fratricide, regicide, and mayhem. Certainly one and maybe both are terribly worried—about something of absolutely no importance. Presently they will both feel better. They will have washed their minds.

He occasionally writes of chess in Reading Notes.

In a chess game the player of the white pieces moves first. There are 20 different possible first moves; he may take his choice. Correspondingly, there are 20 different replies to this first move possible to the opponent on his first move of the black pieces. For his second move, white has 25 or more possibilities; black has an equal number. For the third move, there are at least 30 possibilities for each. This means that after the third move, there are $20 \times 20 \times 25 \times 25 \times 30 \times 30$ or over 200,000,000 possible different arrangements of the 32 chessmen on the 64 black and white squares. The average chess game runs to 30 or more moves!

Obviously, the theoretical complexities are beyond our comprehension. Yet chess is playable by an intelligent child. How so? Through trial and error and through rational processes, chess players have discovered patterns and favorable probabilities. No good chess player uses a third of the twenty possible first moves, and to all of them there are certain well-known "advisable" replies. Yet no two chess games are alike. If we concentrated our attention upon the differences, we should have to attempt to comprehend infinity; if we concentrate upon the similarities, we can go only a little way.

There is always this problem of whether to look at differences or at similarities. When we say that a horse is a horse and not a cow or a turtle, we have already made a classification. But no two horses are alike, not even two horses of the same variety and breed. We can concentrate upon a particular pet pony or upon racehorses or upon quadrupeds or upon mammalia or upon movable objects. But we can never concentrate too long on either the similarities or the differences, or we become lost. Our attention must go back and forth from the general to the particular, from the class to the species, to keep us oriented.

Dr. Reuben Fine, the clinical psychologist [of New York City], is the same Reuben Fine whom all chess players know from his fine, classic analyses of the game of chess. He is a relative, as some may remember, of our colleagues and former associates here, Henry and Milton Wexler, and may have been inspired by them to enter his present career. In *Acta Psychologica* (1965) he presents a subjective (he calls it introspective) account of blindfold chess playing. He himself played only private games during his visit here—not blindfolded. Georges Kaltanowski, who is famous for his blindfold playing, stayed with us several days and permitted Dr. David Rapaport [a world-famous psychologist] to make many psychological tests on him to see if we could learn how it is done. We didn't. Dr. Fine carries the investigation forward in a most interesting way, but he concedes that it needs more study.

(Just for the annals of history, I want to record that through some accident of fate or skillfully masked courtesy on the part of [Georges] Kaltanowski, I managed to tie one game with him here while he was playing a score of others, blindfolded!)

An inveterate bridge player, Dr. Karl often enjoys a Saturday after-noon game with former governor Alfred Landon, editor-publisher Oscar Stauffer, and other friends in Topeka. The following note to a friend and professional bridge player, Arthur Glatt of Lincoln-wood, Illinois, written September 9, 1967, shows that Dr. Karl is an optimistic bidder as well as an excellent player. By hand, on the typed letter, he added, "If my opponent hadn't led the ace of spades, I would have gone down."

My partner and I made six hearts on the following hand with three aces out against us.

            Clubs   K x
            Diamonds   Q 10 9

OF SYCAMORE TREES AND SIX NO-TRUMP

Spades   K Q 8 4 3
Hearts   A 8 3

Clubs   Q
Diamonds   K x x x
Hearts   K Q J 10 9 7 6 5

The left-hand opponent led the ace of spades. (Thanks!) I discarded the queen of clubs. This alarmed him and he led the ace of clubs which, of course, I trumped. I threw off the diamonds in my hand on the king of clubs and high spades from the dummy. (The spades were divided 4 : 4.)

Since Dr. Karl often plays in partnership with his wife, Jean, he is interested in the way other husband-wife teams have made out. He says:

I read somewhere recently that playing tennis with your wife is very dangerous psychologically to the welfare of the marriage. For a man to be beaten by a woman in a physical contest is demoralizing in a peculiar way—like mama spanking you or at least giving you a shake. Psychological losses are not as traumatic, such as being beaten at bridge. But some men take these losses very hard nonetheless.

In one or two of my books, I have referred to the famous Kansas City case of the woman who shot and killed her husband at the bridge table because he played the hand poorly and went down. Many wives and husbands don't shoot each other dead as the result of misplays, but they bawl each other out, call each other "stupid," and humiliate each other in many ways. I've sat through some painful sessions of this kind. Everyone knows at least one couple who shouldn't play together, where the poor, patient husband or wife takes a verbal whipping after every hand.

Mr. Culbertson, on the other hand, as the following [*Reading Note*] shows, was always kind to his wife at the bridge table.

One of my Christmas presents was pretty well described by its title, *The Bridge Player's Bedside Companion*, edited by Albert Ostrow and illustrated with some microscopic cartoons by H. T. Webster. It was given to me by Marty Mayman, who was most discriminating in so doing, for I should probably never have bought it and I should have missed a most delightful book, full of interesting hands, stories, materials, and just all kinds of things.

But from the standpoint of a psychiatrist, and I presume I must always come back to that whether I want to or not, I most enjoyed the history of the extraordinary organization and selling of the game of bridge to the United States public by Ely Culbertson and the way in which he exploited his own very considerable skill and his wife's cooperation in hurling out challenges and successfully defending them.

Among other things I was struck by his record for *always* speaking sweetly and kindly and gently to his wife, even when she misplayed, which was not very often. Some thought she was a better player than he, and he shrewdly declined to deny this; to have denied it would have been unnewsworthy; not to do so furthered the rumor and added more publicity value to their matches. The author of the article about him is quite sure, however, that he did not believe she was. The details of various of his contests are given, including some of the hands on which various great experts made boners. In one contest Sidney Lenz got so angry at Jacoby's "psychic bids" and bawled him out about them so, that Jacoby resigned from the contest.

Puzzles and games are close intellectual allies to another of Dr. Karl's favorite pastimes: reading and reviewing mystery stories.

Dr. [Lewis] Robbins lent me *The Moonstone,* which is almost the granddaddy of all mystery stories, in a way, although written by Wilkie Collins after Poe's *The Murders in the Rue Morgue.* . . . For those who don't want to plow through nearly 500 pages of interesting but, to our present tastes, pedestrian sleuthing, the upshot of it all is that the villain who committed the crime didn't know that he had committed it, but once this becomes an inescapable conclusion, he sets out to ascertain how he could have done it, and becomes also the hero. Very psychiatric without saying so.

Strike for a Kingdom (1950) by Menna Gallie is a mystery story laid in a Welsh mining village. As a mystery it is a little weak; as a picture of dreary Welsh life, it is impressive. I carry in my memory one paragraph where Gwen who was sitting by a dying villager "began to sing in a harsh, cracked whisper a little Welsh folk poem:

"My heart moves as heavy as the horse that climbs the hill,
And I can't for my dear life pretend to be happy.

OF SYCAMORE TREES AND SIX NO-TRUMP

You know nothing of the place on which my shoe is pinching.
And many, many troubled thoughts are quite breaking my heart."

Arthur Upfield, the Australian who has turned out sixteen mystery stories, has now written one, *Death of a Lake,* in which the murder is of minimal importance. The whole story is written about the gradual evaporation, in continuous heat and drought, of a large lake in western Australia. Everyone knows it is soon going to be a dry hole, and the increasing human anxiety plus the concentration of wildlife of all kinds makes it very, very eerie. It gives one a horrific impression of Australia. Even our local heat was coolness after reading this.

One psychological detail: The author never mentions *smell.* Can you imagine what the complete progressive evaporation of a five-mile lake would mean in the way of dead fish, turtles, and so forth? He describes vividly the death of literally millions of birds and rabbits and fish but, as I say, never one word about the smell!

Another—profounder—passion of Dr. Karl's is music. His love of music goes back to boyhood. He explains:

We always got up at 5:30 A.M. and we boys practiced from 6 to 7. I practiced the piano, my brother Edwin the violin, and my brother Will, the cello. Father played the flute, only he didn't often practice.

We had a family orchestra. We held forth, usually with a great deal of quarreling. We'd quarrel over triviality—Edwin turning a page too soon or one of us playing a phrase that sounded wrong. Mother was our pianist and peacemaker.

Dr. Karl studied piano for seven years and violin "for a little while." One of his psychoanalysts, he said, told him he should have been a musician. Talking of opera, he said recently:

Lucia has always been one of my favorite operas. In medical school, I used to get a group of the boys around me, play the main themes, and tell the story in between. I always thought it so ridiculous, however, that the theme, "What Restrains Me at Such a Moment?" should have been set to such a sweet, resigned melody. The melody at that point doesn't say "What keeps me from stabbing these devils?" It says, "Well, it's a pity, all this how-to-do. How did it all come about?" Or "The jig is up." Or something else rather serious but resigned. Once the sextet gets going, there's a little more agitation and the boys grab their swords, half unsheathe them, and step forward in a very phallic manner, which always makes me laugh (at the opera), because it's so obvious that nobody's going to stab anybody or penetrate anybody or do anything but pose. But decked out in a lot of bright colors and fluffy finery, the fantasy rolls merrily along. Up to the mad scene.

Then, if any scene is not "mad," this is it. Lucia warbles sweetly, in several registers, to prove she's better than the flute and can last longer. It's sweet, it's cute, it's pretty. I love it. But what's it got to do with madness? And why should she have gone mad anyway? She got rid of an impossible husband rather roughly (stabbing him on their wedding night). But what's a little homicide in a tragedy like this?

The real tragedy is that nobody gets what they really want. Those that didn't do homicide tried suicide a little later. "Life's impossible—get me death in some form," they say. All this to the most tinkly, harmonious, melodious music. As if the composer says, "These are dreadful fantasies you're having, it's a dreadful life you have to live, but let's put a good face on it and make it colorful and melodic."

I look down from that plush box at those thousands of rapt listeners—and reflect, "What are they coming here for? What delights them? The color? The pretty sounds? The acting? Is it the flash of romance and love and the illusory ain't-life-beautiful feeling? Or the death and disappointment and the ain't-life-awful feeling? My, but real life is so much better."

My favorite melody in *Lucia* is that last sentimental ditty. And I am cross with myself even now for being flippant about it. But here's this pretty girl tripping around almost gaily in a bridal nightgown in front of an audience and pleading so sweetly for us to "Leave But One Tear of Sorrow On My Untimely Grave."

Well, this is a modest enough request, made in all sincerity, but in an acutely sentimental daze. Nobody on the stage is weeping or seems likely to weep, nobody in the audience is weeping or seems likely to weep. There are no tears shed, in spite of her plea, because (a) she hasn't died yet, (b) it's late enough in the evening so nobody thinks her death untimely, (c) there's no grave in sight, and (d) it isn't clear why she's predicting her own death or what she dies of. And that lovely little tune, that sweet, lyrical, if somewhat simplistic, theme, keeps running through your mind even the next day, and one thinks, "Poor thing, up there in the Scottish highlands, there are not many men around so she can have any hopes of a better deal on her next lover."

OF SYCAMORE TREES AND SIX NO-TRUMP

If I'm so dissatisfied with Donizetti as a funeral music-man, what kind of music would I have written for a poor girl who didn't know which way to go or how to get there? I would have written frantic music that just tears your heart.

Chopin was different. His death melodies didn't often get off the ground; when they did, they crashed into beautiful chords. But Beethoven was just so naturally optimistic that when he started out to write a sad theme, it sometimes escaped from him and became joyous. Take the "Appassionata." He no sooner gets one pessimistic phrase out than he decides there is some hope. And up and on we go, gloriously. By golly, there's more than hope in Beethoven—there's achievement. What starts out to be a dirge winds up being great thoughts, the birth of a new idea. Somebody disputes him then in the counterpoint. But he argues right back. He wins the point. And we go on to the next variation. Not one of Beethoven's symphonies gets very graveyardy except the third and even that is never very convincing. There was never a time when Beethoven gave up hope—in his music. And if anybody ever had good reason for losing hope it was he. And if he didn't, why should we—any of us?

CHAPTER THREE

Psychiatry in America

Dr. Karl traced the history of psychiatry in America—and of his own pioneer role—in a speech at the Freud Centenary Celebration of the American Psychoanalytic Association in Chicago on April 28, 1956. The speech, entitled "Freud and American Psychiatry," was published in the Journal of the American Psychoanalytic Association, *October, 1956. In going over it for this book, he edited slightly his reference to the patient he calls his "critical point," a patient he compares to Freud's Dora. Dr. Karl's treatment was successful. "She completely got over her sleepwalking and her other symptoms and sent me several other patients," he recalls.*

Dr. Karl was one of three speakers at the plenary session of the Freud celebration. The other two were Dr. Ernest Jones, a biographer of Freud, and Robert Wälder, an internationally famous psychoanalyst. Of the invitation to speak at this session, Dr. Karl says, "Although I was president for two terms, participation in this memorial was one of the greatest honors paid to me by official psychoanalysis."

When I was invited to join with Dr. Wälder in flanking the address of our distinguished visitor, I sought the counsel of friends regarding the most appropriate material for the occasion. It was their advice that inasmuch as I had been selected to speak for my American colleagues, I attempt to trace some of the peculiarly American de-

velopments of the work of Sigmund Freud whose centenary we celebrate. So I shall offer some reminiscences and observations, making
no apology for the personal flavor that is bound to color such a report. To an audience of psychoanalysts I dare not stress either my
humility or my pride.

I shall skip lightly over those troubled days of our association's
adolescence and concentrate rather—in good psychoanalytic style—
on our childhood and on our marriage. I shall emulate the anonymous author of the Second Book of Maccabees, who wistfully recorded
that ". . . having in view the . . . difficulty which awaiteth them
that would enter into the narratives of the history, by reason of the
abundance of the matter, we . . . have taken upon us the painful
labor of the abridgment [finding] the task . . . not easy, but a matter
of sweat and watching. . . . Yet, for the sake of the gratitude of the
many we [resolved to] gladly endure the painful labor, leaving to the
historian the exact handling of every particular, [endeavoring] . . . to
avoid a labored fullness in the treatment. . . . Here then let us begin . . . for it is a foolish thing to make a long prologue to a history
and to abridge the history itself."

Some of my colleagues will recall that I was in that little group
of worshipful disciples who sat at the feet of Ernest Southard. His
death in 1920 left us highly charged with the exciting notion that the
human mind could be an object of scientific study. This, to be sure,
had been given to psychologists by William James, Josiah Royce, and
others, but to the medical men it had not as yet been given at all.
There was no mention of the human mind or any of its functions in
the medical textbooks of the period in which I went to medical school.
Patients had no minds. Neither did employees, nor yet criminals, nor
indeed anyone except psychology students and their experimental
subjects.

It was this anti-psychologism which Ernest Southard, pathologist
though he was, most vigorously combated. Psychological phenomena
were exciting and intriguing data, and data as considerable and significant as cellular data and tissue data. He was fond of emphasizing
the principle of *bonum ex nocentibus*—good arising from evil, the
sweet uses of adversity. "From the study of the mentally ill," he used
to say, "we shall learn about mental health; from the study of the
mentally retarded we may learn something about the learning process."
In the midst of a veritable shower of new ideas, new projects, new
contacts, and new honors, Southard died suddenly at the age of forty-
three.

This was psychiatry at its best in the area where, a few years previously, Freud had brought psychoanalysis to America. Southard's disciples were shattered, and scattered, by his death. But they continued his ideas. Harry Solomon went sturdily on with the neurosyphilis researches, Lawson Lowrey developed the outpatient multidiscipline idea in the form of the child-guidance clinic, Mary Jarrett and Marion Kenworthy developed psychiatric social work, Myrtelle Cavanan continued neuropathological research, Alvin Mathers turned to medical education (in Canada), Frankwood Williams became medical director of the National Committee for Mental Hygiene. I came west to Topeka to join my father, who had known and admired Southard, and—later—my brother Will. Working together, we tried to put into effect the things Southard had taught us.

There were, of course, other foci of psychiatry than Boston in America, and my father insisted that I travel about the country a month each year to visit them. So in 1920 or 1921 I met Adolf Meyer, Smith Ely Jelliffe, Adolf Stern, A. A. Brill, Philip Lehrman, C. P. Oberndorf, and many others. I recall that Meyer received me while he ate his lunch—a sandwich and a glass of milk. When the lunch was over, so was the interview. Years later I came to know Dr. Meyer better and to realize how much he gave to American psychiatry. But it was difficult for him to communicate his thinking or his real friendliness. Consequently, his disciples were fewer than his wisdom deserved.

Jelliffe, on the other hand, was extremely articulate and gave me a royal welcome. He and his wife invited me to dinner and took me with them to the theater and a nightclub (quite an experience for a Kansas boy in 1920). They insisted on my canceling my hotel reservation and staying with them. Jelliffe talked to me incessantly about Freud and Jung and psychoanalysis and complexes and libido, always as if they were most respectable and timely topics; this was most astonishing to me. It had not been so in Boston. It was not so in Baltimore. But ah, New York!

This most erudite of American psychiatrists, definitely one of our psychoanalytic patriarchs and the father of American psychosomatic medicine, thus became my second psychiatric guide, and my first psychoanalytic mentor. Together with Brill, Lehrman, Stern, Taneyhill, Kardiner, and others, we attended a meeting of the American Psychoanalytic Association in Boston to hear Horace Frink, just back from Vienna, recount behind closed doors his personal experiences in analysis with Freud. All of us—including Freud—looked for

52

great things from Frink, whose book *Morbid Fears and Compulsions* was, and still is, one of the clearest and best-written expositions of psychodynamics. His subsequent decline was one of the early tragedies of American psychoanalytic development.

I never learned who Jelliffe's analyst was. Oberndorf recorded that he and Jelliffe had some hours with Paul Federn in May, 1914, just before the war broke out, and I believe he had some more analysis in Europe. I myself had a few hours with Jelliffe and, subsequently, with Albert Polon, one of the early American workers and one who, like Southard, died in his youth.

In between these rather frequent excursions to Boston, Baltimore, Washington, and New York, I was in Kansas, and quite busy for a young doctor. We were all neurologists *or* neuropsychiatrists in those days, and I was the only "neuropsychiatrist" in a very wide area. Neurosyphilis was one of our most common diagnostic problems, and those of us who could detect it and knew something about the new "wonder drug" arsphenamine had something useful to offer the general practitioner. Untreated syphilis was then very common, and hence acquired and congenital neurosyphilis were quite abundant. (Freud once remarked how many of his neurotic patients came from syphilitic fathers.[1])

Psychotherapy was almost unknown. In Philadelphia the Weir-Mitchell complete-rest-and-force-feeding treatment was still in use for the neuroses and mild depressions. A few colleagues used hypnosis or Dubois' re-education technique or various placebo procedures such as faradic or Geissler tube stimulation. The state hospitals were in a most pessimistic mood of therapeutic nihilism; no one was assumed to recover from mental illness of any kind except by accident or the grace of God. But pinpoint diagnosis, with the brilliant example of the prosperous and rather contemptuous neurologists before us, was earnestly striven for.

Each spring the meetings of the American Psychiatric (and each winter those of the Orthopsychiatric) brought me east again. More and more we heard from the obstreperous and preposterous Freudians. Fancy a sober scientific assemblage where the program was about "Hallucinations in Disseminated Sclerosis," "Alzheimer's Disease in a Woman of 30," "The Effect of Influenza upon Dementia Praecox," and fancy the impact of having "Pop" Brill pop up with some psychoanalytic interpretations! What was the world coming to when

[1] Sigmund Freud (1905): Fragment of an Analysis of a Case of Hysteria, in *Collected Papers*. London, Hogarth Press, 1925, Vol. 1. See footnote pp. 28–29.

these New Yorkers could come to a dignified meeting and begin talking about sex—and *such* sex! (Remember, there was no sex in medicine at that time. Look for yourself. Look in Osler, look in Cecil, look in Oppenheim. You will find nothing. Sex didn't exist.)

This is a situation the flavor of which is very difficult to recapture without producing a caricature. Please believe that we were not complete fools, nor as prudish as this may sound. But everything *looked* different. James Harvey Robinson's *Mind in the Making* was literally *thrilling* to us; we were all reading it. And these psychoanalytic concepts—even the basic ones of an unconscious (we said subconscious) part of the mind, of symbolic values, of sexual development—all of these were controversial topics.

Gradually, of course, they began to sound a *little* less shocking, absurd, and unreasonable—especially to the younger men—and then the early ridicule gave way to scorn and angry moral denunciation. No doctor with academic or social aspirations could afford to be associated with psychoanalysis. This, of course, made it all the more attractive to some alert and independent and, we must add, rebellious souls who were involved in a contemporaneous wave of intellectual enlightenment which came with—not necessarily from—psychoanalysis. An element of martyrdom, which was more theoretical than actual, furthered the spirit of adventure.

William Alanson White, the lifelong friend of Jelliffe, and an eloquent leader of American psychiatrists, maintained an urbane optimism regarding the growth and integration of all things psychiatric—the psychiatry of Kraepelin, the psychiatry of Southard, the psychiatry of Adolf Meyer, the psychiatry of Jung, and even the psychiatry of Freud, Jelliffe, and Brill. His diplomacy and political leadership had much to do with the realization of this amalgamation. He was friendly with them all—the conservative hospital superintendents, the dignified neurologists, the effervescent and often provocative psychoanalysts, and the youngsters like myself who didn't know *what* we were. It was he who engineered the affiliation of the American Psychoanalytic and the American Psychiatric Associations and, with Brill, fathered the psychoanalytic section in the latter organization; it was he who proposed Sigmund Freud for the Nobel prize.

I can recall how exciting it all was. There were fireworks at every meeting. No one could answer Jelliffe; he bowled them all over with his greater knowledge, greater vocabulary, greater memory; but they couldn't always understand him. Brill could be understood, however, and answered—but not silenced. Sometimes he left himself wide open to counterattack, but never to refutation. The opponents of psycho-analysis sometimes managed to make some of the new theories look pretty ridiculous. Some remarks of White's made in 1914 are rather refreshing to read even after the passage of all these years:

> The thing that psychoanalysis did for psychiatry was to open a door to the understanding of the patient which strangely had always heretofore been closed; and one reason that it had always been closed was that the physician had never paid very much, if any, attention to what the patient said, putting his remarks down as of no significance because they were crazy or incoherent. Much less did the physician in the old days ever have the slightest idea that these crazy, incoherent remarks might by any chance have a meaning. Psychoanalysis oriented the physician toward his patient in an entirely different way . . .

> "Dr. B—— has presented certain cases, certain clinical records and dismissed the subject by saying the whole thing was absurd; he did not bring forth any specific argument. A society of this sort should be the proper arena where such things should be threshed out on scientific merits; prejudices should not enter into the question at all. I am a psychoanalyst; I want the truth and I am willing to welcome any light that may be thrown upon the situation . . . I have no doubt that many hypotheses will be laughed at in years to come as being in fault, perhaps some of them ridiculous, but what we want is their correction at this point; we want more light; we want more truth; it does not do any good to call them absurd and let the matter go at that . . . those facts must receive some interpretation; if our interpretation is wrong, there is a right interpretation, and I ask the people who criticize the move-ment to come forward and tell us what all these things mean. We offer our explanation; we are willing to withdraw if we are wrong.
> "I trust this society will maintain an open attitude toward this subject." [2]

I can remember my conversion—the moment in which the forces of repression yielded to the mounting pressure of what we call reason and insight. My critical-point case—my Dora [one of Freud's first pa-tients]—was an intelligent, good-looking woman. She was also a per-

[2] William A. White: *Forty Years of Psychiatry*. N.Y. Nervous and Mental Disease Publ. Co., 1933 (double quotations from Discussion of "A Criticism of Psycho-analysis" by Dr. Charles W. Burr. Proceedings Amer. Medico-Psychological Assn., Vol. 21, 1914, p. 322).

sistent sleepwalker. I made a careful examination of her and came to the conclusion that the diagnosis was either (1) epileptic equivalent or (2) hysteria major.

I imparted to her this great piece of wisdom. But she said she didn't care what the diagnosis was; she wanted treatment. She said it was very embarrassing to wake up prowling around in her parents' bedroom, looking for something—she didn't quite know what—that her father kept hidden and which really should be hers and would change her completely if she could acquire it. This reminded me at once of some "nonsense" I had read recently in psychoanalytic journals (particularly an article by Karl Abraham in the new *International Journal of Psychoanalysis*. It was on penis envy in women—an astonishing, even repellent notion, but logically presented, and calmly. But it was, of course, obviously absurd). I wrote Jelliffe about my patient. I told him I had no couch, but that we did have a chaise lounge. He wrote back for me to use anything, just get her to talk and "you listen!" This wasn't at all difficult, and I listened to her for two hours at a time once a week. Soon I had heard enough to make me go out and buy all the books on psychoanalysis that I could find. (As I look back on my notes of this and some of the other "wild analysis" I did in those days, I wonder if I do as well now.)

All over the country physicians like myself were wondering where to obtain systematic training in this new method and whether it was true, as rumored, that a personal analysis was a prerequisite. We did not know then how the New York Psychoanalytic Society had been almost torn asunder over this very question in what Oberndorf describes as "one crisis after another for five years." A few of us could afford to go to Berlin or to Vienna; a few were victimized by the three-month analysis promised by Otto Rank. Formal training was begun in New York in 1929, and in 1930 Franz Alexander came to Chicago and offered didactic analysis to a group of us who subsequently (1932) assisted him with Lionel Blitzsten and Ralph Hamill and Tom French in organizing the second American Psychoanalytic Institute.

From here on it is unnecessary for me to recount to this audience how systematic psychoanalytic training developed throughout the country, *universitate nullo modo adjuvante* (without benefit of or help from the medical schools or universities). Gradually psychoanalytic concepts began to prevail more and more. In 1930, in the first edition of *The Human Mind*, which I wrote for the profession but which seemed to appeal even more to laymen, I said that "practically no intelligent and informed scientist today disputes the main thesis and findings of psychoanalysis." My whole book implied that psychoanalysis was even then the essence of American psychiatry. I was violently attacked for this by one of my old friends and colleagues, who sent out a questionnaire to members of the American Psychiatric Association to prove that most psychiatrists did *not* accept psychoanalysis. Nevertheless, today American psychiatry is one based on a psychoanalytic theory of personality. The old Kraepelinean terms have largely disappeared. The Meyerian *terms* were never widely used, but the Meyerian *ideas,* translated by W. A. White, "dovetailed into those of Freud, the one for diagnosis, the other for treatment, and both for a new personality theory. The pseudo-conflict was thus resolved. Historic vestiges remain; some psychiatrists emphasize adaptation, and some adjustment, and some relationships, and some repression. Some speak of the 'total personality' and some of the 'character structure.' But regardless of how they *speak,* most psychiatrists now *think* in terms which express the combined ideology of Freud, Southard, and Meyer!" [3]

In European countries one often hears reference to "depth psychology," and there is an emphasis upon the science of the unconscious, of symbolism, of symptomatic acts, and so on. *Here* the emphasis is more upon ego psychology, "defenses," relationships, and reactions. Instead of depth psychology we speak of dynamic psychiatry, an expression rarely heard, I believe, in Europe. This is related, I think, to an important influence of psychoanalysis upon American psychiatry which may seem at first paradoxical. For in spite of the chauvinistic, doctrinaire attitude of "psychoanalysis-is-the-only-worthwhile-treatment" assumed by a few very zealous leaders and very recent institute graduates, one effect of psychoanalysis has been to renew hope and interest in all psychiatric therapy. The very "success" of psychoanalysis as well as its "failures" has inspired this. Shock therapy, drug therapy, and surgical therapy have likewise had their successes and failures, and all this has served as a stimulus to the more careful selection of cases for each of these therapies.

Moreover, there has been a greatly extended use of the various adjunctive therapies in psychiatry in most American hospitals. Much is made of the concept of "milieu therapy"—the beneficial effects of a proper hospital atmosphere, routine, and personnel structure. Psycho-

[3] Karl Menninger: Contribution of Psychoanalysis to American Psychiatry, *Bull. of the Menninger Clinic,* 18:87–90, 1954.

therapy of other types than psychoanalysis has been greatly broadened, and the use of group psychotherapy, as so beautifully developed in England, is another growing field. All these have developed from the impact of the optimism, the rationalism, and the new concepts which psychoanalysis gave us.

Psychoanalysis has changed (American) psychiatry from a diagnostic to a therapeutic science, not because so many patients are cured by psychoanalytic technique but because of the new understanding of psychiatric patients it has given us, and the new and different concept of illness and health. Old names die slowly, but the essential namelessness of mental illness became palpable to us in the light of Freud's great discoveries. We know now that in the unconscious we are all mad, all capable of a madness which threatens constantly to emerge—sometimes does emerge, only to be tucked away again out of sight, if possible. To understand this in one's self and to improve one's methods of controlling one's own madness are essential to understanding it in others whom we essay to help.

Thus the prerequisite of a personal analysis, which so disturbed our psychoanalytic beginnings, has turned out to be the keystone of the psychoanalytic movement. More and more clearly we recognize that Freud's greatest achievement was his courageous self-examination, his unparalleled self-psychoanalysis. More than anyone who ever lived, he followed those great historic adjurations, "Know thyself" and "Physician, heal thyself." Because of what Freud discovered, no psychiatrist today can ever again be quite so much at the mercy of his own unconscious as in the days before Freud undertook this historic task and unveiled his revolutionary findings about the human personality for us all to see and to test and to work from. All of the enormous influence that psychoanalysis has had upon America, upon our sociology, our anthropology, upon psychology, upon literature, upon art, and, above all, upon medicine—all of this stems from the new conception of the nature of man to which Freud introduced us.

The question remains as to why the American soil was so fertile in its reception of Freudian discoveries and hypotheses, contrary even to *his* expectations. We may not and would not forget, of course, that Americans are not only the sons of New Yorkers and Virginians, but of Englishmen and Dutchmen and Scots and Africans and Germans. We should not forget, also, that America has been the beneficiary of Europe's tragedies. To our shores there have come many teachers from the Old World who are now to be accounted Americans.

They brought to us learning and wisdom; their idealism and scholarliness framed our psychoanalytic institute programs. In a hundred years of development, the medical schools and universities had not evolved a single systematic course of training in psychiatry until after the psychoanalytic institutes had shown the way, and it was upon the pattern of psychoanalytic training that courses of instruction for psychiatric residents were developed. For such fortuitous traits of open-mindedness, practicality, romance, adventure, optimism, ingenuity, or whatever it may have been (and others may judge this better than we) which permitted us to make such use as we have of Freud's great gifts transmitted to us by these men, we may also be humbly grateful. For it was out of fire and ashes, out of self-destructive rage and sorrow and heartbreak, that our powers of helping our stricken fellow man have been thus extended.

Thus, again, *bonum ex nocentibus.*

Members of this audience will know how strongly I am convinced of the usefulness, the operational "truth" of the Empedoclean-Zoroastrian-Freudian dualism, and how I believe that, in a sense greater than he himself realized, Freud interpreted the microcosm of the personality in terms similarly applicable to the macrocosm of the universe. Freud aspired to keep his data and his formulations as free as possible from unsupported hypotheses and uncontaminated by mystical belief. Yet he must have realized that even the belief that we can or should or do help a fellow creature is unprovable, and represents an act of faith. In this his native optimism overtook the philosophical detachment toward which he consciously aspired. In all his ruminations about the multiple functions ascribed to that internal governor of our lives, the ego, he must have reflected upon the enormous dependence he was placing upon what he called the intellect. Freud was no gnostic, and, for him, reason and intelligence included that mother-wit whereby the ego exhibits the very stuff of life in so manipulating its controls to make the best of every bad bargain and by reconciling conflicting demands at a minimal sacrifice, averts the disintegration of the organism. It is this economic aspect of psychoanalytic personology which most interests me today because from it, I believe, can be derived not only new concepts of the human situation and of those disabilities which we call illness and pain and misbehavior and crime, but new blueprints for the effecting of *social* change as well as *individual* betterment.

Southard was an optimist; he saw great possibilities in a better understanding of motives and thoughts and feelings and behavior.

He believed Freud to be a pessimist, who found too much that was dark and unlovely in the depths of the human heart. About this I think my first teacher was mistaken. Freud was a great optimist. He struggled to control too great an expectation from man or life; he strove to be as honest as it is possible to be. But had he lacked faith and hope he could not have gone on; he could not have borne his great sufferings or withstood the impact of his great discoveries.

It is a reflection of Freud's basic faith and optimism, as much as of his courage, that he could face the destructive essence of human personality and assign it a basic role in our existence. Perhaps it was the bravest thing he ever did. And, even in his discouragement over the outlook for civilization, he did not fail to add at the end of his essay about it that "Now it may be expected that the other of the two heavenly forces, eternal Eros, will put forth his strength so as to maintain himself along side of his equally immortal adversary."

It was his optimism that Freud bequeathed to America; and it was the optimism of our youthfulness, our freedom from the sterner, sadder tradition of Europe, which enabled us to seize his gift. It appealed to the idealism of American doctors; it was a new way of helping people and building a better world. Freud was optimistic about human beings being able to *help themselves*. His was an optimism which flowed into action and discovery, and this, too, struck a responsive chord in a pioneer country where we feel that there is nothing which we cannot accomplish if we but put our minds to it. It mobilized the forces of Eros and Agape in the lives of professional workers, and gave them a rationale and a program. It conceded the inevitability of death, not by ignoring it, but by identifying it in all its penultimate manifestations and declaring war against it. For it identified love with life, and death with hate. The clinical axiom "You can live if you can love" came, thus, not only from the New Testament but from the new psychology, and not only from religion but from medical science.

It is for this that American psychiatry thanks Sigmund Freud on his one hundredth birthday, him and all those who, like Ernest Jones, brought it to us from him.

Dr. Karl conceived and spearheaded the development of the Menninger School of Psychiatry, which began with the enlarged residency training program at the (then) Winter VA Hospital, later affiliated with the Topeka State Hospital, the Menninger Children's Hospital, the C. F. Menninger Memorial Hospital, and others. It became the na-

tion's largest formal school of psychiatric training. More than one thousand alumni are practicing in the United States and foreign countries. The philosophy of the school—as formulated by its chief founder— was summarized in the initial catalog in this way:

The residency training of today goes far beyond the apprenticeship system of the 1920's which, for all its advantages in the way of personal contact and counsel, would be totally inadequate for the needs of present-day physicians. The field has expanded greatly; the subspecialties are numerous; the theory, as well as the practice, has become much more complex. To insure adequate preparation of the physician seeking to become a psychiatrist, the educational methods and scope of training must reflect this expansion and maturation.

The *practical* goal of training may be stated simply: it is to convert a physician who has had general medical training into a qualified specialist in that field of medicine which is related to the diagnosis, treatment, and prevention of mental illness. By official standards, this means three years of supervised practice and clinical instruction as a hospital "resident" plus at least two years of "experience," and then the successful demonstration of the candidate's proficiency before examiners of the American Board of Psychiatry and Neurology.

These, however, are but the mechanical steps in a process. What are the *theoretical* goals of the process of psychiatric education? What characterizes a well-trained psychiatrist? How is this training best provided?

Any comprehensive answer to these questions would have to begin with formulations regarding character, integrity, intelligence, sensitivity to human suffering, and numerous other such attributes necessary to psychiatrists, attributes which antedate and transcend all medical training. The psychiatrist must be, in the platonic sense, a *good* man. By definition, he is also a scientist, committed to open-minded but critical search for empirical truth. Further, he is, *a priori,* a physician dedicated to the care and treatment of sick people. And, for reasons to be offered later, he should be a man of broad cultural interests and background, conversant with the principal social, scientific, literary, and artistic developments of his own time and of the past.

If an applicant for psychiatric training does not have these assets by the time he has finished medical school, it is probably too late for him to acquire them. Psychiatric training leans heavily upon them and should foster their development. Over and beyond this, psychiatric training will aim at two specific objectives: first, the development of a certain philosophy, a certain point of view, a certain scale of values; second, the transmission of technical experience and knowledge to the point that the novitiate can cope, competently and responsibly, with psychiatric problems.

Psychiatry contemplates the human being as an entity, subject to scientific study and therapeutic ministration only if psychological, social, and cultural factors are given status equivalent to physical and economic factors, and only if all of these factors are considered in their interacting and interrelated aspects. Expressed simply, the psychiatrist must avoid that "certain blindness in human beings" of which William James wrote. A psychiatrist is alert to inner unexpressed feelings of people. He can and must identify himself with the sufferer. The feelings of a nun at prayer, a child at play, an old man intently watching a television screen, a patient weeping in his pillow—these and a thousand other states of mind and feeling he must strive to comprehend. He is no less interested in the peculiar antics of a two-year-old child than in the dramatic assaults upon the community of a psychopathic criminal, no less concerned for a woman covered with the scabs and serum of weeping neurodermatitis than for the soldier screaming that he cannot shoot the enemy.

The psychiatrist must have such self-possession that even the most bitter personal attacks on him by a patient are felt neither as insult nor as injury, but as evidence of a kind of perverted trust. He must not have contempt for any clinical phenomenon, no matter how unpleasant, or for the most unprepossessing patient, remembering always that the stone rejected by the builders may become the headstone of the corner.

Furthermore, he must believe in the inherent capacity of even the sickest individual for reconstruction. Without such confidence he will not be able to sustain the discouragements of the short-term view which his day-to-day experience provides. He must believe that people *can* be understood, and that they are thereby helped. He must believe that only in re-examining his efforts constantly in the light of results obtained can he discover and affirm workable principles. He must become convinced that long-term results are more important than immediate results. He must believe that the mentally ill *can* be helped, and that they *should* be. . . .

The psychiatrist as a person is more important than the psychiatrist as a technician or scientist. What he *is* has more effect upon his patients than anything he *does*. Because of the intimate relationship of patient and psychiatrist, the value systems, standards, and ideals of the doctor are very important. To be sure, these are for the most part features of character which become part of the man before he goes to medical school. Selection of those persons most likely to become good psychiatrists is a responsibility of the School of Psychiatry, but those selected should be reminded frequently of this elementary fact: their effectiveness as clinicians and therapists relates in large measure to the stature and breadth of their own personalities.

Hence, throughout the training period in psychiatry, emphasis on general culture should be implemented by courses, seminars, lectures, and recommendations concerning reading which focus upon the relation of psychiatry to philosophy, sociology, anthropology, and religion. It might be too broad a statement to say that no doctor can become a good psychiatrist if he has not listened at fairly frequent intervals to some of the world's best music or read some of the world's best poetry. But it certainly could be claimed that lack of general acquaintance with the best formalized expression of human emotions seriously compromises a psychiatrist's therapeutic effectiveness. Many psychiatrists in the early days of their training need to be directed to a better acquaintance with the Bible, Aesop's Fables, Grimm's Fairy Tales, and Dostoevski's novels rather than to technical treatises on Gestalt psychology and psychoanalysis.

The concept of personal development just referred to should not be taken as one representing only the pleasurable and satisfying development of the doctor's own personality. Only if the acquisition of technical skills proceeds in a context of general cultural enrichment will the young psychiatrist be likely to develop a sense of social responsibility which is both his inheritance and his obligation by reason of professional selection and training. *For unto whomsoever much is given, of him shall much be required.*

To this end, the psychiatric student must obtain and retain a vision of the broad areas of human activity beyond the doors of office or hospital, in which areas his special insight and knowledge and skills can be effectively applied to the understanding of human motivation and adjustment. How to coordinate his professional interests and activities with those of teachers, ministers, and leaders in all areas of public service is a problem which he should be made to feel is his responsibility, one tacitly assumed by him when he made the decision to study psychiatry. To help him in this direction, a psychiatric training program should include opportunities for observing and discussing with those concerned the relations of psychiatry to the work of ministers, industrialists, lawyers, judges, and others. . . .

The problem of guidance emphasizes the tremendous importance of the teacher's role in a psychiatric training program. The phenomenon of identification, which occurs between parent and child, pupil and teacher, is repeated in the relation of the psychiatric resident to his instructors. One teacher is likely to become the student's ideal and toward this ideal he will consciously and unconsciously strive throughout his life. Hence, the character of the teachers, and the opportunities afforded to residents for becoming personally acquainted with them, assume great significance in the consideration of educational goals. The continuous dedication of the teacher must be insured by the setting up of guarantees that he may be free to teach and act according to his ideals. Regarding himself as the perennial student, he will be inspired, rather than deterred, by the eternal dilemma of the teacher, whether to present the clear, simple, but inaccurate, fact or the complex, confusing, presumptive truth.

It is important that the psychiatric novitiate be exposed by plan and design to the right doctors, the right atmosphere, the right books, the right topics of instruction, the right staff instructors, the right patients and that he be exposed to all of these at the right time. There always will be differences of opinion among thoughtful teachers as to the meaning of the word "right" as here used. But it is a step forward to recognize that whatever is considered "right" must be that to which the psychiatric resident is systematically exposed. . . .

Dr. Thomas W. Salmon, a noted psychiatrist, once referred to psychiatry as "the Cinderella" of the medical specialties. On May 10, 1938, Dr. Karl gave an after-dinner speech, entitled "The Cinderella of Medicine," at the annual meeting of the Medical Society of New York. He sought on this occasion to describe the role of psychiatry to physicians who had perhaps some skepticism about this relatively new discipline. Looking back over this talk today, he says, "It sounds shockingly naïve now. I am embarrassed by much of it." Yet, at the time, it was needed, and it is of interest today for showing, by comparison with the address that follows it, the actual length of the road that Cinderella has traveled from kitchen to palace.

I shall begin what I am to say, with a special version of one of Aesop's fables.

Six blind men sat by the gate of a great city as an elephant was led slowly past. Inspired by scientific curiosity of the highest degree, the six blind men rushed forward to palpate the great beast and to determine the nature of his being.

The first man's hand fell upon the elephant's tusks. "Ah," said he, "this creature is a thing of bones; they even protrude through his skin." Later on, years having passed, this man became an orthopedist.

At the same time the second blind man seized the elephant's trunk and identified its function. "What a nose!" he exclaimed. "Surely this is the most important part of the animal." Accordingly he became a rhinologist.

The third man chanced upon the elephant's great flapping ear and came to a similar conclusion; for him the ear was everything, so he, in time, became an otologist.

The fourth blind man rested his hands on the huge chest and abdomen of the elephant. "The contents of this barrel must be enormous," he thought, "and the pathological derangements infinite in number and variety." Nothing would do but that he should become an internist.

One of the blind men caught hold of the elephant's tail. "This," he said, "would appear to be a useless appendage. It might even be a source of trouble. Better take it off." This blind man became a surgeon.

But the last of the six men did not depend upon the sense of touch. Instead he only listened. He had heard the elephant approaching, the rattle of chains and the shouts of the keepers. It may be that he heard the elephant heaving a great sigh as he trudged along. "Where is the creature going?" he asked. No one answered. "Where did he come from?" he asked. No one knew.

Then this man fell into a deep reverie. What was in the elephant's mind, he wondered, in having left wherever he was and having come to this great city. Why does he submit to the indignities of our curiosity and the slavery of chains? And while he was wondering how to find out the answers to these questions the elephant was gone.

This man became a psychiatrist.

The other blind men were disgusted at this impracticality. They turned their backs upon their visionary companion. What difference does it make, said they, what the elephant's purposes may be? And his chains—they constitute a legal not a medical problem. The important thing is to recognize the animal's structure!

Then they fell to quarreling among themselves as to whether the elephant's structure was primarily that of a nose or that of an ear or that of a tail. And although they all differed flatly from one another on these points they all agreed that the psychiatrist was a fool.

It would be pleasant for me to assume that this allegory no longer represents accurately the attitude of the specialties of medicine toward one another and toward psychiatry. In some respects I think that the proper continuation of the allegory would represent the six blind men taking counsel with one another and making some concessions that the elephant had ears as well as a nose and that he had purposes and feelings as well as tusks and a tail. The tendency in all scientific research is to lose one's perspective in the intensity of one's special interest. Psychiatrists may do this no less than surgeons or otologists.

But in the main it is true that physicians have forgotten or ignored or repudiated the psychological factors in their patients. Modern medicine is based upon three basic sciences—physics, chemistry, and psychology. Of these chemistry is the oldest. For many centuries it completely dominated medicine. The physics of the body were considered unimportant and physical methods of treatment were considered unethical, undignified, unscientific. It was only in very recent times, relatively speaking, that some members of the barber guild became surgeons, that bonesetters became orthopedists, and that stone crushers became urologists. It was only in recent times that the mysticism and magic that permeated the recipes of the pharmacopoeia were purged by the cold light of pharmacological science. But it has been still more recent that psychological data have assumed some recognized validity of their own and ceased to be a vague compilation of theories, variously derived from philosophy, religion, and superstition. A systematic physics of the body was arrived at before a systematic chemistry, but both became the common property of physicians long before a systematic psychology was known to anyone.

It cannot be said that psychology has been incorporated into medicine as yet, either in theory or in practice. Medical science has long since become so great in its scope and complex in its detail as to favor the development of three kinds of physicians, those depending chiefly upon physical concepts, especially in their treatment methods—and here I have in mind the surgeons; those depending chiefly on chemical measures—and here I have in mind the internists; and those depending on psychological methods—and here I have in mind the psychiatrists. What a physician should be called who utilizes all three of these basic sciences in his work I do not know, unless it would be that we come back to a new and prouder use of the simple word "physician." In that case what I am extolling are not psychiatrists but that kind of a physician, one for whom physical, chemical, and psychological data have equal validity.

As a general thing, however, I am afraid this does not prevail. Patients are much more apt to get good physical and laboratory examinations than to get good psychological examinations or good psychological treatment. I have previously made the statement that if a psychiatrist were to make a diagnosis of appendicitis on the basis of a psychological examination alone he would be justly criticized; yet many doctors are quite willing to make a diagnosis of psychoneurosis on the basis of a physical examination alone.

Suppose I should ask you—and you are representative, progressive physicians—did you in examining that patient yesterday make any psychological examination? Did you, for example, ask him anything about his dreams? No? Why not? Are they not a part of him, a product of his anatomy and physiology and psychology? Meaningless? Negligible? Compare the reactions of a practitioner of medicine fifty years ago when a youngster, recently from medical school, proposed that he examine his patient's urine. "What? Urine? I *did* examine it—it was dark and stank. What more is to be examined? Urine is of no importance—it's only an excretion, to be thrown out quickly." And can you imagine the old fellow's scorn when his son diffidently asserted that it was considered by some doctors to be really possible to examine urine with a flame, with chemicals, and with a microscope—for the purpose of understanding better the organs and the human being from which it came?

And is it really so very different from the proposal that dreams, too, can be analyzed—if one studies the technics?

I am reminded of course that there are practical reasons why surgeons, dermatologists, and others feel justified in omitting some of the technic of a complete personality inventory. "Psychiatrists," they say, "are overwhelmed with too many data. They can't use all they have. We don't have time to get so much information about the patient. A patient might die while we are getting it. Furthermore it is unnecessary for the determination of the best practical treatment in many cases."

I won't deny the fact that short-cut methods of examination are desirable. What I deny is that one has any right to make this short-cut method at the total expense of the psychological factor. If a man breaks his leg, it is perfectly true that he doesn't want his surgeon to spend three or four hours getting a family or social history or making an intelligence test or analyzing dreams before he puts the leg in a splint. On the other hand, a complete omission of the psychological factor might lead, and I think often does lead, to serious errors in the treatment. Such an investigation in this case, for example, might prove that the man had broken his leg while in a fit of rage, trying to kick his dog or his child, or that his insurance policies paid him $500 a month disability, or that this was the fourth time that he had fallen in this particular spot and the second time he had sustained a fracture in such a fall, suggesting that there was something more than mere chance involved. In other words, a broken leg is a piece of local destruction and may be a covert form of self-destruction. One can confine himself to merely repairing the destruction as a carpenter repairs a broken joist and wait for the next piece of self-destruction or the next accident or the next infection—or one can look at it in the broad sense and compare this with other self-destructive events in the life of the individual and relate them to some more fundamental patterns.

All this sounds so logical—at least *I* think it sounds logical—that the question ought to be, why is not psychiatry the queen of the medical specialties—in a sense the mother of them all, the integrating and synthetic phase of medicine itself? Or at least why is it not better integrated with the rest of medicine? To some extent, as my brother Will has said, the psychiatrist himself is responsible for this. For many years he contented himself with his assigned but very limited task of looking after an esoteric group of individuals in a secluded cloister on the periphery of a village. He spoke infrequently and then chiefly about such imponderables as dementia praecox and depersonalization, sometimes about dairy barns. He seemed closer to his patients than to the profession and the rest of life.

Thus for years psychiatry remained, as I have indicated in the title, the Cinderella of medicine. She sat alone by the fire in the kitchen, while her proud sisters Ophthalmology and Pediatrics strutted in the parlor. Sister Surgery was there, too, forgetful of her humble origin in the barber-shop, and Mother Obstetrics was never reminded of her poor relations, the Midwives.

When, by the Fairy Godmother's aid, the transformed Cinderella appeared at the Great Ball (the war), she outshone all her sisters. It was there she won the Prince's favor (popular esteem), and thereafter she came out of the kitchen and consorted with her fashionable and now deferential sisters, and at last married the Prince. It was Thomas Salmon, of New York, who first used this figure, a man whose broad vision, whose keen mind, and whose winning personality did much to favor the ascendancy of this Cinderella. And while it is true that the laity has assimilated the principles of psychiatry more rapidly than have some parts of the medical profession, I do not think it was the public alone whose good graces put psychiatry where it is today. I think the intelligent, honest realization of an important portion of the medical profession itself that the psychological factor in medicine could no longer be ignored, forms our most dependable support. Some have felt, not without justice, that psychiatry has been oversold; this is true if one means that a greater need for it exists than our present supply of psychiatrists can fill.

For it was inevitable that science should have gradually displaced the ancient superstitions and taboos attaching to the medical man whereby it was inconceivable for him to be imperfect. So long as the medical man could not bear to examine his own psychology he could not logically concede it to have any importance among the clinical data of his patients. Among the discoveries of Freud, perhaps the greatest are those pertaining to the scientific study of the emotional bonds which develop between the patient and the physician. So long as it was taboo for the doctor to ask himself, "Why am I a physician? Why am I interested in disease? Why does the specialty of pediatrics appeal so to me?" and similar questions, it was necessary also to avoid, "Why did the patient expose himself to syphilis? When did the gastric ulcer patient begin to hate his wife? What is the purpose of this woman's illness?"

For are not the wishes, the dreams and desires, the fears, and hates and envies of a patient as much a product of his being as his urine, his blood, his spinal fluid?

Are they not as deserving of analysis and as amenable to treatment measures?

What I have been saying may have carried some of you beyond your convictions or my persuasions, so I shall pursue that line of thinking no further, because it is not necessary to explain why psychiatry, the Cinderella, left the kitchen and married the Prince. The fact is that she has done so. If you doubt this, reflect upon the fact that in several medical schools more time is devoted today to the teaching of psychiatry than to the teaching of surgery, that more hospital beds are filled with psychiatric patients today than are filled with all the medical and surgical and tuberculous and orthopedic and all other cases combined. That the state of New York spends many thousand times as much upon the care of psychiatric cases as upon the care or prevention of medical and surgical diseases of all other types. And if you reply that this is because of the social importance of psychiatry I should reply that all

disease has social importance and that the failure as physicians to recognize this has laid us open to criticism and to error. I do not mean by
this to indicate my approval of the state care of the ill. It does not have
my approval. I only mean to remind you that the state has for a long
time been in the business of caring for some of the ill and that this
some is a much larger number than many of you realize. As a psychiatrist in private practice, I can get no satisfaction out of the fact that
the state is my largest competitor and that although we are friends, we
are not cooperators. And I strongly feel that had we physicians recognized from the first that *psychological and social factors are a part of
medical science* that we could have made a better arrangement for the
care of the mentally ill than now exists and better arrangements for
other illnesses that now threaten. Those of you who fear that state
medicine will compete with private initiative in other forms of illness
might take this as a warning. I must tell you in frankness that some
physicians whom I have heard loudly declaiming against state medicine, sometimes do everything possible to prevent a patient from receiving the psychiatric care he needs and resort in the end to sending
him to a state hospital without any inkling of the inconsistency of this
program. It is this very inconsistency—this blindness to the psychological and social aspects of the human being, a blindness of which a
few of our colleagues seem even to be proud—which is one reason for
the rise of state medicine.

I am sorry to have injected this serious note into the hour of re-
laxation afforded by this banquet after the heavy program of the day.
You see, I have had some theories about the instinct toward self-
destruction, the way in which man fights against himself. I have extended it from clinical phenomena such as martyrdom and suicide to
social phenomena such as crime and even to nations warring against
nations, and against themselves. Our profession, too, sometimes betrays
this human trait of fighting against itself. As a psychiatrist my daily
occupation is the recognition of such tendencies and the outlining of
programs for their circumvention or redirection. You must forgive me
if I cannot resist the application of my professional technics to the
problems of my own—our own—profession.

I do not know what the future of psychiatry will be. I would
certainly not leave you with the impression that we psychiatrists have
so great a lack of modesty as to assume to guide the development of
all medicine. We have no monopoly on the comprehensive study of
the human being, unless by neglect you force it upon us. From the indications of your courtesy in having invited me here to speak for my

fellow psychiatrists and having listened so graciously to my strictures and suggestions, I have the impression that you have no wish to do so. On behalf of Cinderella, ladies and gentlemen, my appreciation and my compliments!

On September 30, 1968—almost exactly thirty years after giving the Cinderella talk—Dr. Karl came to grips with some of the critical problems of modern psychiatry in an address entitled "Psychiatry in a Changing Society," to the 20th Mental Hospital Institute. The speech was reprinted in the February, 1969, issue of Hospital & Community Psychiatry, *a journal of the American Psychiatric Association. Dr. Karl considers this one of the more important speeches he has ever made, and he is developing the ideas in it into a full-length book, to be entitled* Whatever Became of Sin?

Talk of change is always timely, because as a science, psychiatry must change continuously and does—and we are aware of the changes. At times it seems to be changing too rapidly; we wonder if we can keep up. We see changes in the modalities of treatment—psychological, social, chemical, and physical. Each has its successes, each has its failures; we seek the best combinations.

Perhaps the greatest current change may be our restatement of diagnoses. That is very popular in some quarters, but you all know how I feel about psychiatric name-calling—that psychiatric diagnosis should not mean attaching to the patient a label, one of many collected by a committee and put in a book and forced on residents who are told they must find a number and a label to fit every patient they are treating, or else report to the record clerk in the morning. It seems to me wrong, and I must therefore speak out, for us to brand for life with a pejorative, eternally damning label people who come to us innocently and wistfully asking for help. I must confess that I urge a little enlightened civil disobedience in that matter to all the residents I teach.

I still think it is more useful to stress the degree of disorganization that exists within the organism in relation to the particular environment to which it is trying to adapt. We should note the fluctuations and the forms of that disorganization, rather than trying with pompous fatuity to use such ancient and outworn labels as psychotic, neurotic, or psychopathic. I notice that designating someone as having a borderline personality is becoming the most popular of all. Surely we all have borderline personalities. I border on several different personalities I could describe, and you do too. I like being a borderline personality, but all those other diagnoses seem cruel and damning. We as psychiatrists and psychiatric associates should not continue to use them, even though today's fashion demands that we find a symptom, label it, and put it in the computer quick. That is surely not the function of a psychiatric physician in a troubled world.

Now let us flex our minds a little and consider the philosophy of psychiatry. Surely psychiatry is something more than the specialty to which weary internists refer recalcitrant patients or to which frightened families dispatch alarming relatives. What are we trying to do, we who have seen and worked with strange people all our professional lives? Are we trying to change people, or persuade them to try a different way of life? Are we trying to do something to them, to manipulate them or their environment in some way?

There are some rather puzzling problems that face every psychiatrist, myself included. As psychiatrists—with all our years of experience in working with unhappy people, miserable people, people we hope we can help to a better way of life—what do we have to offer when we are asked what we should do about the great world problem of hunger? I don't think we can say, "Oh, that belongs to the medical department on the second floor, not to us." What do we have to say about poverty, the inequality of the distribution of the world's wealth, which no one any longer ascribes merely to the high IQ of those who accumulate much of it? What about the squalor, the rats and the vermin, the crowding and indecencies of our cities? What about the unemployment and the alcohol and drug addiction all over the country?

What do we say about stealing, robbing, and cheating, which make up about nine-tenths of the incidents of crime, a statistical fact usually overlooked by the newspapers and the statisticians? Most crime is simply a matter of taking something that belongs to somebody else. Is that a psychiatric problem, a problem of education, or perhaps of religion? Is there some kind of error in our notion of what property is? Is stealing actually a normal process for anybody who is strong enough to do it? Is it really the pure demonstration of rugged individualism: take what you can get? Is it normal or is it abnormal? Is it a symptom or is it not? What do we psychiatrists think about it? We don't often say.

What about the assaulting, raping, and killing that goes on? Not as much as the alarmists think, but still too much. The rate of murder in Chicago, I learned, is just about the same as that among the Eskimos. There is no evidence that violence is increasing radically, but because of better communications and more crowding, people think it is.

What about the chronic embitterment that pervades a large element of our population—embitterment with silent projection or noisy protests? I must confess that I am on the side of a good many students who say that the faculty will not listen to them until they are aggravated and depressed and frantic, driven to the point of doing some disgraceful and regrettable things. What about the people who are not heard? And what is "not hearing"? Is it a symptom in itself, a symptom with which many of us, even psychiatrists, are afflicted?

What do we say about overpopulation? There are 300,000 births every day. Even if we concede 100,000 daily deaths, 200,000 more people are accumulating on earth every day. That would make a good-sized city: by the end of a week, it would be somewhat larger than Washington; by the end of a month, several times the size of Chicago. Do we psychiatrists say, "Well, that's beyond our field"? We can't say that. We are already committed to the fact that psychiatrists are concerned with the troubles of human beings. We can't sidestep that trouble. We have to face it. We have to have an opinion.

What do we think about the continued use of war to settle problems? Freud expressed himself about it in his correspondence with Einstein when he said, "Thus there is but one sure way of ending war and that is the *establishment, by common consent, of a central control that shall have the last word in every conflict of interests."* Do we today have a different view? Have we, with the aid of educational television and other means, communicated any recommendations about war? Or are we leaving it entirely to the politicians? Do we have to call war, violence, hunger, and poverty "symptoms" before we can be professionally concerned with them? What is the nature of those various misbehaviors, those difficulties with living?

As scientists, we are traditionally careful to keep value systems out of our thinking. We do not permit ourselves to say this is good, that is bad. We don't hate syphilis; we just fight it. We don't dislike delusions; we just point out to the victims that they are mistaken. We don't condemn suicide or drug addiction; we just recognize their existence and seek reasons for them. We take the attitude that we must not make a moral judgment about the goodness or badness of behavior.

But I wonder if we are not kidding ourselves, because I doubt if anybody would proclaim the virtue of syphilis, delusions, or suicide. But perhaps nobody wants to proclaim them evils either. Well, I will. I take the position that we should make some moral judgments. That in itself is a moral judgment. I think we deceive ourselves in attempting to maintain an objective, scientific detachment about those problems—unless we are doing research from which we must necessarily exclude all prejudgments. But most of us are not in research—that is a rare, precious, honorable, and difficult calling. Most of us are on the firing line, not in the research laboratory, and we have to have views and profess them. And I think we do.

What I'm trying to say is that with 200,000 more people appearing on our earth every day, the handful of psychiatrists, social workers, and clinical psychologists isn't going to be able to keep up with the clinical load. So what are we going to do? We are going to have to think in terms that we have previously found unacceptable. I think we are beginning, perhaps rather sheepishly, to make common cause with our colleagues, the sociologists, whom we have always snubbed. We are saying to them, "Perhaps you do have a few things to teach us. There are some facts about social structure that do not appear in the individual directly, but that do affect him. We need to learn from you something about what happens to people when they collect in groups." We have, moreover, said, "Some of you, unclinical, unmedical, and unenlightened as you are, might even be helpful to a patient now and then, properly controlled, of course, and with very careful safeguards."

I think we might even have to approach the theologians, who have thought about some of the human problems for a long time and who just might have something useful to say to us about the people they have tried to steer, encourage, and support for all these years. They know something about people. Today I'm going to borrow something from them, a tabooed word, sin. I believe in sin. I have seen it; I am seeing it, in various guises.

There is the sin of elective ignorance, which is not limited to the Germans in Hitler's war against the Jews. The sin of elective ignorance, as you all know, is in America too. People have said, "Well, I didn't know such things were going on in the snakepits." And "I didn't know such terrible things were going on in our prisons" . . . "in our slums." We in Chicago are uncomfortable about the article "The Worst Jail I Have Ever Seen: Cook County Jail," in the July 13, 1968, issue of *Saturday Evening Post*. If you haven't already read that description of sin, you should.

I am already on record as opposing the sin of vengeance. It is interesting that vengeance was so extolled, popular, and admired only a century ago, while today it is more of a secret sin. Everyone denies nursing vengeance. It is especially denied, it seems to me, in regard to those convicted of crime. Of course only those who *fail* in crime are convicted; the poor, the weak, the inadequate, and the black are mostly the ones who are convicted. Nine-tenths of all offenders don't go to jail, but vengeance is wreaked upon those who do.

Some of us remember how it was in the state hospitals only a few years ago when patients were frankly regarded as mean, recalcitrant people who had to be slapped around. Don't forget George III of England, a very remarkable king, who suffered from a curious delirium [cause is now known almost certainly to have been a genetic disease, porphyria] in his later years. The records show that his attendants slapped the king "as flat as a flounder" for some of his impudence. Now if you can slap a king to the floor, what can you do to the average citizen who is lunatic? You know what vengeance was inflicted on the sick who were in prison as witches or criminals, and later on the patients in state mental hospitals. You know that it didn't all disappear a few decades ago.

Then there is the sin of exclusive tribalism. Maybe you call it the country-club complex or racism or bigotry. I am proud of my tribe. I am very proud to be what I am, to be a member of all the groups I belong to and contribute to, but that doesn't mean that the man who is not a member of my tribe is a wicked fellow who must be ignored, despised, or exterminated. At one time there were areas in this country where one tribe of Indians would kill the members of another tribe on sight. In other areas, neighboring tribes traded with one another, and occasionally united and fought a common enemy together. In one or two instances, as with the Hopi and the Tewa, one tribe took in another and shared living space with it. Not tribalism as such, but the exploitation of tribalism, the expression of human hatred in and by groups—those are what we have to think about and disavow.

Shall I speak of the sins of sloth, of indolence, of greed and its corollary, stinginess? How many patients have you seen whose sickness was expressed in incredible stinginess? They can't let anything go lest they disintegrate. "I cannot afford to, I cannot think of giving to, the Community Chest. I can't think of giving away money. Somehow it terrifies me." Is greed a borderline syndrome?

An extraordinary pecuniary value is of late attached by some sufferers to our services. Psychiatrists just out of residency can sometimes anticipate an income greater than that of psychiatric administrators with many years of experience. Young men who are not necessarily the best trained and who have had no experience are offered so much money that the spirit of medical service is impaired—corrupted, I would even say. I deplore the change in the ideal, the image, of psychiatrists. I deplore its effect on the teaching of psychiatry. I deplore it, too, because I fear it will attract the wrong type of persons into psychiatric training. It dislocates the emphasis of our profession and encourages the sin of psychiatric arrogance. We may find ourselves guilty of the great transgression, that of being presumptuous. If power corrupts and absolute power corrupts absolutely, such affluence also tends to corrupt, and it takes a very strong character indeed to resist such corruption.

But there are other sins to mention. As a conservationist, I must speak of the sin of wastefulness. One of the dreadful things happening to our country at present is the pollution of our air and our water, and the depletion of our soil and other natural resources. It has taken many years for us, despite our intelligence, to observe how self-destructive we are in ways not only ugly but lethal.

How de we combat our problems? First of all, we can speak out against self-destructive habits we have noted. We can work against them, we can talk and teach against them. We can strive to teach the alternatives: to replace labeling by understanding; selective ignorance by information; and cynicism, depression, and tribalism by cultivated trust in mankind. We can exalt the glories of work, of generosity, of love and beauty as essential to a healthy way of life. We can talk less about mental illness and more about what constitutes mental health.

In place of despair, we can substitute hope—if we remember that, as John Donne said, "Love cures all sorrow." But with that love and hope has to go the conviction that although our society is not sick, we have some afflictions that we must eradicate. There are forces contrary to those of self-destruction, and if we do not deceive ourselves, we can help not only our nation, our people, and our patients, but also ourselves and our science, which has gone far beyond the state of merely declaring a patient committable or detecting the presence of a phobia. We must see the full picture of expanding human development in our country and in the whole world of which we are a part.

The development of psychiatry and—again—the all-important role of hope in effecting cures were treated by Dr. Karl in the article he prepared for Dr. Leo Bartemeier's 75th birthday, when a group of papers presented to him by his friends appeared as a book, Hope, Psychiatry's Commitment, *published in 1970. Dr. Bartemeier has been president of the American Psychoanalytic Association, the American Psychiatric Association, and the International Psychoanalytic Association. He and Dr. Karl are old and dear friends; they often refer to each other as "broth-*

er." Here is Dr. Karl's contribution on the occasion of the "Festschrift":

And now along comes this wonderful invitation to say something in a collection honoring Leo Bartemeier!

Brother Leo has *always* listened to my associations and outpourings. When I would tell him my wild ideas and dreams, long ago, he would listen and say, "Karl, that's good! You must develop that. Karl, that's great. Do that. I'll help." And then sometimes I did do it, and got all the credit and applause for its success. But back of me, as I always knew, stood Leo Bartemeier quietly smiling and saying, "Karl, that's wonderful!"

This is late thanks to give you, all too small, dear fellow, for all you have done for me these years. I don't know whether it was more faith or hope or love, but I know it was all three. And your friendship was of a very special and indescribable kind.

I want to say something not profound, not world shaking, but something I have been thinking about for a long time. I have not thought it through, but someone may pick it up and carry it further if it is worthy of it. I told Bartie about it on the phone and, as always, he said: "Karl, that is wonderful. Write that!"

So I will—knowing of course that it is not "wonderful"—but possibly provocative.

In the old days psychotherapy was far from being the proud queen she is today and was looked upon by the profession as a kind of permitted quackery, profitable and often successful, but not very dignified and certainly not scientific. If, with the aid of a little brow rubbing or faradic brush or Geissler tube manipulation or other form of hocus-pocus, a patient could be "persuaded" to relinquish a symptom, the result was ascribed to suggestion and assumed to justify the means. Sometimes the doctor tried to fool himself into believing that there was a logical connection between the manipulation and the disappearance of the symptoms, but usually it was a clear case of "tit-for-tat": The patient had tried to fool the doctor with nonorganic symptoms and so the doctor could outsmart and outfool the patient with manipulations and suggestions. The patient was cured of a symptom and the doctor got the credit (and the cash, too). Both the patient and the doctor saved face—and benefited.

Psychotherapy has grown up since then. Nowadays we concede that the patient is *not* deceiving the doctor, but himself; trying to fool the doctor is only incidental to getting some needed attention, some opportunity for protest. The good doctor will not treat him by further deception nor encourage self-deception; he will respond to the plea for understanding and try to *undeceive* him—i.e., if he *wants* it enough.

The new psychotherapy gets much credit for some of these transformations and its users believe that they occur more frequently and for more logical reasons than the "cures" of the old days. This is rudely disputed by some cold, calculating statisticians who claim that about the same number of sufferers recover no matter *what* the treatment method, or even with no treatment at all! But this is but the babble of scoffers and cynics!

There has always been some medical pessimism about the possibility of "changing" the nature or personality of patients. At the tail end of the era of therapeutic nihilism, about 1917, anybody who got well was considered to have done so in some extracurricular way; the recovery was false. To be "converted" as it were to common sense and hence to resuming a rational, healthy way of life was less cure than re-education or reformation.

Freud described this transformation as the overcoming of unconscious resistance to recovery. He worked out a method of facilitating it which took a long time and much training, but it set a pattern or model of scientific procedure. Freud also commented on a kind of change for the better which occurred without much help from the doctor. He called it a "flight into health"! Some people just suddenly seemed to turn over a new leaf and need no more treatment. We all know people who "get religion" and who seemingly change their nature and their behavior pattern.

William James wrote what is perhaps his greatest book, *The Varieties of Religious Experience,* on this subject. Recently I reread it, and also reread Harold Begbie's *Twice Born Men,* which appeared in 1909, also under the title *Broken Earthenware.* Begbie was inspired by James' book. (James refers to the "twice-born.") Begbie relates ten case histories of Salvation Army "Twice-borns"—a prizefighter, a robber, a burglar, a peddler, and other such types. All lived in what the author depicts as an inconceivably dirty, vicious, poverty-stricken part of London. (We would call it a ghetto, today.) Each of the ten characters described in detail was a desperate, abandoned, wretched character with years of drunken fighting, irregular employment, numerous prison sentences, and much senseless beating and public abuse. Suddenly the fellow sees some hope of happiness in identifying himself with the Salvation Army!

The author has a simple explanation for this change of personality, this shift of identification and behavior patterns. Science, he asserts, cannot change a bad man to a good man, but religion (faith) can! Some scientists would maintain the exact reverse of this.

He stresses the loneliness and the wish to belong, and the physical participation in marching and holding meetings or speaking to and for the group. Frequently he mentions the pride of "self-victory" in the utterly different pattern of life when suddenly "elected" and followed, joyfully and consistently. A typical case is that of a boy who ran away from a cold, miserable, dirty slum home at fourteen and joined a circus where he was ill-treated, underfed, and overworked. By audacity, stealth, and cheekiness he held on to his job, but his overuse of alcohol became so bad that he was finally discharged. He lost many successive jobs thereafter. He supported himself mainly by petty theft. Occasionally, utterly destitute, he would offer to eat dead cats for a bribe of twenty cents.

Once, while sleeping in some bushes in a London park, he awoke to find a bank of people gathered around him, and thinking he was about to be arrested, he charged out threatening to kill them. They told him they were having a religious service and invited him to join in it. He stood around and listened to them, gradually felt a desire for "betterment" and began to pray. Subsequently he "joined" this group and continued to work with the organization the rest of his life, marrying another Salvation Army worker and abstaining from all the drinking and other of his faults. A speck of hope, a surrender of willfulness, and a following of the way of Jesus.

We psychiatrists agree with Begbie and the Salvation Army workers (and the Alcoholics Anonymous) in believing that a man *can* change his ways, and that this *can* be assisted by outsiders. But can it be done so suddenly, so swiftly? We all agree that a man must *want* to change. Then, perhaps, even a considerably deformed and disorganized personality can restructure itself and become realigned with society. It does happen; we see others achieve it; we experience the thrill of doing it ourselves. It is from this elation we tend to venture further into new fields of "curing"—at least helping—the unwilling sufferer.

We think we must find ways to circumvent the reluctance to accept help. We must meet his resistance and doubt and even hostility not with promises, which he will suspect, not with deceit, which he will forever resent, not—if it can possibly be avoided—with anything based on force. Yet the necessity must arise of detaining or constraining our prospective beneficiary from leaving us, physically or mentally—even in suicide.

The inescapable conclusion is that we must, sometimes, overcome the patient's intractable self-destructive resistance by more than persistence and patience, but our techniques of insistence must be as skillful as the hand of the surgeon.

Does the public know that we doctors are a little shaken up these days—we doctors, we psychiatrists? It's not because we haven't plenty of patients, plenty of acclaim, plenty of income, plenty of know-how—none of which we had thirty or forty years ago. We have them now, and we have a little arrogance along with them, I'm afraid. We also have a little dismay and a little guilt.

We're dismayed to realize—when we reflect about it—that while our incomes have gone up, we don't seem to be so popular anymore. Our predecessors' great discoveries enable us to do many wonderful things, and yet we aren't the honored profession we once were. Sometimes a little gratitude is expressed, to be sure, but often not even a thank you or a backward look. The government or the insurance company will pay the bill. And while there always seem to be more patients coming, we do not seem to have the friends we used to have.

And although the patients come, it isn't always very willingly. We used to be pretty stuffy about insisting upon our prospective patients taking a suppliant attitude if he wanted our help. His first payment on account had to be an unconditional surrender. The doctor knew what was best; the patient followed orders. It was a basic assumption that the doctor could do no wrong, could make no mistakes. Only some children the doctors expected to treat against their will, children and the mentally ill. . . .

Today we still treat willing patients, but we are constantly reminded of the responsibility we have, toward unwilling patients or potential patients. There are millions of people who ought to be helped but who reject his—or anyone else's—offer. Among the victims of alcohol addiction, that grievous phenomenon which affects five or ten million of our fellow citizens, there are many who partially want help but will not fully submit themselves to medical authority. They retain mental reservations, secretly or avowedly. The success of that worthy organization Alcoholics Anonymous is ascribed by many to the wisdom of its founders in requiring an applicant for help to completely and unconditionally surrender, freely admitting that he can no longer save himself.

Psychiatrists have demonstrated that *some* patients can be successfully treated even against their will. Indeed many have been treated and cured without *initial* cooperation. But in recent years the morality of undesired, unsought treatment has been questioned; the question asked is: *Should* sufferers be forced to receive treatment if they harm no one but themselves? Perhaps a patient is wise in choosing to remain ill, or at least to decline help from a doctor, but on the other hand this stubbornness and arrogance may be the very essence of the patient's illness. . . .

We agree that human nature can be changed. We are almost to the point of agreeing that it can be changed even against the other person's will. But this is very dangerous because it makes us responsible for the direction in which the change is made.

Assuming this responsibility is a solemn task not to be entered into lightly. Effecting this metamorphosis is a difficult task which can be accomplished in many different ways although each of us has his favorite.

Perhaps in another one hundred years we will know which of these methods are the best ones and we will know more definitely their probabilities of success.

Until then, let us keep trying.

Dr. Karl's most complete statement on "hope"—what he called the "essential constituent of both treatment and teaching"—was contained in the first (it later became a tradition) Academic Lecture that he delivered at the annual meeting of the American Psychiatric Association in Philadelphia in the spring of 1959. He says of this event, "It was a large, highly critical but also affectionate audience, composed of colleagues from all over America. It was a great honor for me and I thought very carefully about what I wanted to say. I must have rewritten this speech fifteen times. I discussed the philosophy of hope— the whole question of our identification with the Greek or Hebrew spirit and whether or not hope is an evil, as the Greeks thought, like the lures for bass. Should doctors tell a patient there's hope, or that he is incurable? This applies to mental illness as well as physical. Some doctors give up on the very name 'schizophrenia'; they think it's incurable. We seem to be going more and more toward the Greeks in this. Which is too bad for us."

Dr. Karl's address was simply entitled "Hope."

It is from a background of teaching that the topic which I propose to discuss emerged. I would like to warn you not to expect a scientific analysis of it along conventional lines. The subject does not permit of that; we don't yet know enough about it, and it would be presumptuous to make the attempt. I am not reporting a research or a discovery, and it is no dark hour, calling for exhortation or comfort. I speak, rather, to the point of focusing attention upon a basic but elusive ingredient in our daily work—our teaching, our healing, our diagnosing. I speak of hope.

Long before love became medically respectable, long before Sigmund Freud demonstrated it to be a basic consideration in psychiatry, philosophers and poets and the common people of the world knew that it was essential to our mental health. Perhaps the most beautiful essay ever written was about love and its manifestations in personality.

To that essay was appended a footnote which is often quoted as if it were a summation. It is true, observed the writer, that there are other permanent goods in the world beside love: there is, for example, faith, and there is hope. "But," he added, "the greatest of these is love."

With this famous concluding phrase most psychiatrists, I presume, would agree. Most of us, I think, would also agree to include faith— the faith that sustains our belief that existence has meaning and the faith that our concern for one another reflects the concern of a Creator.

Our shelves hold many books now on the place of *faith* in science and psychiatry, and on the vicissitudes of man's efforts to *love* and to be loved. But when it comes to hope, our shelves are bare. The journals are silent. The Encyclopaedia Britannica devotes many columns to the topic of love and many more to faith. But hope, poor little hope! She is not even listed.

I confess I was astonished to discover this. And yet, I realized that this avoidance of the theme reflected my own attitude. Time was when for this occasion I should have chosen as my subject "Love" or "Hate" or "Conflict" or "Instinct" or "Sublimation" or "Symptom Formation" —but never such a thing as "Hope." It seems almost to be a tabooed topic, a personal matter, scarcely appropriate for public discussion. And yet—since when has psychiatry eschewed examination of our innermost thoughts and feelings? Should we not adhere to our professional habit of self-examination and contemplation? If we dare to hope, should we not dare to look at ourselves hoping?

This is not the way I began to think about the topic. Nor did I come to it fresh from struggles with Kierkegaardian logic, or from brooding over Greek pessimism, or from apprehensiveness concerning the muddled management of unsettled world affairs. It was all in the day's work, so to speak, some preoccupations with the motivations of the young doctors I teach. The miracle of growth has long intrigued me: the growth of the child, the growth of plants, the growth of cultures, and the growth of young psychiatrists. I have seen one after another young doctor step forward, fresh from his internship or from his military duty, to enter the mysteries of psychiatric training. I have seen these young men approach the abstruse and puzzling material of our field of medicine with resolute courage—let us say, rather, with hope.

But behind the façade presented by these acolytes there are often tumults of conflicting voices, fearful insecurity, and bold overself-confidence. The dramatic picture of psychiatry fascinates them, the reputed resistance to treatment challenges them, the multiplicity of method appalls them. They are assigned to wards filled with vacant or frantic faces, turned now upon "the new doctor." It is usually long after their initiation into the uncanny world of mental illness that they can distinguish the dynamic process, or would have the personal experience of interaction with a recovering patient.

Nevertheless, the novitiates assail their tasks headlong, sometimes with a *furor therapeuticus*. There is nothing mercenary or aggressive about this. They are struggling to become effective in a new kind of relationship with patients. Sometimes they go too far; they presume; they expect or promise too much. More often frustration, sad experience, or self-depreciation erodes the confidence required for persistent effort, and the little candle of hope, which for awhile burned so brightly, weakens, sputters, and goes out. We see the beginning of a repetition of scenes so common 25 years ago—hopeless physicians presiding, passively, over hopeless patients. "Psychiatry," we will hear, "has been oversold. The enthusiasm of inexperience only awaits the disillusionment of time. It is enough if we bestow kindness and wait for the inevitable. Hope is for the hopeless, and for fools."

We would like to think that the young men who pass through our training programs mostly emerge with certain limits put upon their expectations and certain guards upon their implied promises, but with the flame of their hope unextinguished and unextinguishable. We like them to believe that there is no patient for whom something helpful cannot be done. But we also like them to realize that the changes the patient desires in himself, or the physician desires in his patient, may not be the ones which come about, may not even be, in the long run, the changes that it was best to have sought for. It is a responsibility of the teacher to the student, just as it is of the young doctor to his patient, to inspire the right amount of hope—some, but not too much. Excess of hope is presumption and leads to disaster. Deficiency of hope is despair and leads to decay. Our delicate and precious duty as teachers is to properly tend this flame.

I propose, therefore, that we examine this essential constituent of both treatment and teaching. How shall we think of it? Is it something which *deserves* our concern as scientists? Or only as philosophers and poets? Is it only an epiphenomenon of life and the healing art? Do we, perhaps, tacitly ascribe hope to temperament, a sort of fringe benefit deriving from certain fortuitous congenital arrangements of glands and neurons? This is slight improvement upon the humoral theories of sanguinity and melancholy treasured by our forebears. If we ascribe hope, as some psychoanalytic writers have done, to recollections of maternal infallibility and recurrent oral gratifications, what combination of these experiences shall we regard as optimum? Others have seen in hope a prevailing note of fear, a counterphobic denial of the horror and despair born of self-destructive trends or of the imminence of existential doom.

More congenial to my thinking is the ascription of hope to the mysterious workings of the repetition compulsion, the very essence of which is a kind of relentless and indefatigable pursuit of resolution and freedom. I would see hope as another aspect of the life instinct, the creative drive which wards against dissolution and destructiveness. But some will say, with Freud, that this is only our speculative abstractions to supply a model for practical thinking and behavior. Our mythology, he called it.

Here we might pause a moment to consider another mythology about hope. Pandora, it will be recalled, was an agent in the infliction of revenge of mankind. Curiosity led to Pandora opening the box from which all the evils now in the world emerged. Biting, stinging creatures flew through the air and attacked mortals; but remaining behind was one good little sprite, man's consolation, Hope. But if Hope was a blessing, why did she remain in the box? And if, on the other hand, she was an evil like the rest, perhaps even the worst evil of all, why did she not fly out with them and begin work?

The Greeks mostly did consider hope an evil. The Greek philosophers and the later Greek literature tended more and more to the view that since fate was unchangeable, hope was an illusion, "the food of exiles" (Aeschylus) and, indeed, "man's curse!" (Euripides). Quotations from Solon, Simonides, Pindar, Thucydides, and others say this in different ways. The Greek feeling about hope is vividly expressed in

Anouilh's adaptation of Sophocles' *Antigone,* where, referring to herself, the heroine cries, "We are of the tribe that asks questions, and we ask them to the bitter end—until no tiniest chance of hope remains to be strangled by our hands. We are of the tribe that hates your filthy hope, your docile, female hope; hope, your whore. . . ." [Which Creon interrupts with "Shut up! If you could see how ugly you are, shrieking those words!"]

From this one can see that it was intrepid indeed of St. Paul, writing to Greek friends, to declare that hope should stand along with love. In this Paul was loyal to his Hebrew heritage (Psalms 42, Isaiah 40) as well as his Christian convictions. For while the Jews were, to be sure, people of faith, they were also at all times a people of hope who, despite tribulation, clung to the expectation that the Messiah would come and the world get better. Hence, with the spread of Christianity and the dispersion of the Jews, hope had its missionaries, and Paul was one of them.

Martin Luther, like St. Paul, shook his fist at Greek fatalism and declared: "Everything that is done in the world is done by hope." Samuel Johnson opined that "where there is no hope there can be no endeavor," and our own countryman Emerson took up the cudgels for hope: it is by his hope, he said, that we judge of a man's wisdom. "You cannot put a great hope into a small soul," said another (Jones) and Tennyson's words, "The mighty hopes that make us men," now echo in our ears.

But many poets have tended to accept (rather bitterly) the fatalistic if not cynical view of the Greeks:

"Hope—fortune's cheating lottery, where for one prize a hundred blanks there be." (Cowley, 1647)
"Worse than despair, worse than the bitterness of death, is hope." (Shelley: *The Cenci,* 1819)
"Hope is the worst of evils, for it prolongs the torment of man." (Nietzsche: *Human All-too-Human,* 1878)

I have had some patients who agreed with these poets. Partly that is why they were patients. But when I searched the literature for some kind words about hope, I experienced some uneasiness lest I find that very little (that my colleagues would accept) had ever been said for hope! And very little I found, indeed. But the cupboard proved not to be entirely bare. Particularly Dr. Thomas French, in his five-volume examination of the psychoanalytic process, has dealt extensively with hope as the activating force of the ego's integrative function.

Twenty years ago Mrs. Menninger and I submitted the thesis in *Love Against Hate* that hope was the dim awareness of unconscious wishes which, like dreams, tend to come true. We said,

> There is no such thing as "idle hope." The thoughts and hopes and wishes that we entertain are already correlated to the plan of action which would bring these about, even though the whole project is ultimately renounced as too difficult or too dangerous. . . . This essential identity of hoping, wishing, purposing, intending, attempting, and doing is a little difficult for the practical common-sense man to grasp, because for him it makes a great difference whether a thing is executed or only planned or only hoped for. There *is* an external difference, to be sure; and there is an internal difference, too. But internally, (psychologically) from the standpoint of *motive*, there is no difference. There is a difference in the *fate* of the impulse, the degree with which it is correlated with reality, inhibited by internal fears, supported by other motives, etc.— but the motive force is the same. . . . The hopes we develop are therefore a measure of our maturity.

At that time it seemed to me that education best expressed the hope of the human race. But today I think I see the expression of hope in many clinical phenomena, as well.

Each of us here who has been in practice more than a decade has seen the "hopeless case" recover. And we have sometimes seen, or so it seemed, that a mother's or father's indomitable hope was a factor in this recovery. True, we have also seen hope deferred making the heart sick. But hope must be distinguished from expectation. "We are saved by hope," wrote St. Paul to some Roman Christians, "but hope that is seen is not hope: for what a man seeth, why doth he yet hope for?"

Nor is hope identical with optimism; optimism always implies some distance from reality, as Marcel points out, so that obstacles appear attenuated. The optimist, like the pessimist, emphasizes the importance of "I." But hope is humble, it is modest, it is self-less. Unconcerned with the ambiguity of past experience, hope implies process; it is an adventure, a going forward, a confident search.

When Doctors Bartemeier, Romano, Kubie and Whitehorn and I went to the European Theater of World War II for my brother Will and the surgeon-general, we arrived at the Buchenwald prison camp a few days after it had been entered by our armed forces. What I remember most vividly of that terrible place was something we didn't actually see. But we heard it at first hand. The night before we got there, our U.S. Army doctors had given what they called a "smoker" for the physician prisoners they had discovered and released. It was a kind of unearthly medical society meeting. Army rations were put out as refreshments, with some wine and tobacco, incredibly relished by the emaciated but overjoyed guests. Communication in words was imperfect because of language difficulties, but the spirit was unmistakable. The members of a fraternity were reunited. And in the spirit of the fraternity, experiences were exchanged.

These doctors, prisoners along with all the others, had followed the same routines of 4:00 A.M. rising, shivering roll calls, day-long drudgery on the Autobahn, shivering roll calls again, and finally a cold bowl of thin soup. They were starved and beaten and overworked like all the others, with no reason to expect any other fate than the miserable death and cremation which they observed about them daily.

But now comes the surprise. At night, when the other prisoners were asleep, these thin, hungry, weary doctors got up and huddled together in a group, and talked. They discussed cases. They organized a medical society. They prepared and presented papers. They made plans for improving health conditions. Then they began to smuggle in materials to make various medical instruments. And finally they built, of all things, an X-ray machine! The pieces had to be found somewhere; they had to be stolen, they had to be concealed in the prisoners' clothes; they had to be carried back to the prison on the long, weary marches after work. The guards had to be bribed or otherwise thrown off the scent. But little by little, with the aid of some engineers and electricians among the prisoners, these doctors put together a workable X-ray machine and used it, secretly, at night, in their efforts to ameliorate the lot of their fellow prisoners. This was what dedication to medicine and humanity could do—*kept alive by hope.*

But, someone who remembers may ask, bitterly—what of the thousands who died miserably for *all* the hopes they nurtured? Even here I would not concede that hope had altogether failed. I would believe that hope had sustained them in their martyrdom, and that their hopefulness, however frail and tortured and ultimately defeated, was communicated on down through prison generations to those who were ultimately freed and brought us the record of this medical miracle. Who can read the eloquent last messages of the condemned as collected by Gottwitzer, Kuhn, and Schneider and published as *Dying We Live,* and fail to catch a spark of hope from them?

Confirmation for the sustaining function of hope in life has recently come from a most unexpected quarter—the psychobiological laboratory. At the annual convention of the American Psychological Association in September, 1956, Curt Richter of Johns Hopkins reported in an unpublished manuscript an astonishing phenomenon.

It was simply this, that when placed in certain situations which seemed to permit of no chance for escape, even vigorous animals gave up their efforts and rapidly succumbed to death. This was observed experimentally in both laboratory rats and wild rats. "After elimination of the hopelessness feature," reported Richter, "the rats do not die . . . (indeed, the speed of their recovery is remarkable). A rat that would quite certainly have died in another minute or two becomes normally active and aggressive," swimming vigorously for fifty to sixty hours. Richter emphasized that not the restraint alone, nor the immersion, nor the exposure, nor the trimming of whiskers will explain the phenomenon. It is, he insisted, the loss of hope.

Richter added some confirmatory data from other fields and suggested an extrapolation from his laboratory observations to explain the occurrence of sudden death in rabbits, chimpanzees, foxes, raccoons, some birds, musk oxen, otters, mink, and even human beings. "Some of these instances," he said, "can best be described in terms of hopelessness, all avenues of escape appearing to be closed."

This is not an isolated observation or hypothesis. For example, from a large amount of psychosomatic investigation Engel and his associates in Rochester, New York, considered that what they describe as "helplessness" and "hopelessness" reflect a necessary if not a sufficient condition for the development of organic disease.

And then there is the Queequeg phenomena of "Voodoo Death" in Moby Dick which Walter Cannon and others have amply substantiated with authentic data from primitive societies. No doubt most of us can recall instances in which the loss of hope seemed to accelerate the arrival of death for a patient. There are many such stories, unconfirmed of course but highly suggestive, in the daily press. One that appeared in the *Topeka Daily Capital* of April 2, 1959, with a dateline from Tucson, Arizona, had the headline "Blasts End Mother's Will to Live." It reported:

Twelve days ago, Mrs. Helen E. Hopke lay in her bed fighting to stay alive to see her daughter's wedding.

Incurably ill for the past five years, Mrs. Hopke had been indirectly responsible for the meeting about a year ago of her daughter, Rose Marie, 20, and the girl's intended husband, Arthur Woodrow Hudson, 26.

Rose Marie had acted as nurse and housekeeper to her bedfast mother. While buying medicine she met Hudson, a pharmacist in a local drug store. Friends said it was the girl's first romance.

They also said all that kept Mrs. Hopke alive in recent months was the thought of the impending marriage.

The 56-year-old mother heard the couple enter the house laughing and talking about the April 4th wedding. She heard them enter the next room.

Their chatter ended in three blasts from a shotgun.

Police said Hopke, opposed to the marriage, wanted his daughter to continue to care for her mother. He became enraged at reading the wedding notice in the paper, shot the couple, then turned the gun on himself.

Rose Marie was taken to one hospital where she is recovering. Her mother was taken to another.

Tuesday night, Mrs. Hopke died.

All of these things seem to me to support the theoretical proposal that hope reflects the working of the life instinct in its constant battle against the various forces that add up to self-destruction. It would be too narrow to regard it as a form of refined narcissism since, as Marcel points out, there is something essentially unnarcissistic and beyond self in hope. One sees this in the hopefulness not of the patient but of the physician. How much our patients do for us doctors!

We in Kansas have lived through the experience of a state hospital revival. Although we have built almost no new buildings, and although our admissions have increased tenfold in fifteen years, our once over-crowded patient population has steadily diminished until we now always have available empty beds. We have even closed some wards as unneeded. We are proud of this, and proud that the voters and officials of our state appreciate it, and consider the cost per *stay* more significant than the commonly used cost per day. A distinguished governor visited us for several days, determined, as he said, to "discover the secret." "Our state has more men and more money than Kansas," he said. "Why can't we do these things?"

He didn't discover the secret partly because he didn't believe what we told him.

Many of my colleagues in this audience may not believe it now, either. But we consider the crucial element in the Kansas state hospital program to have been the inculcation of hope. Not in the patients directly, but in the doctors and all those who help them, in the relatives of the patients, in the responsible officials, in the whole community, and *then* in the patients. It was not just optimism; it was not faith; it was not expectation. We had no *reason* to expect what happened, and what still happens, and our faith was only that which all scientists share. But we did have hope.

We had more than hope, you will say; we had had experiences which encouraged hope. But these experiences were themselves based partly on hope, confirming the assumption that hope fires hope. This is not a conscious process, or at least not entirely so. I have wondered if we might perhaps understand the placebo effect in this way, a transmitted hope or reinoculation, as it were? In control research studies of the new drugs, for example, patients who receive only placebos sometimes show much improvement. In one study that I know about, testing an excellent drug, more patients in the group which had only placebos were able to be discharged from the hospital than from the group of those who got the actual remedy (although a larger number of the latter showed marked improvement).

Another phenomenon that is perhaps related to hope is the sudden improvement and even recovery of patients who have been for a long time fixed, as it were, at low levels of organization and regression. A new doctor arrives, or a new aide, and the patient promptly and most unexpectedly begins to recover. But it is also true that just the opposite occurs: A patient on whom intensive efforts have been made fails to respond and is given up in despair, dismissed by her physician or removed to a custodial hospital. We have all frequently seen this result in a prompt improvement and even recovery. Perhaps we could regard this as an awakening of dormant hope by a desperate and unintentional shock-type method.

Whatever the explanation offered for such phenomena, to invoke suggestion or coincidence (whatever *they* are) will not suffice. There is more to it. And yet we doctors are so schooled against permitting ourselves to believe the intangible or impalpable or indefinite that we tend to discount the element of hope, its reviving effect as well as its survival function. Because of the vulnerability of every doctor to the temptation of playing God and taking the credit for the workings of the *vis medicatrix naturae,* we are necessarily extremely cautious in attributing change to any particular thing and least of all to our own wishful thinking.

There are many sufferers in the world, and there are many who seek to afford them relief. Among the latter there are those who use intuition and magic, and there are those who attempt to derive basic principles checked by experiment and observation, which we call the scientific method. For the former group, healing is more important than truth; for the latter, truth is more important than healing. Indeed, the search for truth, the desire to heal, and the earning of one's living are three persistently conflicting forces in medical practice.

In the daily performance of healing acts, the scales are weighted heavily against scientific truth. Patients long to be deceived. Driven by pain and desperate with fear, they are ready to seize at "straws of hope." They prostrate themselves before the doctor; they queue up in weary, straggling lines awaiting the opportunity to submit themselves to humiliations and new sufferings, or even to hear a few words of reassurance. Besieged by such multitudes of petitioners, often with gifts in their hands, the doctor, knowing his limitations, must try to be patient, kind, and merciful—but simultaneously "objective" and honest. The desire to bring comfort, the need to earn one's living, the suppressed longing for prestige and popularity, the honest conviction of the efficacy of a pill or a program, sympathy for the pleading sufferer—all of these throw themselves upon the scales in the moment of decision. Every physician in the world has heard the devil whispering, "Command that these stones become bread . . . All these things I will give thee if thou wilt fall down and . . ." And sometimes he falls down. He exploits the patient's hope.

Against such dangers there have been for twenty-five centuries an oath of loyalty, a tradition of humility, and certain maxims of practice. One of the latter is the putting of diagnosis before treatment, empiricism before hope. Even in prescientific days it was indefensible for a doctor not to indicate some comprehension of what one claiming to be a healer was dealing with. For the patient, even a diagnosis offered *some* hope, since it showed that his condition was not unique. But for the doctor, who was better acquainted with the implications of a diagnosis for which he had no real treatment, the temptation was ever present to neglect diagnosis in the interests of hope, or at least in the interests of treatment.

It should be remembered that there were once many different kinds of competing healers. There were the apothecaries who in 1617 were granted a charter permitting them to sever their two hundred year association with the grocers. There were the various trade guilds: the barber-surgeons, midwives, and bonesetters; and then there were the physicians, with their plasters and clysters. All were busy "treating."

Out of this confusion, under the leadership of a gallery of immortals on pillars erected here and there over a wide area, there slowly arose the magnificent edifice of modern, scientific medicine. The elimination of superstition and magic took a century, but the purge strengthened medical science mightily. Thousands of remedies were tested, found wanting, and discarded. Many improvements in diagnostic techniques and instruments were introduced. Treatment, except for the most superficial palliation, was apt to be regarded with great suspicion, while the memory of recent quackery, pretention, and deceit was fresh.

In psychiatry, the efforts of our predecessors to bring order out of the apparent chaos of the phenomena of madness were reflected in assiduous efforts to describe disease entities, to name them, to identify them, to graph them, and to seek for "etiologies." This was the traditional concept of diagnosis and it offered little to justify hope. The broken or misshapen personalities coming under medical observation were described or christened with tens of thousands of names and groupings, painstakingly put together by assiduous workers, only to be discarded by those of a later generation. These old labels, like epitaphs on tombstones, may be read with sober reflections that life is short and the art long, that our grasp of human phenomena is limited and narrow, and that our concepts are ever changing and unclear.

Once diagnosis in the sense of recognizing, naming, classifying, and distinguishing between different forms of behavioral disorder seemed of fundamental importance. The best psychiatrist in my early days was one who could most convincingly distinguish between some of the many varieties of "paranoia" or "dementia praecox," a term introduced 99 years ago by B. A. Morel in 1860 describing the mental condition of a boy of 14 years, or "psychopathic personality." Some of my colleagues "discovered" new varieties of these; I even thought that I did.

Today it seems to me most important that we *not* do that. Our impressive labels only reify and freeze a phase of a process; they misrepresent our modern concepts and they strike a blow at hope, and hence at treatment. Words like *non compos mentis* or "responsible" and "irresponsible" really indicate only whether or not we think an accused person is able to appreciate being executed. "Psychotic" and "neurotic" cannot be competently defined, since what they mean at any one moment depends upon who is using them to describe whom. Many of us have urged their abolition, but they persist as weapons in scientific name-calling. Some colleagues incline to label "psychopathic personality" all patients who admit having broken the law. And surely it is more than a little disturbing to us all to contemplate the results of the recent researches by colleagues Hollingshead and Redlich exposing the fact that what one gets called by psychiatrists depends to a degree upon what class of society one comes from.

But over and above the matter of social and political and medical misuse of terms, these diagnostic designations belie the progress we have made in understanding the nature of illness. A name is not a diagnosis. It does not determine treatment. Its original purpose, perhaps, was to distinguish between wise and foolish expectations, but its net effect has come to be that of destroying hope.

Today there is a trend away from names, states, and entities and toward dynamics, relativity, and process. Just as the nature of matter has assumed a new aspect, so the nature of disease has come to be understood differently. The only entities in disease, said Allbutt long ago, are the individual patients, Smith and Jones, in certain phases of their being. "Diseases are not specifics such as cats and mushrooms; they are 'abnormal' *behaviors* of animals and plants." Today we are following Allbutt.

It is the privilege of some of us to be *called* doctors. And if the peculiar phases of existence which Jones and Smith are experiencing lead them to approach us in the belief that we can help them, they can then be called patients and their afflictions may be *called* disease. But we cannot discharge our responsibility by "calling." We may not exorcise Smith's afflictions by giving them a name. That is not the basis of our hope, and if it is the basis of Smith's hope, it is one we should not exploit.

It is our responsibility as physicians to instigate some change in the relations of Smith to his environment—directly if possible, indirectly and gradually most likely. To do this we must attempt to understand the man, how he has become what he is, what goes on inside of him, what goes on around him and how these interact. By observing the internal and external processes we can discover what in his world is good for Smith and what is unbearable, what damage he inflicts upon himself and others, and what potentials within him remain underdeveloped. And here enters in hope, for we acquire, thus, a rationale for therapeutic intervention.

This is what we now call diagnosis. It were better to call it diagnos*ing*, to indicate its transitive, continuing nature, its look toward the future rather than toward something static or past. Diagnosing is the first step in a cooperative relation between patient, physician, and environment working toward the betterment of a situation, especially as it affects our patient. This is based upon hope, hope implicit in our effort and hope nurtured in our patient.

The practice of medicine today is vastly different from that of a hundred years ago when Samuel Gross wrote (1861):

> It requires no prophetic eye, no special foresight, to discover that we are on the very verge of one of the most fearful and widespread revolutions in medicine that the world has ever witnessed.

That revolution came about (Dr. Earl Bond reviewed it this morning) but not so soon as Gross expected. Yet it is hard to believe today that there was ever a time when a doctor had to defend himself to his colleagues if he claimed to have cured someone. In those days hope was faint and precious. Today it seems sometimes almost as if hope were considered unnecessary.

The revolution that elevated our medical profession from a discouraged, submerged state to a progressive and confident one was partly the result of new discoveries, and partly from the recognition of psychology as one of the basic medical sciences, along with physics and chemistry. This came about from the experiences of World War I, and from the discoveries of Sigmund Freud. The latter were introduced into American psychiatry about 1920, the way prepared for them by J. J. Putnam, Ernest Southard, Adolf Meyer, William A. White, A. A. Brill, and Smith Ely Jelliffe.

I cannot describe all of these old friends here, but I must say a word about Southard, because he was my teacher and because above all men I have known, and entirely out of keeping with the spirit of his day, he placed great hope in psychiatry. He said here, long ago, in *1919, remember:*

> May we not rejoice that we (psychiatrists) . . . are to be equipped by training and experience better, perhaps, than any other men to see through the apparent terrors of anarchism, of violence, of destructiveness, or paranoia—whether these tendencies are showing in capitalists or in labor leaders, in universities or in tenements, in Congress or under deserted culverts. . . . Psychiatrists must carry their analytic powers, their ingrained optimism, and their tried strength of purpose not merely into the narrow circle of frank disease, but, like Seguin of old, into education; like William James, into the sphere of morals; like Isaac Ray, into jurisprudence; and above all, into economics and industry. I salute the coming years as high years for psychiatrists!

These "high years" really began after Southard died. The public had been alerted by the literary dissemination of the discoveries of Freud and also by the growing "mental hygiene movement." Most doctors had had almost no psychiatry in their medical school training. Twenty-five years after Southard had spoken those prophetic words—and died —we were in the midst of another World War. There was a shortage of psychiatrists. To enlist interest and recruit doctors, I visited medical schools over the country and talked at length to students, deans, and faculty members. I found that a common objection to entering psychiatry was an impression that our patients "never get well." It is such a hopeless field, they said. Penicillin and the other miracle drugs are more definite and exciting than the dreary wards of state hospitals, filled with silent, staring faces.

We can see, now, that these students had been shown the wrong side of psychiatry, its failures rather than its successes. But one thing struck me then which has remained in my mind indelibly. I perceived vividly how hopelessness breeds hopelessness, how the nonexpectant, hope-lacking or "unimaginative" teacher can bequeath to his student a sense of impotence and futility, utterly out of keeping with facts known to both of them! Surely even these misled students knew that *some* psychiatric patients recover, even if they didn't know that the vast majority does so. But like their teachers, they adopted some of the very symptoms of their patients: hopelessness and goal-lessness! Physicians in state hospitals at that time did not expect their patients to recover and were a little surprised when recovery occurred. Some superintendents quite unabashedly announced (published) recovery rates of 5 percent per year!

This experience only reinforced my conviction that hope, that neglected member of the great triad, was an indispensable factor in psychiatric treatment and psychiatric education.

At the end of the war, veterans requiring continued psychiatric treatment began returning to this country in large numbers, and at the same time the physicians who had seen these phenomena of stress and overstress develop and recede were demobilizing. Many of these doctors now sought to learn more about this psychiatry which seemed so important in understanding these cases. During the first few months of its existence, the Menninger School of Psychiatry received over six hundred applications. Other training centers were similarly flooded.

Some of them no doubt came into psychiatry because of an awareness of their own threatened disorganization and the dim realization that this human-all-too-human tendency was one against which penicillin and heart surgery and all the discoveries of modern medicine offered no protection. By Freud, discoveries of quite another sort had been made and knowledge of them had slowly become common property. These discoveries promised no miracles, no instantaneous cures; they did not seem to justify hope. In fact, Freud was frequently accused of a devastating pessimism. Surely hope has rarely entered medical science through so narrow and tortuous a crevice. But it did enter and its rays transformed the face of modern psychiatry in our lifetime. A whole new viewpoint in medicine developed, one that gave authority and technique to efforts at systematic self-scrutiny, a kind of extended and continuous diagnostic case study.

In a way it seems curious that the psychoanalytic process, which is so obviously diagnostic, has generally come to be called treatment. Diagnosis is the hopeful search for a way out; but the setting forth on the way which one discovers and the unflinching persistence in making the effort—*that* is the treatment; that is the self-directed, self-administered change.

The psychoanalytic treatment method is a great discovery but this is not what changed psychiatry. It was the new understanding that psychoanalytic research gave us concerning men's motives and inner resources, the intensity of partially buried conflicts, the unknown and unplumbed depths and heights of our nature, the formidable power each of us holds to determine whether he lives or dies. It was the realization that we must encourage each individual to see himself not as a mere spectator of cosmic events but as a prime mover; to regard himself not as a passive incident in the infinite universe but as one important unit possessing the power to influence great decisions by making small ones. Wrote William James:

> *Will you or won't you* have it so? is the most probing question we are ever asked. We are asked it every hour of the day, and about the largest as well as the smallest, the most theoretical as well as the most practical things. We answer by *consents* or *non-consents* and not by words. What wonder that these dumb responses should seem our deepest organs of communication with the nature of things! What wonder if the effort demanded by them be the measure of our worth as men!

"Ye shall know the truth and the truth shall make you free," said another wise One. For this emancipating truth Freud searched not in physics or chemistry or biology, but in the tabooed land of the emotions. From the Pandora chest of man's mind, full of harmful and unlovely things to be released upon a protesting world, there turned up—last of all—Hope.

Selfishness, vengefulness, hate, greed, pettiness, bitterness, vindictiveness, ruthlessness, cruelty, destructiveness, and even self-destructiveness—all these are in us. But not only those. Invisible at first, but slowly pervasive and neutralizing came love, and then—perhaps because of it—came faith, and then hope.

Love, faith, hope—in that order. The Greeks were wrong. *Of course* hope is real, and of course it is not evil. It is the enemy of evil, and an ally of love, which is goodness.

Freud's great courage led him to look honestly at the evil in man's nature. But he persisted in his researches to the bottom of the chest, and he discerned that potentially love is stronger than hate, that for all its core of malignancy, the nature of men can be transformed with the nurture and dispersion of love.

This was the hope that Freud's discoveries gave us. This was the spirit of the new psychiatry. It enabled us to replace therapeutic nihilism with constructive effort, to replace unsound expectations first with hope, and then with sound expectations.

This is what it did for us, for psychiatrists. And for our patients—miserable, apprehensive, discouraged, and often desperate—what can we do better than that? What can we do better than to dispel their false expectations—good and bad—and light for them a candle of hope to show them possibilities that may become sound expectations?

And we who are teachers—can we do better by our eager, young seekers for the keys to wisdom than to help them sharpen the accuracy of their expectations without extinguishing the divine fire?

But there are many people in the world who are neither our patients nor our students, and who are nonetheless filled with great apprehensiveness, partly from ignorance and mistrust of one another. They are afflicted with great suffering which all our discoveries have not ameliorated, and awed by vast discoveries which none of us fully comprehend. Some of them look to us for counsel, to us whom they have so highly honored and so generously rewarded with prerogatives and opportunities. They are our friends, our brothers and sisters, our neighbors, our cousins in foreign lands. For these people—for them and for ourselves—are we not now duty bound to speak up as scientists, not about a new rocket or a new fuel or a new bomb or a new gas, but about this ancient but rediscovered truth, the validity of Hope in human development—Hope, alongside of its immortal sisters, Faith and Love?

CHAPTER FOUR

Indomitable Spirits

"Twice in my life I have been in the presence of very great men," says Dr. Karl.

The first time was in 1934 when he visited Freud in Vienna with Dr. Franz Alexander of Chicago, who founded the Chicago Institute for Psychoanalysis.

The second time was in the summer of 1949 when Dr. Karl sat beside Dr. Albert Schweitzer at supper in an inn near Aspen, Colorado.

He compares these two occasions in a hitherto unpublished manuscript.

I offer these observations and impressions with a reluctance not born of modesty. Schweitzer was in this country in 1949 for only a few weeks. He was written up by numerous journalists in vivid, skillful, and convincing words. As I read their reports I had a growing respect for the skill of the artisans of this sister profession. Their verbal sketches conveyed pictures of Schweitzer's personality after only a brief exposure, like a rapid Kodak picture, whereas we psychiatrists work like artists over a canvas, using much time and labor, paying close attention to many details; even after we have finished the picture, the meaning of it may elude the painter. I, as only the amateur photographer, am keenly aware of the difficulty, the impossibility of quickly encompassing and comprehending another human personality, in such a way that it can be rendered into adequate words. One cannot, like a physician or a newspaper reporter, subject such individuals to systematic interrogation. One can only observe facial expression, small acts, responses and reactions to a few topics of conversation and minor details of everyday life, such as attitude towards time, food, putting on one's coat, walking through a door.

There is an aura about great individuals created by legend and report, by phantasy and by observation. This aura is distracting. It becomes confused with impressions that originate with oneself; these too one feels.

As I sat beside Schweitzer, who has been compared to Goethe, to Gandhi, and even to Jesus, it was a little startling to hear him order his fried eggs; it was a little disturbing to find myself intrigued by his old-fashioned wing collar and bow tie slightly askew. I made conventional remarks and asked a few obvious questions, reproaching myself for not being able to formulate questions worthy of a mind and vision so great as his and an opportunity so unique.

Fifteen years previously I had spent about the same amount of time with Sigmund Freud in Vienna. On these two occasions I was in the presence of very great men, and because they were both (at the time I saw them) about the same age, and because I had much subjective interest in both, it was inevitable some comparisons should have occurred to me.

I had every reason, every conscious reason at least, for placing a far higher value on the personality of Freud. I remember the visit to his home quite well. He kept me waiting for over an hour while he argued in private with Dr. Alexander who had gone inside the house ostensibly to introduce me. I waited in the garden talking with Dr. Ernest Jones and Anna Freud.

I had been told Freud was very punctual, so I was considerably nettled by the long wait. Later Dr. Alexander told me it was Freud who had detained him, discussing in anger certain developments in America concerning psychoanalysis. America was one of Freud's deep and inexplicable prejudices, and it was perhaps unfortunate that such an argument preceded my entrance since, unlike Dr. Alexander, born in Hungary, I was a native American. However, Freud proved to be so gracious during the interview that I could not have detected the alleged prejudice from anything he said to me. Perhaps a bit from what he didn't say.

Few colleagues had supported Freud's unpopular death instinct theory, and no one but myself had made self-destruction the subject of a book. Freud made no reference to this, which disappointed me. We spoke a little of the applications of psychoanalysis to more serious psychiatric conditions than the neuroses, the "psychoses." Freud expressed polite pessimism about this, saying, "I've never had much experience or success with doing so. But one can try."

Freud was a bit angry; Freud was in pain. (He went through twenty-eight operations and never took anything to kill the pain in his jaw except aspirin.) He bore his pain with incredible bravery; he was extremely reserved about mentioning it or allowing anyone to suspect he suffered, if possible. But it must have shortened his temper.

But what impressed me about Freud was the *inner* pain which he was obviously suffering, underlying his gentleness and sweetness, a kind of inner pain that may have derived in part from the content of his great discoveries because, like the atomic physicists, he may have felt his discoveries transcended comprehension of the effects and their control by the discoverer.

The feelings I carried away from my visit were tinged with sadness. While he concealed from me his bitterness toward America, and was most courteous, yet it slightly ruffled me that he had kept me waiting over an hour while he argued in private with my introducer. My narcissism was also slightly injured, as I said, that Freud made no reference to my published efforts to support his great but not popular death-instinct theory.

I went away from Freud with the impression I had been with a very great man, a great man who not only was tired but sad and suffering, who was perhaps faintly cynical about the purpose of my visit and knew that he had done me a favor by granting an interview which gave him little pleasure.

On the other hand, visiting with Schweitzer was as if everything pleased him. He was full of joy, not sorrow. Though he was about the same age as Freud, his spirit was much younger. He mentioned several times that he had so little time left to live and so much he wanted to do. He was alert and lively; his eyes twinkled, he made little jokes and smiled or laughed heartily with others. He repeatedly exclaimed about "how far" I had come just to see him (it was some seven hundred miles; I had gone about five thousand to see Freud).

There was another difference. Freud was a fighter: Schweitzer was not. He was a persistent and indefatigible *worker* with great versatility and virtuosity in music, theology, medicine, and surgery. Freud lacked the versatility; his virtuosity was in one or two fields. Freud carried that virtuosity further than Schweitzer has carried any of his great talents, for Freud discovered the instinct of aggression, its universality, its potentiality for evil, its susceptibility to control by the forces of love. Also, Schweitzer gave the impression of having no prejudices in the world, except the prejudice against evil, whereas Freud gave the impression of possessing many bitter prejudices—prejudice against America, against physicians (although he himself was one), prejudice against Christians (although he himself followed no Jewish observances and was Jewish only in the sense of ancestry and some cultural conditioning). Freud knew nothing of Protestant Christian theology, nothing of the Chinese, nothing of sports and games, very little of music and, in the opinion of many, very little about children.

When Jean and I went to see Schweitzer, we were kept waiting for a time outside the little guest house where he and Mrs. Schweitzer were staying as visitors in Aspen. Artur Rubinstein and Dimitri Mitropoulos, also after a long wait, had been invited in to speak with him for "a few minutes." These minutes had lengthened into an hour. The hostess, and later the host, went in to speed the departure of our little party. But once inside the little house, they too disappeared.

Finally, when it was almost dark, the door of the house opened and Dr. and Mrs. Schweitzer came out and went directly to the car. They bowed, smilingly, during the formal introductions. Immediately afterward they began to chat freely and informally as we entered the car and drove away.

"Ah, yes," said Schweitzer, "you are my colleague. But my dear colleague, you came so far to see me?"

This was said so warmly, so simply, so genuinely, that all deprecatory replies regarding the insignificance for a Middle Westerner of a journey to Colorado from Kansas seemed ineffectual. Schweitzer continued to express surprise and pleasure in being so honored, so admired. He spoke a little in English, mostly in French, then later in German. We drove a short distance to a mountain inn. There we filed into the dining room and took our places at a longish table.

At the head of that table sat Albert Schweitzer. THE Albert Schweitzer. One of the greatest living men. I sat beside him on his right. I thought of how the lips that had uttered profundities and wisdom for the whole world were now engaged in sociable chatting and little jokes; the hands and fingers that could play one musical instrument better than anyone else in the world were now spreading butter on a piece of bread. His eyes twinkled, he smiled frequently, and laughed aloud. Eager to make clear something he had said which

I had not fully grasped, he reached across playfully to a woman companion and thumping her on the arm called out vigorously "Interpreter! Interpreter! We need you again, interpreter!" He addressed me often as "dear colleague."

Hoping to learn something of his reconciliation of psychiatric and religious theory, I mentioned the emphasis psychiatrists had given Freud's concept of the function of love. To this he only nodded and smiled, then brought the discussion back to very practical matters by asking my opinion of the atabrine psychoses (caused perhaps by too much quinine) which he had observed and with which he had had so much difficulty because of his limited psychiatric hospital space. (He said he had only one room for such patients.) During the dinner I mentioned my efforts to maintain a private wildlife refuge. He was much more interested in this and nodded eagerly, saying, "I do the same thing myself, you know. I let all the birds and animals and weeds grow unmolested in our tract. Except for the plantings, of course, the orchards and the gardens." I asked him if this little tract didn't extend out into the whole vast jungle, and he vigorously assured me it did not, that the French government had given him a definitely restricted area. He said laughingly that the insects took full advantage of this wildlife refuge and harassed everyone constantly because there are no screens and the temperature is always about the same, 85° Fahrenheit, day and night; it is very humid, there is almost never any breeze. This makes it uncomfortable for human beings, but apparently very comfortable for insects.

I asked him about the personality traits of the natives. He emphasized first what we all know but tend to forget, namely that Africans are of many kinds. He said he was qualified to speak only of the natives in his particular area. Among these he differentiated between those who had been exposed to the so-called civilization of the French colonials and those who had not. For the most part, he worked with the latter whom he described, without either bitterness or amusement, as characteristically unreliable and unpredictable. For example, if he himself would hoe and dig in the garden ordering them to do the same, they would follow and imitate him. But if he left the garden to go to the hospital to perform an operation, they would lay down their implements and fall asleep or leave even though they had been told many times that their comfort, even their very existence, depended upon their working. The concept of work as necessary for survival or because others requested it or because it yielded benefits for the future, seemed not to be grasped by them. They worked only because of immediate return or because they were forced to do so. In psychoanalytic language, they illustrate what one might call an almost complete absence of super-ego. Schweitzer mentioned that even those natives whom he had trained for many years to perform certain tasks well under supervision could not be relied upon to carry on these tasks the minute the eye of authority was turned elsewhere.

Although I had read this in his books, I was very much impressed by his telling of it because it brought home to me vividly how reconciled this great man is to work himself, for the work's sake. It is difficult enough for most people to conceive of giving up all the ordinary compensations for labor, secondary though they may be—material reward, barter value, prestige—but it is even more difficult to imagine sustained, self-sacrificial work of this kind being carried on without hope either of gratitude on the one hand or of permanent character alteration on the other. I have not seen this stressed in any of the comments about Schweitzer's work in Africa; the privations, the discomforts, the loneliness, the difficult climate—these and other hardships are often mentioned. But to think of a man working for people who are essentially children and very young children at that, and children who learn very slowly, if at all—children who see no necessity for expressing permanent gratitude—seems to me a particularly heavy burden.

But Schweitzer seemed to enjoy doing things for people. This was illustrated rather vividly by his autographing experience. Efforts were made by the authorities at Aspen to keep him protected from the throngs who wanted to meet him. An effort was made to hurry him out the back entrance of the inn to a waiting car, but a young woman in the front row reached him before his escorts did, and handed him her program for an autograph. His sponsors urged him not to start such a precedent, saying it would tax his waning strength and limit time for other activities far too greatly. A crowd now gathered about him, waving their programs and copies of his books they had bought. He turned to his friends and said, "For some strange reason these people want me to write my name for them. Surely that isn't much to do. I'm glad to do it," and for over an hour he smilingly complied with requests for his autograph.

This episode and others like it might indicate that Schweitzer was not the humble, modest man that some have described, but a man who got a great deal of pleasure out of acclamation and popularity. This is not my impression at all. It is obvious he got simple pleasure out of the fact that people wanted him to do something he could do, and it seemed to make little difference to him whether that was a surgical operation in Africa, an autograph in Aspen, or the rendition of a Bach toccata in London. I think of him as a shy and gentle man, rather slow-moving but very alert mentally. In view of his enormous virtuosity and versatility, to say nothing of his sudden worldwide popularity, it seemed to me his humility and modesty were outstanding.

Dr. Karl wrote formal tributes to Freud on several occasions. The first was an article in The Nation, *October 7, 1939, titled "Sigmund Freud":*

At midnight, September 23–24, 1939, Sigmund Freud died in London in his eighty-fourth year. His death came as a great relief to those who knew how the cancer which had afflicted him for sixteen years and which had necessitated operation after operation and caused him constant unalleviated pain had within recent months extended beyond the reach of surgical or radiological relief. It is an eloquent, though incidental, testimony to the heroic qualities of the man that during all this period his only medication was an occasional tablet of aspirin. Only within the last few hours of his life was any morphine administered, and despite incredible suffering, to which was added the sorrow of exile and the loss of many friends, he had continued to see his patients and to work on his manuscripts until a few weeks before his death.

The solemn magnificence of this brave and losing battle of an indomitable spirit with an inexorable physical process reflects at the same time the theme and the vitality of his life work. His greatest concept was that of the instinctual conflict between the will to live and the wish to die, the life forces and the death forces. In his early years he passed productively and brilliantly through the phase of laboratory interests and then through that of clinical medicine (neurology), and made great and lasting discoveries in each of these fields. But he was not satisfied with these; he became interested in the more fundamental factors that served to determine not only disease but health, not only symptoms but behavior, not only pain but sorrow. And for the next three decades of his life he studied the phenomena of what he later called the life instinct, which shows itself most directly in the impulse to love and to reproduce. For this he was reproached and ridiculed by those many for whom the conventional attitudes of hypocrisy, prudery, and salaciousness impelled the relegation of sexuality to the role of a dirty and inconsequential incident of unfortunate biological necessity. When as the result of indefatigable patience and unflinching courage he had gained for his views the recognition and acceptance of scientific leaders, he turned to the consideration of the malignant force which battles against this life instinct. Man, he said, is his own worst enemy; warring constantly against the instinct to live and to let live, to love and to create, is an instinct which has as its object the return to inorganic insensibility; it is this instinct in the direction of death from which arise our hates, our bitterness, our suffering, our sicknesses, and our demise. This concept of hate aroused the same resistances and refutations as had his earlier concept of love, despite such frightful confirmations of it as the activities of the Third Reich.

It is a presumptuous thing to comment on the life of a genius upon the occasion of his death. Freud is not a man about whom one can write a few casual words, a few comments of praise, a few notes of criticism, and feel that an appropriate gesture has been made to his passing. For Freud was not an ordinary man; he was not an ordinary scientist. He was so nearly unique an individual that it is difficult to find anyone with whom to compare him. No one in the field of psychology ever attained to a fraction of his stature. Among medical scientists almost none can be said to have approached him in brilliancy, originality, or influence upon medical practice. Perhaps no other one individual in the field of science lived to see the thinking of the entire world so profoundly modified by his discoveries within his lifetime as did Freud. Galileo, Dalton, Lavoisier, Darwin, these and others contributed discoveries which greatly modified our thinking and our ways of living, but the effect was more gradual in its permeation. For not only medical science and psychological science and sociological science, but literature, art, anthropology, pedagogy, and even popular speech show the influence of Freud's discoveries and show them in unmistakable terms.

All that Freud did stems from one simple discovery, a discovery based on knowledge which many had possessed before him. This was the knowledge that beneath the surface manifestations of human life there are deeper motives and feelings and purposes which the individual conceals not only from others but even from himself. Freud discovered a method for ascertaining and eliciting this hidden material; he called this method psychoanalysis. By means of it he and many others working with him gradually accumulated a considerable body of systematic knowledge about the unconscious processes of the human personality; this body of knowledge is also called psychoanalysis. It is psychoanalysis in the former sense which trained physicians use for the relief of suffering and maladaptation in their patients, and for further research in the study of personality. It is psychoanalysis in the latter sense which has come to modify the trends of literature, science, and philosophy.

It was from the fruit of his methodological discovery that Freud learned to understand technically, and hence usefully, the concept of ambivalence—although as a matter of fact this particular word was not coined by him. He became able to understand and to help others to understand that just as back of life there is always death, so back of professed love there is always some hate and back of professed hate always some love. More clearly than anyone else he saw how stalwartly the human mind defends itself against the acceptance of unpleasant truth. This helped him to be tolerant in the face of the ridicule, the misrepresentation, the distortion, the bitter and unscientific refutation of his theories which they initially aroused throughout the world. He reminded himself and his students that all scientific discoveries which diminish the feeling of self-importance in mankind stimulate resentment and incredulity. And so, were he alive, he would not be dismayed by the astounding ambivalence revealed in some of the contemporary comments upon his life. It would neither surprise nor disturb him that a great newspaper (*The New York Times*) should have published—on September 25, 1939—an editorial ostensibly commemorating his death but actually vilifying him, misrepresenting him, speaking of "his colossal self-satisfaction and his natural intellectual arrogance," declaring with pompous inaccuracy "that psychiatrists still dismiss him as unscientific," flagrantly misrepresenting the facts about his last published book, and ending with the awkward and dubious compliment that he "was the most effective disturber of complacency in our time."

It is true that Freud was never happy in his feeling toward America, and even his best friends, many of whom were Americans, were never able to fully understand it or to alter it. He felt that we were characterized by an "unthinking optimism and a shallow activity." He was always suspicious of the popularity his theories and techniques acquired in this country. It is an ironic paradox that America should today be the country in which his theories are best known and most widely accepted. This is true not only of the general public but of medical scientists.

Sigmund Freud finally succumbed to death after many years spent in deflecting it from others. He was subject to prejudices and complexes although he spent his life in eliminating them from others. But these things do not detract from his greatness; indeed, it can be fairly said that he gave evidence of fewer prejudices and fewer complexes than most men, just as he retained his grasp on life longer than most men. What cannot be conveyed in words is Freud's ineffable modesty and gentleness and essential sweetness of character, for he had the qualities of the true scientist, and he never for one moment forgot that he was only a passing observer. To the eternal blessing of the human race, his sharp eyes and his great mind made his observations uniquely effulgent.

Another tribute to Freud appeared in the Bulletin of the Menninger Clinic, *September, 1949:*

Some centuries before Christ, it occurred to some wise Grecians that the honor we do others is in part for our own sake, and Ben Jonson cast this thought in his romantic idyl:

> I sent thee late a rosy wreath,
> Not so much honoring thee
> As giving it a hope that there
> It could not withered be.

It is in this spirit that the editors of the *Bulletin* and the cooperating committee from the Topeka Psychoanalytic Society have dedicated this number to the memory of Sigmund Freud. The honor we can offer him is nothing compared to the support which his eternal spirit gives to our own work, our thinking, and our ideals.

It is for our own sakes, not in a ritualistic compulsion, that we call to mind in thoughtful reflection the solemn events of ten years ago. On March 13, 1938, a cable was sent to Professor Freud inviting him and his family to become our permanent guests and to continue his work here in whatever way he desired. All the world knows how he was able soon after this to get out of Austria and spend a little over a year of refuge among friends in London. In May of 1939 one of us, representing the American Psychiatric Association, cabled him this: "Your fellow members assembled here in convention unanimously express their gratification at your safe arrival in London and send best wishes." Four months later he was dead.

Few of us realized the physical suffering that accompanied the distress of those later years of his life. Dr. Max Schur has written a note to the *Bulletin of the American Psychoanalytic Association* incident to the death of Dr. Hans Pichler, who died in Vienna in

February 1949. The last of the twenty-eight operations by Doctor Pichler was performed in London in September 1938.

At the time of Freud's death, there appeared an editorial in *The New York Times* (September 25, 1939) which seemed to many of us to be misrepresentative, demeaning, and patronizing. "Psychiatrists," it said, "still dismiss him as unscientific." The editorial ended with the awkward and dubious compliment that "Freud was the most effective disturber of complacency in our time." This editorial angered many of us. It was answered in a spirited and eloquent way by Dr. Smith Ely Jelliffe and of course it was eclipsed by many other memorial notices far more complimentary.

But as the years have passed and the world has grown more troubled rather than less, that description of Freud as "the most effective disturber of complacency" seems—to the writer, at least—to have taken on a new and stronger significance. For perhaps, of all the deadly sins in a sinful world, complacency is the greatest. The complacency which springs from the assumption that man is a rational creature and that science is the answer to everything (or else that religion is), the complacency of intellectual arrogance, the complacency of emotional isolation and social indifference—these are complacencies which need disturbing and which Freud did disturb profoundly and, let us hope, irrevocably.

In these days when peace of mind and peace of soul are held up as desiderata of the highest order at the very moment that millions are homeless and millions are hungry and millions are in slavery and millions in fear—surely we need to fear the dreadful disease of smug complacency and restless pursuit of an illusory peace. Freud did much more than disturb our complacency. But that alone is a great heritage.

A third tribute appeared as an introduction to a special Freud memorial issue of the Bulletin of the Menninger Clinic *in May, 1956:*

One hundred years ago now a child was born in a humble home in the hinterlands of central Europe who grew up and became a doctor and a research scientist. His discoveries and proposals changed the thinking of the whole world within his lifetime. This did not make him less humble; he bowed his head lower and through suffering and exile worked all the harder. Not to Isaiah nor to Jesus nor to Plato, not to Empedocles nor to Galileo nor to Newton was it given that they should live to see the effects of their discoveries and their teachings. But Freud may have thought of Moses who changed his world but lay down in a lonely foreign grave, or of Alexander, who conquered everyone except himself and died in disappointment and defeat far from home, or of Columbus, who found a new world but died in chains in the old one.

But revolutionary and world-shaking as were his discoveries and postulations, perhaps Freud's most long-lasting influence upon those of us who follow him lay in his character. His persistence in the pursuit of enigmatic and mysterious data, his conviction regarding the reality and lawfulness of psychic phenomena, his belief in the curability of the "hopeless" neuroses, his humility in the midst of renown, his courage in the face of disaster, his patience in the grip of suffering—it is these which now three generations of followers have consciously and unconsciously taken unto themselves and into themselves as ideals. If we are less assiduous than he in the pursuit of truth, less modest in the proclaiming of it, or less effective in its application, count it our lesser stature, not our lesser aspiration.

We are a sentimental species, and proud of our time-binding faculty. So we "celebrate," as we say, in our quaint human fashion, the double decimal of the circuits of our planet about the sun since the mother of Sigmund Freud first gazed at her newborn child and wondered, as mothers do, what he and the world might do to one another. More than anyone who ever lived, that child was to show us how "as the twig is bent the tree's inclined." And so on this anniversary we honor a great tree of many leaves but we honor also that mother and the father and the others who together bent that twig in that village in another part of our planet one hundred years ago.

Another "great tree" was Havelock Ellis, who died just two months before Freud. Dr. Karl paid tribute to him in the July 22, 1939, issue of The Nation:

Havelock Ellis died in England on July 10 at the age of 80. He was described by the New York *Herald Tribune* as a psychologist and sociologist, by the *Times* as an essayist and philosopher, and by *Time* as an editor and sexologist. Perhaps in other journals it will be recorded that he was a poet, an artist, a physician, a psychiatrist. Such designations are correct, but even taken all together they are inadequate, for Havelock Ellis had the versatility that is the blessing of genius.

Most of those to whom his name is familiar know only about one or two aspects of his life. Some think of him correctly as a pioneer in the study of sex; others esteem him for his literary grace and his gift as a critic; few remember that he was a successful editor and still fewer that he was a physician and a psychiatrist; only his intimates knew that he was an excellent cook as well as a charming host. He himself might have put first among his attainments that he led a full, a rich, and a happy life. He believed, in the words of the Numidian Bishop of Hippo, that one should "love and do what you like," and he practiced this.

As a thoughtful boy of sixteen, Ellis dedicated himself to the study of sex at the period in life when other youths are solving their adolescent struggles by indulgence in political and religious fervor or by ostentatious rebellion against custom and social orthodoxy. He pursued this idea with scientific detachment and with unfaltering courage in the face of bitter and slanderous opposition, indifferent alike to applause and praise on the one hand and abuse and criticism on the other. Substantially, Ellis did three things. In the first place, he made a careful, thorough, and honest collection of data relating to a phase of biology which the hypocrisy and prudery of medical science had, until Ellis, caused to be ignored for the most part. In the second place, he evolved and advocated a hedonistic philosophy of life tempered if not determined by the sane, scientific attitude toward sex which his studies engendered. In the third place, he presented his scientific findings and philosophical beliefs to the world with that artistic combination of directness and delicacy which made them acceptable to non-scientific readers.

It is inevitable that Havelock Ellis should be compared with Freud. Like Freud, Ellis was scientist, physician, psychiatrist, psychologist, philosopher, and essayist. Like Freud, he bravely but modestly stuck to his principles in the face of persecution. Like Freud, he was vastly and widely misunderstood. Like Freud, he recognized the importance of sex. While Ellis was saying that sex was the center of life, Freud was saying that the sex instinct should be called the life instinct. Freud has acknowledged his indebtedness to Ellis for several ideas and terms. But their ways parted, for Freud is primarily a clinician, and this Ellis never was. While Freud worked with patients, Ellis worked with ideas. Both had the ideal scientific attitude, but of the two only Freud used the traditional scientific method. Even Ellis's celebrated *Studies in the Psychology of Sex* was chiefly a collection of data. They had no practical applications, no therapeutic usefulness. Freud looked at the same data, not in large collections but in individual instances, and asked, "Why should these things exist in this person? Why does he feel or act as he does?" And then he proceeded to find out. What Freud did was to explain the why and the how of the facts which Ellis tabulated. On the other hand, while the work of Ellis supplied no means for understanding or relieving the individual, it formed the basis for a philosophy of life which benefited and enlightened the entire world, and thus prepared the way for Freud's work with individuals.

It seems extraordinary today that the leading British medical journal, the *Lancet*, refused to review a scientific study of homosexuality by a medical man (Ellis) and explained this in an editorial entitled "The Question of Indecent Literature," declaring that it had not been published under the proper auspices. To this Ellis made reply that none of the medical publishers whom he had approached were interested in the publication of such a book. By others than the medical press the first volume was called "a wicked, bawdy, scandalous, and obscene book." Even *The Nation* of those days commented rather haughtily if not contemptuously that frequently in the volume "one comes upon remarks that suggest a paean upon sex, scientifically, philosophically, and poetically."

How does it come about that some individuals, such as Ellis and Freud, can have so completely escaped those psychological fetters which bind all of us? The answer is not easy to give. This much one can say, however, that there certainly was in Ellis a highly developed sensitiveness to the principles of dialectics, to the recognition of truth in the opposite. Early in his life he wrote that there were few questions about which, after a study of both sides, he did not come to a conclusion "totally opposite to the orthodox one which I have always been taught to believe true." Discussing this further, Ellis said that he felt sure that he was not actuated by any spirit of perversity, but on the contrary was frequently "convicted" in spite of himself and "made miserable." To one psychoanalytically oriented this accidental substitution of the word "convicted" when he obviously meant to write "convinced" suggests how strongly determined this attitude was by emotional factors. It is significant that Ellis, who led a most idealistic sexual life, should have written the world's greatest treatise on the abnormalities of sex. Olive Schreiner once wrote that Ellis was like a cross between a Christ and a faun. But all this does not explain him; it only indicates that it was out of vast internal contradictions that there grew an outer life characterized by a magnificent unity of purpose and spirit.

Dr. Karl has devoted a large part of his life to teaching psychiatrists, and he remembers fondly the men who influenced him at the outset of his own career. One of them was Dr. Elmer Ernest Southard, who urged him to return to Topeka, saying, "Go out there to the people you know and try to help them." Here, in a review of The Open Mind, *Frederick P. Gay's biography of Southard, Dr. Karl tells what his early teacher meant to him. The review appeared in the* Psychoanalytic Quarterly, *Volume 8, 1939.*

In the early years of this century there flashed across the horizon a bright star in the field of psychiatry, a star that blazed brilliantly, briefly, and disappeared as suddenly as it had come. The light of the star went out in 1920 when Elmer Ernest Southard, one of the youngest professors in the three hundred years of Harvard history, died at the age of forty-three.

It was a brave and ambitious task that Professor Frederick Gay of Columbia University set himself when he essayed to write the life of his friend. Yet he has done it faithfully and accurately. If his compilation of facts lacks something of the scintillating spirit or the warmth of feeling characteristic of the man whose life is recorded, this must be charged up to the inevitable difficulties of describing the soul of a genius.

There can be no doubt of Southard's greatness measured by his breadth of vision, by his capacity for stimulating and inspiring his students and colleagues, and by the amazing fertility of his investigatory curiosity. The man who was not only a pathologist, a psychiatrist, a hospital executive, and a teaching professor, but a philosopher, a philologist, a psychologist, a poet, a chess champion, a sociologist and, above all, a charming, gracious human being is a personality too rare and precious and extraordinary to be registered in the cold lines of print of a formal biography. In his few brief years Southard attracted to himself and inspired a large number of disciples with whom he dealt with a never-failing kindliness, with that extraordinary technique which so few professors have of making subordinates feel that their ideas are brilliant and important. Often he would take an idea diffidently tendered by one of them and perhaps almost valueless at the beginning, mold or polish it into something of worth, and give it back to the author without the slightest intimation that anyone but that author deserved credit for the product.

The innumerable facets of his personality as seen by his intimate friends, his colleagues, his students, have been patiently collected and recorded by Professor Gay in a book which every man who knew Southard will want to possess, and which every man who would know the determining personalities of American psychiatry will feel obliged to read.

To readers of the *Psychoanalytic Quarterly* it is an interesting speculation as to why those two leaders, Southard and Freud, never met, and what would have happened if they had. In spite of Southard's nominal rejection of psychoanalysis, one of the reviewer's friends is convinced that although he had not publicly acknowledged his intellectual acceptance of psychoanalytic principles, he had long recognized their validity. I knew him very well, and I do not quite believe this; for it must be said that strictly speaking the title Professor Gay has given this book is not accurately descriptive of Southard. Southard had a brilliant, a versatile, a profound, a cultivated, and a productive mind, but not an open mind—an open heart, but not an open mind. This is one of many ways in which he resembled Freud. They also shared the same personal charm and graciousness, the same self-effacement, the same joy in the discovery and elaboration of new ideas, and the same prejudice against foreigners. And just as Professor Freud has never been able to bring himself to feel quite right about America and Americans, so Professor Southard had a definite prejudice against Europeans and against ideas originating and developing in Europe. He would have pointed to the present political developments there as evidence for the justifiability of his prejudices. Psychoanalysis was one of these European ideas, and Southard rejected it instinctively (I use the word in its conventional, not its scientific, sense). Furthermore, I do not feel it is disloyal for me to say that Southard was essentially a "superficialist" in the sense that he felt that the nature of things was patently apparent even on the surface if one but looked carefully. He regarded the tendency to sneer at the obvious as a kind of blindness. It required courage for him to say that he could detect pathological changes by the manual palpation of the gross naked brain, and it required courage for him to say that one could see from the very reasons alieged by employers for the discharge of certain employees that the latter were sick. Freud too bespoke the significance of the obvious; for example, the psychopathology apparent in everyday life. But where Freud depended upon deep subsurface analysis, Southard depended more directly upon deductive logic and philosophical extensions, especially by analogy. In this sense Freud is, of course, much the greater scientist; but whereas Freud nominally rejects philosophy and exalts empiricism, Southard, although trained in the mechanics of empirical science to a far greater degree than Freud, preferred the philosophical disciplines to those in which he was trained.

And it is extremely interesting that Southard, who sparkled with life, whose whole career was characterized by an optimistic vivacity, should have died so young, while Freud, whose sober realism led the optimistic Southard to describe him as a pessimist, Freud, who wrote of death, who gave us that magnificent conception of the death instinct, lived, in spite of suffering and sorrow far beyond that to which the average man is exposed, to almost twice the age at which Southard died.

And of Dr. Smith Ely Jelliffe and Dr. Peter Bassoe, two more men who, as he said, "greatly influenced" his life, Dr. Karl wrote in the Bulletin of the Menninger Clinic, *November, 1945:*

I should like to write a very personal memorial notice concerning two great men in our field of medicine, both of whom contributed much to it and both of whom greatly influenced my life and therefore had a direct connection with the institutions and organizations with which I am connected.

My teacher, Ernest Southard, died in 1920. His brilliant and catholic mind was nonetheless capable of stubborn prejudices, and one of these prejudices was against psychoanalysis. Yet it was through him that I had met Smith Ely Jelliffe of New York, one of the most vigorous and most gifted of the protagonists of psychoanalysis at that time. Dr. Jelliffe was like Dr. Southard in his catholicity of mind and in his brilliance; he was less philosophical than Southard but more erudite and far more experienced clinically. I remember with deep gratitude how he took me under his wing after Southard died—me, a youngster fresh out of my hospital training, unknown to anyone in the field. Dr. Jelliffe introduced me to people, to experiences, and, above all, to ideas. He took me into his home, where I was impressed no less by the thousands of volumes of neurologic and psychiatric wisdom than by the infinite variety of home-made wines and liqueurs and the enormous collections of fungi, mosses, and pressed botanical specimens.

It was Jelliffe who introduced me to clinical psychoanalysis; prior to that time I had known only the published material of Freud, Jones, Brill, Frink, and others. In those days a personal analysis was not regarded as a necessary prerequisite to the clinical practice of psychoanalysis, and it was Jelliffe who first encouraged me to try the experiment of listening for a time to free associations and judging for myself whether or not they had any clinical meaning. I recall a private meeting of a few psychoanalysts in New York to which Dr. Jelliffe took me, at which one of the members of the group described in considerable detail his own personal experiences in analysis with Professor Freud, subsequently discussed by all those present as if it were an ordinary clinical case.

In those early days of psychoanalysis Jelliffe always stood for an open-minded consideration of the theories and findings of all workers. He was regarded by some as being Adlerian and by others as being Jungian. I think he did give considerable weight to the ideas of these men, particularly Jung, but basically he was Freudian in the best sense of that word. As he grew older he became more and more definitely so. In fact I recall very clearly his angry reaction to an article of Jung's which we read together; what he objected to were certain claims of Jung for priority which he said actually belonged to Freud.

Dr. Jelliffe saw no borderline between medicine, neurology, psychiatry, and psychoanalysis. This seems obvious enough today, but in 1920 this was more than heresy; it was either "dilettantism" or "psychosis." I have heard Jelliffe described by envious and hostile critics as belonging in both categories. Nothing could be more inaccurate. The profundity and orderliness of Jelliffe's investigations were evident in whatever field or aspect he wrote about. He was an exceptionally fine neurologist and an exceptionally fine psychiatrist and an exceptionally fine internist. He knew all these fields just as he knew the fields of mycology, botany, geography, chemistry, and many others. He knew the essential contribution of every European worker in neurology and psychiatry and knew most of the leaders personally. His reading was prodigious and his memory equal to his voracious reading.

It is apt to be forgotten in these days of "psychosomatic medicine" that Jelliffe was writing about the emotional factors in physical disease thirty years ago. When he suggested (1916) that psoriasis might be a "hysterical conversion syndrome," or that tuberculosis was in some degree amenable to psychotherapy (1919), or that psychogenic factors were present in multiple sclerosis (1921), bone disease (1923), hypertension, urinary-system disorders, and many other "somatic" conditions (1925–1935), he was laughed at; he was maligned; he was ignored. But he was also respected, listened to, and imitated. Psychiatrists began to think about the possibility that their field extended beyond the description of delusions and hallucinations. He and his longtime associate, William Alanson White, and their mutual friend, A. A. Brill, were the real fathers of psychoanalysis in this country; and Jelliffe should be regarded as the founder of psychosomatic medicine and credited with the introduction of the term.

Dr. Jelliffe died on September 25, 1945, after a long illness against which he battled with great courage. His funeral was held in his home at Hulett's Landing on Lake George, and he was buried near there in the forest, among the trees he had seen grow from sprouts. In this quiet spot (his wife writes) "the winds alone will move the trees to sound, and summer rain will fall and winter snow; the small animals he loved will scamper over him. His frantic seeking for knowledge, his bright spirit will rest. Surely he will now know all that he sought."

Only a few weeks after this one great tree had fallen, the thin forest of our medical leaders was depleted by the fall of another giant.

Peter Bassoe, who died in Chicago on November 5, 1945, was a man very different in type from Smith Ely Jelliffe but similar in being a great leader, teacher, and friend. Dr. Bassoe was a neurologist, pure and simple. He never laid claim to any considerable knowledge of psychiatry although he was always interested in it and never displayed the depreciatory attitude toward it which used to prevail in some neurological centers. For many years he edited the *Yearbook of Neurology and Psychiatry* with eminent fairness to the latter field. Thousands of medical students learned clinical neurology under his tutelage. He contributed many original articles of significant scientific value. But in my own opinion, his greatest contribution was the inspiration given to his many colleagues by the strength and beauty of his personal character.

My personal association with Dr. Bassoe began shortly after I had met Dr. Jelliffe. In the winter of 1921 I called upon him in Chicago and was most hospitably received. He showed me his work in the Rush Medical College and the Presbyterian Hospital, with which he was long associated, and took me to his home in Evanston where I became well acquainted with his wife, herself a physician, their son, and their four daughters. Dr. Bassoe and I talked about the formation of an organization of neurologists and psychiatrists practicing in the Middle West. He endorsed the idea heartily and suggested a list of men who might form the nucleus of such a body. At our first informal meeting in St. Louis in 1922 he presided and was unanimously chosen temporary chairman and later elected our first president.

The Central Neuropsychiatric Association thus born grew to be a sizable body; I have often heard it described as the liveliest neuropsychiatric organization in the world. Whatever success it has achieved is certainly to be ascribed in large part to Peter Bassoe, who was present at every meeting since its formation, served on almost every committee, counseled every president and secretary. All of us will remember him as a kindly, wise, gentle, fatherly man who was fair to everyone, considerate of everyone, friendly to everyone, a man who never did a mean or selfish thing in his life, who never expressed an ungenerous or bitter sentiment. He was able to do this without swerving for a moment from his scientific ideals and his professional work.

This is what we shall remember.

For another pioneer in psychoanalysis, Dr. Abraham A. Brill, Dr. Karl delivered the following tribute at the annual meeting of the American Psychoanalytic Association, May 15, 1948, in Washington. It was published in the Bulletin of the Menninger Clinic, *September, 1949.*

Because I knew him for many years, and sat with him at many meetings of the American Psychiatric Association and the American Psychoanalytic Association, I feel qualified as well as honored to fulfill a request to speak a few words at this annual meeting of the American Psychoanalytic Association about the scientific work of our longtime "permanent president."

Let us remind ourselves today, and let us often remind our children and grandchildren and great-grandchildren hereafter, how much we owe to Abraham Arden Brill. Let us remind them that it was this little doctor with a big heart—born in Austria, an immigrant to America, a boy who arrived with three cents in his pocket, a student who put himself through school and through medical school—that it was this real American who perceived the greatness of Freud's discovery and brought it to America.

Let us remind them that it was he, this indomitable, irresistible, uncompromising little doctor, who gave life and being to psychoanalysis in this country—who first translated Bleuler and Jung and Freud for Americans to read; who fathered the New York Psychoanalytic Society and mothered the American Psychoanalytic Association; who faced with intrepidity and good humor the sneers and jeers, the scorn and calumny of his colleagues to speak out for what he believed, to speak the truth he saw and hoped they might sometime see.

Let us remind ourselves and our successors that the great edifice of psychoanalysis and psychoanalytic psychiatry, which today we eagerly and proudly help to build still greater, was established for us here, with his lifeblood, by A. A. Brill. He taught Americans such everyday words as repression, displacement, transference, abreaction, and the unconscious. He wrote the first English treatise on psychoanalysis, plus 140-odd other books and articles. For many of us in this Association, as we look around each year at the ever-increasing multitudes that flock to these meetings, once so pitiably small and esoteric, the figure of a plump, cheery, energetic "permanent president" will always be visible —sitting at sessions or chatting in corridors, nodding, listening, smiling at us, and ill concealing his pride in the evidence of the rich fruit of his many labors.

If some of his earlier contributions now seem elementary, if some of his presentations and translations have now been superseded, let us never forget that it was with these as an entering wedge that he taught the present teachers of American psychiatry, and thus helped to develop the dynamic psychoanalytic psychiatry of today. Let us not forget also that many of his contributions were keen, novel, original, and of basic importance. With these stimulating, variegated studies, Dr. Brill continued to be engaged up to the day of his death, and they remain for the enrichment of our knowledge.

But the greatest contribution Dr. Brill made to us may well be something beyond these shining landmarks, these patriarchal milestones. I suspect that it may seem to many (as it does to me) that his greatest bequest to us was the example of his indomitably optimistic, honest, and courageous spirit. Death itself had no alarm for Brill. A little over a year before he died he addressed his beloved Vidonian Club on the topic "Thoughts on Life and Death." It is a charming and characteristic essay. In it he described in his fresh lively style a flight of *Ephemeridae* which he had once observed, and added, "We who, to our minds, belong to a much higher stage of evolution tarry on this earth much longer; everything being equal for three score years and ten, but in the end the

> ". . . Earth, that nourished thee, shall claim
> Thy growth, to be resolved to earth again,
> And, lost each human trace, surrendering up
> Thine individual being, shalt thou go
> To mix forever with the elements,
> To be a brother to the insensible rock . . .

"Thus spake a young man when he was only about sixteen years old, in his *Thanatopsis,* in his reflections on death. I have always considered this summation of our seemingly complicated self by William Cullen

118

Bryant the most beautiful and most consoling description of the end-in-view. What could be nicer than 'to be a brother to the insensible rock'?

"As to what happens after we stop breathing, I agreed with one of my favorite authors, Samuel Butler, who said: 'Still, the life we have beyond the grave is our truest life, and our happiest, for we pass it in the profoundest sleep, as though we were children in our cradles. If we are wronged it hurt us not; if we wrong others we do not suffer for it; and if we die, as even the Handels and Bellinis and Shakespeares soon or later do, we die easily, know neither fear nor pain, and live anew in the lives of those who have been begotten of our work and who have for the time come up into our room.' Samuel Butler repeats here what Cicero said long ago and what our own Herman Melville said somewhat differently: 'Since death is the last evening of all, valiant souls will taunt him while they may. Yet rather, should the wise regard him as the inflexible friend, who even against our own wills, from life's evils triumphantly relieves us.' In old Greece it was customary to sacrifice a rooster to Aesculapius when a person recovered from a disease, but when Socrates was about to drink the hemlock he asked his friends and pupils who were with him to sacrifice a rooster when he died, 'Because,' said he, 'I look upon the end of life as a recovery.' . . .

"And so," said Brill, with his famous chuckle, "whether we have passed through life as Vidonians or as criminals, we have all done our best with the means at our disposal. For whatever we did depended, not, as we think, on ourselves, but on accidental factors which we ourselves did not control.

"As you know I have always been deeply influenced by the monistic philosophy of Spinoza, who posits a single substance which he calls God and maintains that everything here is nothing but an accident of the divine substance itself. Man, as an individual thing, Spinoza conceives as an accident or a mode. The modes of Spinoza are to the substance as the rippling *waves* of the sea to the *water* of the sea. . . . Hence when I consider our departed founders"—and here he cites several, mentioning "especially my close friend Jelliffe, that brilliant and versatile mind who was the last of them to leave us; when I think of all these students of the mind I cannot help but return to the closing words of *Thanatopsis* (I have altered the personal pronouns in the quotation from second to first person):

"So live, that when my summons comes to join
The innumerable caravan, which moves
To that mysterious realm, where each shall take

His chamber in the silent halls of death,
I go not, like the quarry-slave at night,
Scourged to his dungeon, but, sustained and soothed
By an unfaltering trust, approach my grave,
Like one who wraps the drapery of his couch
About him, and lies down to pleasant dreams."

Freud's biographer, Ernest Jones, was renowned in his own right. After learning of Jones's death in 1958, Dr. Karl wrote the following, previously unpublished, reminiscence of his meetings with Jones, first in Freud's garden in Vienna and later in the United States.

The night I finished reading the Freud biography by Ernest Jones, word came over the radio that Jones had died. It struck me most sadly, because I had been strongly moved to cable him and tell him what a great deed I thought he had done in thus memorializing Freud. I had that feeling that what we can do to encourage fellow travelers in this valley of life is often too little and too late.

In 1934 Jones and I sat in the garden in Freud's summer home talking with Anna Freud and waiting for Dr. Franz Alexander and Professor Freud to get through their conference. We got started on a discussion of Americans, among other things. I thought Doctor Jones was a little unnecessarily acidulous, but I didn't hold it against him. He declared that I was mistaken about the British being so polite; Americans, he said, were much more so, but the trouble with Americans was that they were so wasteful and destructive.

Eleven years later, during the war, Leo Bartemeier and Larry Kubie and I had dinner with Jones (and some other analysts) in London and on this occasion he was exceedingly truculent. He resented the fact that the American psychoanalysts liked their own journals more than they seemed to like the *International Journal of Psychoanalysis* which, he felt, should remain *the* central organ of psychoanalysis. Unless we Americans supported it, it could not survive. It wasn't the content of the discussion so much as the tone of the discussion that was disturbing—Jones made it so evident that he didn't like us, he didn't like American chauvinism. (Who does?) Jones did not entertain us or offer to do so or show us any special courtesies as most other colleagues did.

Well, I had almost forgotten this incident until he and Mrs. Jones were our guests at dinner in Chicago on his last visit to the United

States in 1956 and he told me with a sigh that he remembered keenly what had taken place in Vienna that afternoon; and that he only wished that he could forget it! I lied and said I recalled nothing regrettable and he said he was glad, and that ended that discussion. I record this for posterity without knowing exactly what it means.

During his visit to Chicago, he and Mrs. Jones expressed the wish to see the archaeology and the dinosaurs at the Field Museum. Dr. Max Gitelson and his wife, Dr. Frances Hannett, and Jean and I took them there. Max had arranged for the curators of different departments to be on hand and give us a personally conducted tour. The things Jones wanted to see were the very things I especially like to see at the Field over and over. This time I couldn't help but keep one eye on Doctor Jones and wonder what he was thinking about as he looked. From time to time he made some comments which I don't recall but which were to the effect that "this is the fate of all of us; I wonder where we are going; dust to dust; all is vanity, saith the preacher." I don't think he said a single one of these particular things but that was the spirit of it and I kept wondering if he was thinking of his own imminent extinction.

As in my previous contacts with him, I noticed his inability to express praise or gratitude. Not that we did anything worth mentioning, but everyone was trying to please him and I don't think any of us thought he appreciated it or felt under any obligation to acknowledge it. I mention this in no grudging way but merely as a characterological observation. I didn't hear him say one word to Max or any of us about any of the scientific work that American psychoanalysts have done or are doing. Of course, compared to what he himself did, or to the magnificent labors of Freud, which he had just completed recording, nothing of ours was worth mentioning except for the sake of politeness. He was preoccupied, I am sure, with the carcinoma of the bladder from which he was suffering.

It seems a little gratuitous to remember these slightly negative things about a man who has left us the great heritage of the biography of Freud, especially the third volume. Violent objection has been taken by some colleagues to his interpretation of Ferenczi's technique and behavior, which he describes as "psychotic"; he speaks also of Ferenczi's longtime "latent psychosis." I think Ferenczi was, if I am not mistaken, Jones's own analyst, and I think Jones might well have pondered long before he made any diagnostic estimates. However, it only bears out my own present convictions, oft expressed, that psychiatric diagnostication tends to become outright name-calling. Words like "psychosis" and "neurosis" have no place in our scientific language. I realize this puts a strain on our verbal ingenuity, and I wish I could have enlisted Doctor Jones in the task of helping us with new verbal constructions.

Jones is gone now; his work is finished. No doubt, like Robert Louis Stevenson's hunter, "he laid him down with a will."

Later, Dr. Karl added:

Feeling a dissatisfaction with what I had written (above) about Doctor Jones, I sent a draft to Max Gitelson, whom I had consulted about many things and asked his impressions of Jones and what I had said about him. It is characteristic of Max, and his wife, Frances, that they saw Jones in a tolerant and kinder light. Actually, Max said, Jones was very tired when he was in Chicago because of the intense activities in New York, and furthermore he was somewhat anxious and depressed because he recalled that forty years previously he had had a rather unhappy reception in Chicago at a lecture delivered in the course of his early barnstorming for psychoanalysis in this country. This memory and the fact that in Chicago, unlike New York, he was not surrounded by old European friends, left him ill at ease until he was quite convinced of his welcome.

Max and Frances saw Jones in Paris afterward and on another trip went to England and saw him in his home, a privilege they will always remember. Max told me Jones was most kindly, simple, gracious, and hospitable. He was extremely grateful for the elevator which had been installed in his house by the generosity of a few friends. Max thinks Jones had difficulty in demonstrating gratitude, but that he gave definite signs of feeling it.

And then again, I thought to myself, how gracious and amiable are most of us going to be at the age of eighty with Mr. Death just around the corner? There are few people who can bear it as Freud did, or who can face it with the courage my own father did. I am deeply indebted to Max for softening my judgment of our great biographer.

And I told him (Max) so before he, too, went away. (I see his dear widow Frances quite often. She is an officer in the International Psychoanalytic Association and I know that pleases Max! I wish I had written a memorial note about Max when *he* died. I was very fond of him; he was a good friend, a *very* good friend of mine, as his widow still is.)

INDOMITABLE SPIRITS

In 1953, before these private reminiscences of Jones were written, Dr. Karl had publicly hailed the appearance of the first volume of Jones's biography of Freud in Reading Notes.

To write a biography of a contemporary colleague who has already taken his place as one of the greatest men who ever lived is a task that only another great man would dare undertake. Dr. Jones has himself contributed many things to science and to the world but this is undoubtedly his masterpiece. It represents enormous research, selection, investigation, and organization, and demonstrates astute and penetrating judgment and interpretation. Its content is clearly indicated by its title. Its clarity and beautiful diction are in keeping with its scope and purpose. No one but Ernest Jones could have written it. And the scientific world, particularly psychiatry and psychoanalysis, will be eternally grateful to him. For every psychoanalyst, for years to come, this book (and no doubt its succeeding volumes) will be imperative reading.

For the first time, perhaps, Freud ceases to be an oracle, a wizard, a saint, a super-father, a Messiah, an obsessional neurotic, or God knows what I and others have made him; he becomes a human being with peculiar incentives and peculiar gifts, who happened upon discoveries which he had the persistence and the brilliance to work away at until they could take sufficient shape for others to pursue the ultimate goals by similar methods.

And of the third and final volume, appearing in 1957, he said:

The magnificent record of the crowning years of a great life, *The Life and Work of Sigmund Freud, Vol. III, The Last Phase 1919–1939,* adds new luster to the names of both Freud and Jones. Few have known, and few can realize even now that they know, what courage and self-mastery accompanied the continued productiveness of this giant among men during sixteen years of agony. Himself living in the shadow of death, Ernest Jones dedicated his last years to recording the life of the man he loved and by whom he was inspired. This volume records not only the events of Freud's latter years, but the detailed medical records of the surgeons. Increased tolerance of personal discomfort is often listed among the evidences of maturity and mental healthiness; on the basis of this criterion, surely Freud was almost the healthiest-minded man that ever lived. In spite of his incessant and ominous pain, Freud worked on, with unflagging dedication. This final volume is the greatest of the three, and completes what will surely long remain one of the most important biographies ever written, and certainly the pivotal biography for the education of every psychiatrist.

A large proportion of Dr. Karl's Reading Notes *down through the years have been devoted to his colleagues. For example:*

Paul Federn was a great character in psychoanalysis. His essential kindliness, his integrity, his earnestness, and his personal charm made him a beloved figure in psychoanalytic groups ever since his early association with Freud. We all admired his courage so much when he came to this country at a relatively advanced age and continued his scientific work, even when his heart was wrung with anxiety; his son was imprisoned in a concentration camp. He continued to work on his special theories about ego psychology and the help that he felt that they gave to the understanding of the proper treatment of psychoses. These are the things he talked to us about here in 1949, and these lectures are included in his book *Ego Psychology and the Psychoses.*

On March 17, 1957, it began to rain and snow in Topeka, breaking a five-years' drouth. A film running in a local theater that week was entitled *The Rainmaker,* the story of an ebullient young man who wanted to believe and achieve the impossible, and who did. He made a disheartened girl believe in herself and, to his own immense surprise, he brought rain!

And also on March 17, 1957, along with the snow and the rain, there arrived in Topeka a very different sort of a person—a modest, quiet spoken gentleman from Philadelphia, the first incumbent of our Alfred Sloan Visiting Professorship. For the next few weeks it rained almost daily, so Visiting Professor Earl Bond, in his typically whimsical way, christened himself "The Rainmaker." It was very apt, too, because like the other "Rainmaker" he made some people believe in themselves and in what they were doing.

Each day he visited with residents and faculty members, addressing the staff, addressing the student body, interviewing patients, and lunching with various groups. The dignity and charm and unassuming wisdom that characterized him impressed everyone. To see a colleague in his fiftieth year of psychiatric practice still eager to learn, still anxious to see patients, still happy to talk with residents, still endeavoring to interpret his experiences, still revising his theories—this was an inspiration to us all.

INDOMITABLE SPIRITS

This was our Rainmaker of 1957, who came and went so gently, leaving a little of himself in the lives of several hundred people who will never forget him.

A kinsman of mine whose family has long lived in Vienna, Dr. Erich Menninger-Lerchenthal, is also a psychiatrist as was his brother, now dead. He contributes to *Die Furche,* an Austrian literary journal, for April 20, 1957, a brief account of the life of Wagner von Jauregg, the only psychiatrist ever to receive the Nobel Prize. Most colleagues will remember his discovery of the efficacy of malaria therapy for brain syphilis. Many would not remember his discovery of the relation of cretinism to iodine deficiency, with the resulting disappearance of this condition in most parts of the civilized world. He is also responsible for important additions to and corrections of the Austrian legal code.

He was a poor boy, in spite of his inherited title, which his father acquired in recognition of distinguished legal services. Wagner von Jauregg chose psychiatry, according to my kinsman, by mere chance. He was an active mountain climber, horseback rider and sportsman as well as physician. His brother was postmaster-general of Austria.

Several times I have referred to that psychoanalytic "character" Wilhelm Reich. He wrote one of our most valuable books on technique, correcting a serious error into which many had fallen. He had received worldwide acclaim only to dive off head first in the direction of Communism, and later in the direction of a delusion about "orgone" sex energy being accumulated from the ether by an empty crate. He was deadly serious about this and attracted quite a few disciples. He stubbornly refused to stand corrected even by the Federal government and installed himself in a strange fortress in the Maine woods, issuing threats and warning bulletins to the F.B.I. about "the Medical Trust." He died in a Federal penitentiary shortly after conviction for using the mail to defraud. His story is rather vividly reviewed by two writers, Brown and Cooley, in the magazine *True* for April 1962. I don't know anything about this magazine but the main outline of this story is not far off and is surprisingly rich in detail.

Franz Alexander, who died last year [1964], had an important relationship with the Menninger Clinic. He was the personal analyst of both Doctor Will and myself, and taught others of our earlier staff.

He came to the United States in connection with the International

Congress of Mental Hygiene in Washington, 1930. He was heralded as a new, young leader who had won Freud's acclamation. Some American physicians had already gone to Europe for psychoanalysis with him, including Lionel Blitzsten and Tom French, good friends of ours in Chicago. In the fall of 1930, Alexander came to the University of Chicago as a visting professor. Dr. Helen McLean, Dr. Leo Bartemeier, and I were among the psychiatrists he analyzed there that year.

Alexander was so successful in attracting the interest of students and faculty that a wave of [jealous] reaction swept him out of the medical school. The next year he went to Boston; the following year he gathered Blitzsten, Hamill, French, Helen McLean, Bartemeier, myself, and others together and with the aid of our contributions and some larger ones from other friends he organized the Chicago Institute for Psychoanalysis. He conceived and built it, and he directed it energetically for the next quarter century. Doctor Will, Robert Knight, Robert Morse. Douglass Orr, and many others of our organization were analyzed and trained at that institute. For five years some of us went up to Chicago for every other weekend.

As Therese Benedek says in her very objective memorial notice in the *Journal of the American Psychoanalytic Association* for October, Alexander's "expansiveness, the source of his indefatigable productivity, made him restive." First psychosomatic syndromes, then the controversial "brief psychotherapy," then the concept of a "corrective emotional experience," then the "manipulation of transference intensity" successively interested him. Benedek thinks that perhaps by moving to Los Angeles he "hoped to re-create an experience of the past, his early (exciting) years in Chicago, by a new beginning."

We here owe much to Franz Alexander for having developed our interest in psychoanalysis. He helped us in the founding of our society and our institute. He gathered many new friends and had many circles of acquaintance, necessarily leaving behind some of the older ones. I shall always remember my travels in Europe with him and Mrs. Alexander, his introduction of me to Professor Freud, our attendance at the Lucerne Congress, and many other pleasant occasions. I think both he and I regretted that this closeness could not have continued. But both our territory and our thinking separated. To him, I think, we here seemed conventional and overly conservative. To us he seemed saltatory and aligned with aberrant and dissident exponents. But he will always be remembered as our teacher, and *the* teacher of psychoanalysis to American physicians: he probably analyzed more of them than all other training analysts put together, up to about 1945.

Lawson G. Lowrey was my friend, my fraternity brother in medical school, my teacher, my guide and my hospital chief. He launched me in psychiatry. He introduced me to [Ernest] Southard. I owe him much. He lived a brilliant, erratic, stormy, stimulating, irritating, disappointing life. Many young psychiatrists owe their start to him. Many social workers ascribe the growth of psychiatric social work with children to his support. Some credit him with developing the team concept in psychiatry. And for all this, he is almost unknown to present-day psychiatrists.

Child Guidance: Lawson G. Lowrey Memorial Volume (1964) contains a brief biographical sketch of Lowrey by Dr. Simon Tulchin, a note of appreciation by psychiatric social worker Frederika Neumann, a brief but eloquent letter by David Levy, and thirty-six selected papers thought by the editors to be representative of the work and the associated workers of Lowrey.

This book is a labor of love; a tribute put together with indefatigable persistence by Lowrey's great admirer and loyal friend Simon Tulchin.

Bertram Lewin is one of the pioneers and pillars of psychoanalysis in America. He achieved his position not on the basis of long monographs or texts but on a deft and elegant skill in presenting his ideas concerning human phenomena, psychological phenomena, and psychoanalytical phenomena as if they all belong together. And don't they?

No other psychoanalyst would write a chapter on the meditations of Descartes, or one on a diagrammatic picture of John Locke's mind, or on the drawings in the Lascaux caves of Spain and southern France. But, in a little book of 120 pages entitled *The Image and the Past* (1968), Lewin tied all these things together around the idea of pictorialization as a human talent.

Lewin was born a Texan, but he adopted New York and later Pittsburgh. A faint flavor of the eastern seaboard psychoanalytic aristocracy pervades this booklet, but it does not impair its elegance or its soundness, and old friends can only applaud the achievement.

Dr. Karl has been close friends with a number of psychiatrists but none perhaps has been more cherished by him than Dr. Leo Bartemeier,

*of whom he says, "A friend like that is like a jewel from heaven. He
will never be properly recognized or thanked for what he contributes.
But I know!" In the September, 1970, issue of the* Bulletin *of the
Menninger Clinic, the lead article was Dr. Karl's "Birthday Greetings"
for the man he often addresses as "Brother Leo."*

Some years ago a boy from Muscatine, Iowa, went off to school at St.
Mary's College in Kansas, a beautiful school in a beautiful setting.
Thirty miles east of St. Mary's another boy was growing up and attending another Kansas college. They did not meet for a number of
years, when both of them had attended universities and medical
schools, served internships and residencies, and gone on independently
to become psychiatrists, a rare profession in those days.

These two psychiatrists—one living in Detroit, Michigan, and one
in Topeka, Kansas—became acquainted in May, 1930, at the First
Congress of the International Committee for Mental Hygiene in
Washington, D.C. This is where I first met Dr. Leo Bartemeier.

I like to think it was not coincidence alone that we had Kansas in
common and that we both loved its landscape and shared its blue
skies and lazy rivers. We Kansans are proud of Doctor Bartemeier
and claim him not only for his numerous sojourns among us but for
his outstanding help and encouragement and inspiration in the Menninger School of Psychiatry, which he helped to found, and the Topeka
Veterans Administration Hospital, which he was with at the beginning,
and The Menninger Foundation of which he has been a trustee since
1944.

In June, 1970, Doctor Bartemeier received a citation and the
singular award of the John Carroll Medal of Merit from the Georgetown University Medical School, his alma mater. And from September 11 to 13 at the Seton Psychiatric Institute in Baltimore, a symposium on "The Future of Man: Psychiatry Tomorrow" is to be held,
honoring him and celebrating his birthday.

He has had many other responsibilities, duties, and honors:
President of the American Psychiatric Association, President of the
American Psychoanalytic and of the International Psychoanalytic As-
sociations, Professor of Psychiatry at the University of Maryland and
Georgetown University medical schools, and Medical Director of the
Seton Psychiatric Institute, Baltimore—these are only a few of them.
But at this time of his birthday festival we think of him as our "Brother
Leo"—a Kansan with lifelong ties to us.

When Doctor Bartemeier presented me to the audience for the

first William C. Menninger Memorial Lecture, May 4, 1968, he said: "How can I introduce my brother—my brother, though we don't carry the same name? We have lived together in many places over the world since that meeting in Washington thirty-eight years ago. This is not the time or occasion for reminiscing about beautiful, harrowing, terrifying experiences together during our sojourn in the European theater of operations in 1945. Nor for relating in the detail they deserve our many hours of joy and worry and work and sorrow in the early formative years of the American Psychoanalytic Association and the Menninger School of Psychiatry. But I have always had great fascination for Karl's vision, his ability to see ahead."

After some more words of sincerest admiration, he turned to me with the kindest phrase of all, "And so, now, brother Karl. . . ."

I quote this to show an outstanding aspect of Dr. Bartemeier's greatness—his enormous capacity for the selfless appreciation of other people. How many great enterprises and wonderful things might have happened in this world had there been more Doctor Bartemeiers to assuage this deep, universal human hunger!

CHAPTER FIVE

Man Against Himself

The aggressive impulse is a powerful part of man's inherent makeup.
Dr. Karl comments, "Freud's followers were quite upset when Freud
changed his emphasis from sex to aggression as the basis of nervous ill-
ness. Just imagine with what dismay his followers must have received
the news, saying, 'You can't change your mind in the middle of things
—all our books and articles are printed the other way. Everything will
be in confusion,' and Freud replying, 'I can and do change my mind.'"
In a Reading Note *Dr. Karl says of aggression:*

Self-destructiveness, which Freud saw as the very core of death
within the personality, manifests itself in each of us in ways easier for
others to see than for ourselves. Not only individuals but groups of individuals, organizations, businesses—*all* of them do things, follow policies and practices in apparent naïveté which observers can clearly
recognize as self-destructive. Even nations do it.

Expanding on this thought in the Kansas State Peace Officer's Magazine, *December, 1950:*

All of us, whether we are doctors, poets, grocery clerks, politicians,
racketeers, drunkards, gangsters, scientists, priests, or police officers,

have within us aggressive, destructive, lawless, cruel, selfish, ruthless tendencies which are capable of coming to the surface under the right conditions.

All the things that we call civilization—the radios, bathtubs, neckties, automobiles, books, paintings, cosmetics—are really just a thin veneer over the basic biological nature of the people who drive the automobiles, use the cosmetics, read the books, and listen to the radio.

I call these aggressive drives "tendencies" to indicate that while they may rarely come to full expression they are always there. Civilization is nothing more than the development of a program for controlling these aggressive impulses. We are constantly losing partial control of these tendencies and requiring help from our neighbors or our police officers or our wives.

"I just don't believe violence accomplishes any worthy end," declares Dr. Karl. Nowhere has he expressed this deep-seated belief more movingly than in his testimony on June 19, 1969, before the Committee on Foreign Relations of the United States Senate. The committee chairman, Senator J. William Fulbright, said that he had asked Dr. Menninger to appear "in the expectation that some of the general insights of psychiatry will assist both senators and the general public in understanding and coping with the outstanding issues of foreign policy," so that "we will be better able to understand the political behavior not only of other nations but especially our own."

In his testimony, hitherto unpublished except in the Congressional Record, *Dr. Karl made the following points:*

To many of us the war in Vietnam seems a prime example of self-destructiveness, one more likely to spread Communism and other evils than to control them. Youths are being sacrificed; money, materials, the country, our own national image, and in many places our goodwill are being destroyed in a continuing, pointless, and—as it seems to many of us—futile military bonfire.

Meanwhile, a general mood of uneasiness, discouragement, and even despair has settled down over the world. Even in these most prosperous times, few people seem truly happy. Busy, but not happy.

Three of our own great leaders have recently been assassinated by restless, disturbed, ill-controlled fellow citizens. These leaders were the heroes of a better day to the young men and women who are growing up now in these uneasy, restless times. And for our young people to lose their inspiration is for our older people to lose their hope. . . .

How better can we [psychiatrists] serve you and our nation than to convince you of the essential identity and similarity of all human beings? Can we also convince you of the universality of aggression and vindictiveness, predaciousness, greed, and envy?

And can we also convince you, paradoxically, of the universality and persistent strength of [self-punishment, self-sacrifice, and] self-destructiveness? Can we convince you [the public] that since life depends upon averting [the consequences of] self-destructiveness [as well as of external dangers], it must depend also upon the control of aggressiveness, which is what civilization is all about?

How, you may ask. You know, I am sure, that there are many known facts and measures and devices available to [one]. The wonderful benefits the National Institutes of Health have discovered are available and the search for new knowledge must continue, but we already possess far more information than we are using. We do know some antidotes. We do know some steps for prevention. We do know prophylactic measures.

Would it help, do you think, Senator Fulbright, to arrange a continuous seminar for your committee, or in your department, led by behavioral scientists, psychiatrists included? These would be for the inculcation and application of some of the information and some of the principles that we already know in the training of young diplomats and specialists in international relations.

It may be that at the present time our usefulness as psychiatrists may be less a matter of technology than [one] of philosophy. I have stated what that philosophy is—one which assumes an essential identity of all human beings and an essential similarity of needs, motives, fears, and techniques of communication, and self-deception with, of course, minor variations of meaning which may be of enormous importance. These, too, can be a matter of study.

Our philosophy puts a high value on mutuality and understanding, on helpfulness, on cooperation, and on conservation rather than upon destructiveness for any purpose.

And because some of us have had long experience in dealing with frightened, desperate, angry, deluded, disorganized, irrational, misbehaving persons, perhaps we might be helpful, like the old chiefs in the Indian war councils, not so much for what we do as for what we have seen and felt, [what we] remember, and what we believe . . .

Civilization is, and always has been, a struggle. From . . . my parents, I know something of what the settling of the West really cost in pain and [privation, in] fear and courage and sorrow. Civilization is a never-ending series of struggles and conflict, but [it should be] conflict to prevent conflict, not to enhance it.

Those of us who are closer to the chronological limits of natural life may feel more keenly a concern regarding dangers which seem to us ominously growing and seemingly irreversible. I mean, destructiveness and self-destruction. I mean counterviolence as a supposed antidote to violence.

Life is too precious to waste or to be wasted. Our country is too beautiful to be selfishly ravished. Our world, for all the scars we have inflicted upon it, is still too wonderful, too magnificent, too holy, may I say, to be destroyed by our sloth, our pettiness, our hates, our heedlessness, or our failure to use our intelligence.

But in Dr. Karl's view, the retreat to isolationism can be as self-destructive as the advance to war. More than thirty years prior to his testimony before the Fulbright committee, he explained why in a talk to the Herald Tribune Forum *in New York. This talk, entitled "Some Observations Concerning War from the Viewpoint of a Psychiatrist," was delivered on October 26, 1938. Today, going back over this text, he says: "Much that has happened since confirms the thought that this is one of the better pieces I've ever written—and I was much younger then. But I still agree with myself!"*

He also notes, "This was spoken—and written—before the women's liberation movement."

I am reminded of the proposal made from time to time that women could, if they really wished to do so, put an end to war. Just how they would go about it is another thing. Mary Pickford suggested that they accomplish it by a sitdown strike. In the famous Greek comedy *Lysistrata,* a revival of which many of you have seen on the stage, the women stopped a war through the power of sex. I have heard it argued that if women could by their disapproval prevent their husbands from flying in airplanes, and many do, they could prevent them from the far more hazardous adventure of going to war.

It is tempting to indulge in fantasies of this kind. Women are so obviously less aggressive and destructive than men, the core of their life is so much closer to creativeness, to the fostering of culture and beauty and children, that it would seem as if they would instinctively perceive the uselessness and the wastefulness and terribleness of war much more keenly than do men and would bend their efforts toward preventing it.

And yet we know that were war to become imminent tomorrow, the excitement and the thrill of it would become contagious and women as well as men would be engulfed in a sweeping wave of popular enthusiasm. They, like the men, would rush forward to do their bit in the great crusade, happy to escape from the petty routine and the personal problems of daily life and merge themselves in a surging mass bound on high adventure. Mothers would boast of the bravery of their sons and flock together in happy eagerness to roll bandages intended for the swaddling of disemboweled soldiers and men without faces. The women would join the men in believing everything evil of those unknown human beings whom they have been told were their enemies, listening uncritically to avalanches of inflammatory invective and palpable absurdity.

Why is it that women, more conservative and more constructive than men, should succumb to these orgies of glorified national self-destruction? Why do the women not follow the example—at least the spirit—of Lysistrata and stop it? Once it could be said that they did not have the power—the political power—but this is no longer true; for today in America they have both. Even more recently it could have been said, and was said, that effective deterrence of war by women was impossible because of their lack of cohesiveness, their lack of organization. But the organizations represented in this audience, and more than ten thousand women they represent, give the lie to that excuse. It may be that women do not realize the power they possess, but this, too, is changing; the coming days and years may see a great giant awakened from his sleep—the organized women of America.

But no amount of organization or determination on the part of women or any other group can avail much toward the abolition of war until we recognize honestly our own mixed feelings about war, and when I say "our," I mean women's as well as men's. I belong to a profession the members of which spend many years in study and painstaking practice in order to relieve a few people of pain and to prolong the lives of a few others. Because we are devoted to the relief of suffering and the pushing back of death, our profession is held in high esteem. And yet the same body politic which believes in us as medicine men, as saviors of the people, as prolongers of life, the same populace encourages the manufacturing of instruments that can deal more destruction in a day than all the doctors in the country could repair in a year. It seems to us paradoxical indeed that people should faint and scream and shudder at the sight of one mangled corpse on the highway and at the same time plan for the wholesale mutilation of hundreds of thousands of other persons, many of them their own flesh and blood.

In the jails of this city tonight there are a few dozen men who are confined there because they have killed or attempted to kill one human being. But in this same city at this same moment there are thousands of men whose entire lives and energies are devoted to the purpose of killing not one but many human beings. While we are here thinking about methods for peace they are concentrating their thoughts and energies on the devising of more ingenious, more destructive, more invincible machines for the ghastly purpose of destroying and muti- lating as many people as possible. These men are not in jail; they are in comfortable homes and apartments; they are in hotels and country clubs, and they stand high in the esteem of society, business, commerce, and politics.

Who are the intended victims of these respectable murderers? Are they mad men about to strangle us in our sleep? Are they savages? Are they gorillas or some other beasts? No, they are simply other human beings like ourselves who have been constrained by their so-called governments to offer themselves as targets for this hideous machinery. It is all very politely done. Those who are to be shot at will be supplied with instruments with which they are to shoot at the others who are shooting at them. The same manufacturers are impartially supplying both sides in order that the merry little game of tearing people apart can go on in all fairness. Our sporting ideals are such that though we sympathize with China, we supply arms to Japan; although we sympa- thize with established government, we supply arms to those who sell them to the Spanish rebels, although we sympathize with ourselves and with those fellow citizens who will ultimately repose as carcasses in the trenches of some future war, we sportingly supply arms to the nations who will probably effect this slaughter.

Why isn't it considered as criminal to manufacture killing ma- chines as it is to do the killings? I mention the politicians and the mu- nition makers not to reproach them alone but to remind you of the inconsistencies, the contradictory attitudes within our culture which will lay the foundation for the next mass homicidal demonstration.

Society seems to proceed on the assumption that it has to inflict this damage upon itself. One would suppose that, in the face of the overwhelming blows man receives at the hands of fate and nature, we would align ourselves against these external forces in a universal brotherhood of beleaguered humanity; instead we divide ourselves artificially into groups and make occasions to fight self-destructively with one another.

Behind the various villains we blame for war—the neurotic statesman, the truculent militarist, the callous munitions manufacturer, the fatuous politician, the paranoiac dictator—behind all these are the self-destructive impulses of the people at large who allow themselves to be maneuvered into death and destruction. And this not alone because they are hoodwinked and fooled and played upon emotionally by eloquent orators or crafty conspirators, but because they carry within themselves inflammable potentialities for destructiveness. We must discard the naïve notion that human beings are dominated alone by the will to live. The behavior of individuals and nations conclusively demonstrates that we are not entirely willing either to live or to let live. The instinct of self-destruction as we see it cropping out in war, in suicide, in crime, and in the addiction to alcohol, in the speed mania, in the neuroses and psychoses—this is not some special devil with which a few individuals are cursed. It is something which is in all of us. It is something which, unrecognized and unacknowledged, we are powerless to combat, a sleeping beast ready to spring into deadly action at a word—ready with the slightest encouragement to wreck all that we held beautiful and living.

What suicide is for the individual, war is for the nation. One might think that we should say that only civil war is really suicide. But all war is civil war from the standpoint of the scientist and the philosopher, and even from the standpoint of the historian. I believe it is generally agreed that there has never been an instance of what one could honestly call victory. We certainly know that the World War was not a victory for anyone. Wars are always not only destructive but self-destructive and by war I mean not only the so-called declared wars but the undeclared wars, the territorial seizures and the regimentation and oppression by armed forces of one group by another. So long as we depend upon military force instead of upon economic boycotts, non-communication, and such civilized techniques for bringing recalcitrant groups into line, we are depending upon a method which encourages the self-destructive instincts. For this reason I consider the fascistic regime in Europe as equivalent to war, a dangerous and aggressive kind of self-destruction from which all of us may expect to suffer and against which the only defense the politicians can think of is a competitive preparation for an ultimate military show-down.

I cannot regard as other than terrified stupidity or cynical hypocrisy the appeals I have read for prayers of thanksgiving for an accomplished world peace at the present time. What peace? It would seem as if such individuals must never have heard of China, of Spain, of Ethiopia, of Austria, or of *Mein Kampf*. The inability to think or feel beyond one's own country would seem to be a form of narcissistic self-absorption closely related to a more obviously malignant mental disease which the psychiatrist sees so frequently in individuals. We are all a part of the world, one people, one species, one kind of organized life. There is only one race and the members of that race are actuated by instincts, needs, and emotions common to them all. Any artificial delineations used as the basis of programs of expansion or of non-cooperation constitute a palpable form of self-destruction. That some in this country exalt as discreet isolationism is nothing but dangerous provincialism, motivated by the same instincts that determine war. Isolation is always self-destructive for the nation just as for the individual.

Finally, I should say that we psychiatrists would expect the most effective opposition to war to develop from an improvement in the interpersonal relations of individual men and women. Resentments that are stimulated in childhood and which churn unceasingly beneath the surface for years, incapable of expression in any logical or endurable way, will always find opportunities to vent themselves upon some person or some group of persons which has been labeled "devil." The Germans, bitterly burdened by their conquerors and then by their tyrannical government, were glad to have first the Jews and later the Czechs pointed out to them as hideous monsters. It was astonishingly easy for us Americans in 1917 to be persuaded that our previous conceptions of the Germans and Austrians as peaceful, charming, amiable people were all wrong, that they were instead, malignant creatures, whom it was proper for us to mortgage our future and sacrifice our lives in an effort to destroy. What this shows is not our gullibility but the high state of inner tension within us, a tension caused by an insufficient neutralization of our silent surging hatreds of one another. It is in this field, the field of personal relationships between individuals, that we can most effectively combat not only war but all forms of self-destruction. I still believe that this, in some way or other, is closer to women's hearts and more likely to be accomplished by them than by men. Eve has been blamed for man's downfall; she may yet accomplish his salvation.

Man's aggressive impulses when they are turned inward may lead to destruction of himself—suicide. In Man Against Himself, *published in 1938, Dr. Karl described the internal war that leads to self-murder:*

It is not difficult to discover in the act of suicide the existence of various elements. First of all it is a *murder.* In the German language it is, literally, a murder of the self *(Selbstmord),* and in all the earlier philological equivalents the idea of murder is implicit.

But suicide is also a murder *by* the self. It is a death in which are combined in one person the murderer and the murdered. We know that the motives for murder vary enormously and so do the motives for wishing to be murdered, which is quite another matter and not nearly so absurd as it may sound. For since in suicide there is a self that submits to the murder and would appear to be desirous of doing so, we must seek the motives of this strange submission. If the reader will picture to himself a battlefield scene, in which a wounded man is suffering greatly and begs someone to kill him, he will readily appreciate that the feelings of the *murderer* would be very different, depending upon whether he were a friend or a foe of the wounded man; those of the man who desires to be *murdered,* i.e., to be put out of his agony, however, would be the same in either case.

In many suicides it is quite apparent that one of these elements is stronger than the other. One sees people who want to die but cannot take the step against themselves; they fling themselves in front of trains, or like King Saul and Brutus, they beseech their armor bearers to slay them.

Finally, probably no suicide is consummated unless—in addition to this wish to kill and to be killed—the suicidal person also wishes to die. Paradoxically, many suicides in spite of the violence of the attack upon themselves and in spite of the corresponding surrender, do not seem to be very eager to die. Every hospital interne has labored in the emergency ward with would-be suicides, who beg him to save their lives. The fact that dying and being murdered achieve the same end so far as personal extinction is concerned, leads the practical-minded individual to think, "If a person wants to murder himself, or if he feels so badly about something that he is willing to be murdered, then he surely must want to die." But the illustration just given is only one of many indications that this is not so. Murdering or being murdered entails factors of violence, while dying relates to a surrender of one's life and happiness. A more complete discussion of both these elements will come later. For the present it is sufficient to make the point that in attempted suicide the wish to die may or may not be present or may be present to a quite variable degree, as may also the other wishes mentioned.

To summarize, then, suicide must be regarded as a peculiar kind of death which entails three internal elements: the element of dying, the element of killing, and the element of being killed. . . .

And in a Reading Note:

I have always said suicide prevention was a public health problem, but the proposition still isn't taken seriously by any state that I know of. In a typical town the size of Topeka, 200 to 250 people will try to kill themselves each year, and of these 10 per cent or more will succeed. This means about one suicide every other week in Topeka.

Dr. Karl would like to see the formation of more suicide prevention clinics, such as the pioneer one in Los Angeles and in other cities. He explains:

We talked and talked about preventing suicide in the old days. It was mostly idle talk. What it came down to was if anybody looked withdrawn and acted strange, we'd say, "Watch 'em. They might be about to kill themselves." This may still be good advice though I don't know how many suicides it prevented. It's a kind of passive prevention. "Watching" them usually means penning them up and taking away drugs and razors. Nowadays anybody can get drugs. And only very disturbed people use razors.

Prevention now consists of trying to get clinically pre-suicidal individuals to accept help while they still can. How? By making verbal contact with someone who is willing to listen or lend a hand.

The suicidal impulse is apt to come in mounting waves, and people can be reached and, after contact with a person who cares and is willing to listen, can often be tided over the period of desperation. We must remember it's the feeling, not the impulse to kill or to die, that leads to the act which does seem definitely impulsive, not something people logically resolve to do.

My whole book *The Vital Balance* is devoted to the theme that there are thousands of ways every one of us uses to avoid suicide.

Mostly these are automatic and relatively remote. But if stresses pile up and the impulse to end the show gets stronger, the devices to ward it off may get stronger. They usually work. But if they don't, despair sets in. Then some kind of termination seems the only thing to do.

I often think that the curious philosophy of the suicidal moment— "There's nothing else to do," "There's no other way out," "I had no other alternative"—ought to attract our attention as inherently morbid. There is *always* an alternative. There is *always* something else to do. To get into a frame of mind in which the hopeless thought dominates is the preliminary to the suicidal resolution.

The desperate loneliness which often leads to suicide was described by Dr. Karl and his wife in an article that they wrote for Ladies Home Journal:

In my files are scores of case histories, the gist of which is "I am lonely and unhappy. I am groping for contacts with fellow creatures that I do not seem able to make." And across the country, in state after state, in schools and offices, in homes, in factories, on farms and in rooming houses, live lonely women.

Here is one who is lonely because she unwittingly repels her friends' advances in friendship. Here is another who is in love with herself so much that she cannot love anyone else. Here is another seeking an ideal she will never find because she has placed her ideal above human possibilities: she does not understand her fellow man at all. Then one who is lonely because she gives too little, and another who is lonely because she gives too much.

We all look for miracles in the relief of our distress, but psychotherapy lays no claim to miracle performings. All it can do is to present certain aspects of the truth and by this, as we are often reminded, some are set free. Loneliness may disappear as you know yourself better and become aware of conflicts within that prevent you from getting close to others.

A sort of incomplete, unconscious suicide is seen in the "happening" of accidents. Freud called them "purposive accidents." Dr. Karl also discussed accidents in an address to the conference on Family Happiness and Security of the Insurance Companies of North America at Disneyland, California, in January 1959. The address, entitled "Mental Attitudes and Safety," was published in the Menninger Quarterly,

MAN AGAINST HIMSELF

Summer 1959, and later reprinted widely in publications of insurance companies and others concerned with the high toll taken by accidents.

Accidents rank third as the cause of death in our country. One would think, naturally, that anything ranking third as the cause of death would be the subject of a great deal of scientific research. Cancer is. Pneumonia is. Tuberculosis has been. But are accidents? I am afraid not! The amount of scientific research into accidents is extraordinarily small compared to the research that goes into the other causes of death. Research into the factors responsible for suicide is another area in which there is a startling paucity of research. Indeed, in all of the fields that touch on human motivation, on psychology, psychopathology, psychiatry—there is relatively little research. It is something that we psychiatrists have always been talking about because we not only know it and feel it, but we deplore it. We think more research in these areas would accomplish much for our country and the world.

We looked up some of the research that has been done on accidents since I myself wrote something about it in *Man Against Himself*, twenty odd years ago, and we were a little startled when we found out how little more was known about the motivation of accidents than we knew then.

Although actuaries compute the expected frequency of accidents on the basis of chance, actually one cannot explain accidents as products of pure chance. The dictionary does this, but you and I know better. We know that relatively few accidents are wholly accidental. If you want to be statistical about it, the number of accidents ascribable to pure chance must be well below 15 percent. Accidents are always partly—I'm going to stop right there—partly what? If accidents aren't due to chance, what are they due to? People have always declined—abhorred—to be made responsible for accidents. "Not me!" "Not my fault," we say. Accidents are caused by fate, by hard luck, by inadvertence or ignorance or carelessness or distraction or alcohol.

Scientifically speaking, none of these are explanations; they are only descriptions of some aspects of some accidents. We are all careless at times. Why was this individual careless just at this critical time? What factors in him contributed to that costly careless moment? Was Romeo, the romantic one, a poor fellow in hard luck? Or was he just too impulsive? He was so impulsive that he had just lost one girl before he met Juliet. Then he impulsively picked up Juliet at a party he wasn't invited to, impulsively not noticing that she was "off limits" for him. He impulsively got his best friend killed and while impulsively avenging that, he impulsively got himself exiled. Then he impulsively rushed home and impulsively jumped to some impulsive conclusions about Juliet and ended the whole thing in a mess.

All this impulsive aggressiveness can be described as hard luck, or you can just say that Romeo was impulsive, or it can be seen as a persistent, self-defeating, self-destructive program.

Shakespeare portrayed another fellow who messed everything up by the opposite technique, by never deciding anything. Hamlet couldn't decide anything, so everybody killed themselves while they were waiting. Now, these "Hamlets" and "Romeos" drive cars, you know. And they kill people. They injure people. They don't exclude themselves from disaster.

You get a hint now, of what we psychiatrists and psychologists perceive in these cases. It is all right to say, "Don't be careless. Don't take three drinks before you take the car out. Watch for the red lights!" These are all good rules, but what is the psychology back of the necessity for having such rules? It is just as old-fashioned today to ascribe accidents solely to these conscious motives as it would be to drive the sort of vehicles we used thirty or forty years ago. We know today something of the great dominating motivation of individuals, shielded or submerged beneath the surface of consciousness. But the viscera of the mind are just as unbeautiful as the viscera of the body, and you won't enjoy looking at them.

The simplest way to put this, unpalatable as it may be to hear it, is that there is a little murder and a little suicide dwelling in everybody's heart. Give them a powerful weapon like a car, inflame their inhibitions or irritations or frustrations, and diminish their suppressive control by means of alcohol or fatigue, and the murder or suicide may get committed.

I have a cartoon from a recent installment of "Peanuts," in which Lucy I think it was, is charging forward saying, "I don't feel very good today and nobody better get in my way." Think of arming a man with 256 horsepower, tease or hurt him a little bit, give him plenty of good victims from which to choose, and your company is going to have some losses to pay.

The other side of that is, of course, that our aggressive, destructive impulses, which have to be kept in control or released in modified or specially directed forms, are accompanied by correspondingly self-punitive impulses. We all punish ourselves. Indeed, the impulse to punish oneself is often just as strong, or even stronger (for some curious reason), than the wish to hurt someone else. I could cite instances about the wife who gets angry and says something cross to her husband; he goes off to the office and she stays home, washes dishes. Still mad, she swipes a knife through her hand and cuts it. I could cite many other such instances, where a self injurious act follows an aggressive act. People come to us clinically who have fallen downstairs under circumstances which make it very clear that they would like to have thrown somebody else downstairs—who have just done something, or said something, or even thought something that aroused enough guilt feelings to precipitate this kind of reaction.

Some of my colleagues started to study what we call psychosomatic medicine by investigating the kind of emotional things that were going on in people's live at the time they developed the illnesses for which they came to the hospital. They got together a group of stomach cases, a group of heart cases, a group of arthritics, etc.

Now we always have to have something to compare our research cases with, "controls" we call them, and in the early days of these investigations the workers said, "Let's take something for our control that is absolutely pure chance. Let's take accident cases." So they took all the accident cases that were brought into the hospital during the same period. Twenty-five heart cases—for example—would be analyzed and compared with the events in the lives of the accident cases.

Imagine! They found this to be no good at all! Ninety per cent of the accident cases had had instances of provocation, frustration, disappointment, etc., just before their injuries, very similar to the events in the heart cases and the stomach cases. In other words, accidents are not controlled by chance as people think. There are unseen things behind them.

An interesting way to point up the tendency toward self-inflicted punishment to fit the self-thought-up crime is the so-called "burglar trap." From time to time some of these cases appear in the newspapers. I happened to notice one such squib many years ago, and I got so interested in it that I subscribed to a clipping service and asked for them. What happens is that somebody has decided that too many of his chickens are being stolen and he contrives a burglar trap so that if anybody comes in, he'll be taught a lesson. He will be shot by a gun triggered by opening the door. He erects it. He sets it. He retires.

And then, he forgets!

You think that this is exceptional. So did I. But when I subscribed to the clipping bureau I got a whole handful. It seems that this is a regular syndrome! The chances seem to be that anybody who would go to such an extent is likely to get caught in it himself!

How many burglar traps we erect for ourselves in the course of a day would be hard to estimate. We certainly do do that sort of thing; everyone does. Figure out just how many traps you have set, with or without being caught in them, and I'll do the same. Only, let's not tell each other.

"Accident proneness" got to be a widely used term some years ago. It was noted that some people seemed to have more than their share of accidents. Here is a clipping about a Californian who spent every tenth birthday during the past fifty years recovering from some major injury suffered in accidents happening on or just before the anniversary. Here is the record: 1890—badly crushed right hand; in 1900 lost a leg in a train wreck; in 1910 hospitalized for five weeks due to an explosion; in 1920, he got into a fight, got knocked out, had the other leg amputated. On his fiftieth birthday he was arranging a deal in his print shop, and while he was handing a pen to the customer to sign the contract, the pen dropped. He stooped to reach for it, missed, and caught his hand in the printing press.

Hard luck champion? The papers repeatedly publish these accounts. . . .

The person who has an accident all too often endangers those around him, as Dr. Karl points out in the following Reading Notes:

I am beginning to get phobic about riding in a car, especially outside the city limits. Two cars crashed on a lonely country road here at Christmas and killed or injured fourteen people. Where can you go with a car safely? Not even on a deserted Kansas lane?

Back in the twenties I wanted to join the staff of the AT&SF (Atchison, Topeka & Santa Fe) Hospital. I felt it might be useful to them to have psychiatric and neurological consultations and interesting, if not profitable, to me. The staff evidently didn't think so, and I was never invited.

But in a chair car one evening, going to see an out-of-town patient, I sat beside the chief surgeon of that hospital and in visiting with him told him I suspected there were some railroad accidents which could be attributed to psychiatric or neurological conditions. I even suggested that the AT&SF ought to have a psychiatrist or neurologist or both. Of course I meant myself. He took my advice, in part; he appointed Dr. M. L. Perry, the superintendent of the Topeka

State Hospital, to be AT&SF consulting neuropsychiatrist and Dr. Perry remained their consultant for many years.

One of my own private patients at the time was a Santa Fe conductor who had become increasingly irritable and disagreeable to passengers—a phenomenon which no experienced traveler would regard as exceptional. This fellow went too far, however, in his offensiveness and indifference to passenger comfort and one passenger brought suit against the railroad and won. The Santa Fe paid the claim but suspended the conductor.

Members of the union's Ratings Committees wanted to be sure of the ground before they applied for his re-employment. They noticed that his irritability and disagreeableness to people had not diminished.

I traveled a good ways to make the examination and, to my astonishment, quickly discovered that the man had general paresis [a disease of the brain usually caused by syphilis]. The railroad never knew how lucky it was that the conductor's rage attacks hadn't gone beyond his offensiveness to passengers before he was laid off.

Dr. Perry found several cases of paresis when he began examinations, and he told me about one engineer in particular whose first recognized symptom was a flock of hallucinations occurring while he was driving his train across western Kansas. He stopped the train and refused to drive the engine any farther; fortunately the fireman could take over both the train and the engineer and did. No one on the train ever knew that anything unusual had ever happened except the brief unexplained stop, and since the railroads never take the trouble to explain their peculiar stopping and starting to passengers—even now that they have modern communication systems—presumably no one became suspicious.

. . . This was many years ago and I recently investigated and found that Wassermann tests are still not made on railroad engineers routinely. . . . How about airplane pilots?

Alcoholism is another way to self-destruction. Dr. Karl remarks in Reading Notes:

Dr. Harry Tiebout, after a long study of alcoholic addiction, proposes in an important article in the *Quarterly Journal of Studies on Alcohol* [1953] that the difference between benefit and no-benefit in treatment of alcoholics relates to a distinction between compliance ("My alcoholism is getting me. I have to have help. I will do whatever you say") and surrender, which is more than a compliant bowing of the head. I am in agreement with this and am very interested in the "conversion point." It seems to me that this is the difference between false and true humility as well as between false and true cure of alcohol addiction. I think it is involved to some extent in all psychiatric treatment, and in religious attitudes also. I have often thought that the meaning of

"My head is bloody but unbowed"

is generally misunderstood. A little bowing of the head might be less spectacular and narcissistic but also less self-destructive. It is a hard problem, this question of pride versus humility. You have to have a certain amount of both, and the question is just how to construct the best pattern.

Man Takes a Drink is the title of Dr. John Ford's book. Father Ford is one of the leading moralists of the Jesuit order and is professor of theology at Weston College, but he has also been a member of the Governor's Commission on Alcoholism in Massachusetts. His book is very simple, didactic, and unequivocal. It is especially good for Catholics who, as Father Ford suggests, sometimes get the notion that temperance, or at least total abstinence, is Puritanical, hence Protestant, hence un-Catholic and hence unrighteous. Well, he scotches that one quickly. Father Ford told me recently that the present leaning of the Catholic moralists was in the direction of regarding alcohol addiction as self-destructive, a violation of the commandment not to kill [one's self] rather than a violation of the rule not to be gluttonous. In other words, as he laughingly remarked, my *Man Against Himself* theme was getting a little clerical support!

Dr. Karl was a pioneer in psychosomatic medicine. In 1934 he wrote an article, "Some Unconscious Psychological Factors Associated with the Common Cold," which has become a classic. It appeared in the Psychoanalytic Review, *April, 1934:*

Every clinician knows that organic diseases often occur under circumstances that make it seem as if the disease served some psychological purposes for the patient. I do not refer to the secondary capitalization of the illness by the patient, with which we are all familiar, seen particularly in the neuroses. Rather I refer to those cases where the illness seems to be, in part, a reaction to a certain event even though the nature of the illness precludes the possibility that such an event alone could have brought on the illness. We know that sore throat is caused by an irritation, usually bacterial; but when a woman who is not subject to them develops a severe sore throat immediately after an episode in which she has maligned the character of a friend, or immediately after a relative has swallowed carbolic acid, or immediately after a fellatio experience, we have reason to support a connection which psychoanalytic research may substantiate.

Much work has already been done in this field through the pioneering courage of Smith Ely Jelliffe in this country, and by Felix Deutsch, Georg Groddeck, and others in Europe. In this brief communication I shall not attempt to review the literature. I shall only mention Groddeck's hypothesis, which is that the libido in some way or other pervades the entire body so that the body may accept or reject an infection in accordance with some instinctive demand. Even though this is not entirely scientific it is, at least, stimulating and fruitful because it reconciles the bacteriological theories of resistance and immunity with the psychological theories of self-protection and self-destruction.

Where should one expect to find more abundant evidence concerning the nature of these unconscious factors in physical diseases than in that most prevalent of all infections, the common cold? We do not know how it is caused, how it is communicated, or how it can be cured. We all know its symptoms very well, both subjectively and objectively, but what are the psychological factors that accompany it? Beyond the well-known descriptive aspects of irritability, sluggishness, etc., I think almost nothing has been recorded.

Yet every psychoanalyst in the course of his clinical work with neurotic patients has the experience time after time of observing the inception, development, flourishing, and decline of a "cold," and in these cases he is able to learn rather completely what the psychological configuration of his patient's unconscious is, both before and during the cold.

Perhaps the reason more has not been written about the subject is that the psychological material does not appear to be entirely constant or identical in all patients, or because the common cold is so ubiquitous that it is often exceedingly difficult to be sure how much the cold is a specific result of particular psychological tendencies and how much it is simply a general and habitual "invalid" reaction to the unpleasant.

I recently had the opportunity to observe the development of a very severe cold of a typical sort in a woman who is not at all subject to colds. This occurred when there was no general epidemic of such infections. It was a matter of common knowledge and remark in her family that she never suffered from colds as other members of the family did. In her entire life of forty years she had not had more than three or four colds. Therefore, it could not be charged that this was simply an habitual response on her part or an incidental event. Nor could it be charged that she was only one of many who were affected by a prevalent epidemic. As will be shown, the cold occurred in such a way as to represent dramatically, in organic terms, certain very pronounced psychological tendencies of hers.

Just prior to the development of her cold she had recognized quite definitely in her analytic work her aggressive tendencies against men in general and her husband in particular, and had had a dream in which she was once more at the deathbed of her younger brother. Her husband was also there dripping something all over the floor which she interpreted to be menstrual blood.

With her associations which dealt with the fact that her brother died of a bladder affliction and that her husband was actually present at his death, I was able to make the interpretation to her that the wish to humiliate me, of which she was quite conscious, was also present in her attitude toward her husband, whom she represented in this dream to be menstruating, and that this wish to have her husband castrated was also present toward the brother by whose death she had been so profoundly moved. She had already recognized before this that her marriage to a man she regarded as cruel had been influenced by the death of her brother since it was a fact that she had fallen in love with her husband at the deathbed of her brother. I asked if it might not be possible that her submitting herself to her husband in marriage had been an attempt to atone for wishing to castrate her brother.

Following this session she returned to her home for the weekend and I did not see her until Monday, when she reported that there was a marked change in her marital relationship, that her husband had seemed unusually loving for the first time in over a year, and that she had mentioned it to him and he had assured her that it was she that had changed and not he.

"But," she said, "*I have a terrible cold.* I noticed as I was leaving here last Friday that my eyes were watering so that I could not see clearly. Now I am having the worst cold I ever had in my life. It was always a proverb when I was a child that I never took colds and I have never had but three or four in my life and this is certainly the worst ever. There must be some psychological cause for it."

After a short digression she returned to the theme and asked me if I had noticed that she had used the expression "took cold." She went on to remind me that I had told her a week or so previously that she had a great wish to take things from people (she was actually taking some money from her brother at the moment and she also referred by this to her wish to take the penis from her other brother and from her husband) and that she had denied this by saying that all her life she had tried not to take anything from anyone and was very proud.

"Perhaps," she said, "you were right after all, that I do want to take things, so intensely that I lean over backward and try to persuade myself that I don't want to accept anything from anybody. But now this cold comes along and I speak of 'taking' a cold and my use of that expression catches my own attention which makes me think that perhaps I have decided I *would* take things from now on."

"And not pretend that you don't want to," I said. (A more appropriate comment might have come from the analyst at this point. From the patient's next remark it is strongly suggested that her use of the expression "taking it" had also the connotation of taking her punishment; cf. the expression "take it on the chin.")

"Yes," she said. "Perhaps this had something to do with my better relations with my husband over the weekend."

"That you were able to be more feminine and take the love he had to offer?" I asked.

She didn't know about that but she did know that she was displeased with this miserable cold, she didn't want to take colds, whatever she took. If psychoanalysis was going to mean that she would lose this immunity to colds which had distinguished her formerly, she didn't like it at all and she didn't want to find out what caused her to have it. But, upon second thought, since it looked as if she had already lost this immunity, she might as well face it; something in her must have changed already.

Here the analyst explained that if the cold represented a greater acceptance on her part, she must observe that she was still able to take only something that gave her distress, i.e., she *took*, but she punished herself for taking. She made no comment upon this and the hour was up.

The following day she announced first of all that her cold was much worse. Also, she wanted to tell me that she had concealed from me the fact that she was expecting her husband and that he would be here on this day, the very day on which her cold seemed to be at its height. She had been planning for his visit for some time.

"It looks as if I felt guilty about having him come and was trying to spoil it," she said. "I am sure that isn't true, however."

She went on to remark that the most conspicuous thing about her cold seemed to be her nose, that it was so red and raw, twice its natural size and running profusely. As she described her nose she suddenly stopped and after a pause remarked that it came to her mind that something which got red and enlarged and discharged mucus made her think of a penis, for which her nose might be a substitute. Now she was reminded again that the way in which the cold was in connection with her dream about her brother's death and her wish to castrate him. But what connection could that have with the coming of her husband? Maybe it was to show him that she was a man and could exert a masculine and controlling influence over him (which, as a matter of fact, she did).

The following day she developed more fully the idea that her red and running nose represented the penis that she had taken from her brother and asked if I thought it possible that that was why she was punishing herself for having it. I agreed, whereupon she immediately returned to the theme that she did not want to lose her immunity. (The foregoing and subsequent material will show that "immunity" is in her unconscious synonymous with virility.) Then she spontaneously recalled something from her childhood which was too terrible to mention. After considerable stalling she said she would spell it. It was the appellation "snot nose." I asked her why this term seemed so objectionable to her. She remembered that certain unkempt, neglected, unloved children whose nasal discharges streamed down their faces were disparagingly referred to by her mother as "snot-nosed children." As she reflected upon the matter she recalled that all these were little girls and realized that it had to do with the extreme disparagement with which she felt that she and other little girls were held by her mother and by society in general. (Back of the feeling that these children were rejected because of their noses was the earlier idea that they were rejected because they were girls and had no penises.)

The following day she began as follows: "What on earth do you think happened yesterday after I left here? I had a terrible hemorrhage from my nose! It bled all over my handkerchief and down on my dress so that I had to change my clothes. I never have nosebleeds and I asked myself, What does all this mean? Then it came to my mind that it was a reaction to what you said about the nose being the equivalent of a penis. 'He says my nose is a penis. Penis, the devil! I have no penis. Look, I *menstruate* from my nose! That shows I am feminine.' "

She wanted to know if people ever did such things as this, that is, reacting with physical symptoms to psychological concepts. Bleeding from her nose that way and getting blood on her clothes reminded her so vividly of menstruation it couldn't be anything else, but she had never heard of it.

Furthermore, there was another development about her cold. She had a cold sore on her lip. It was a large, swollen one. It seemed to be full of a liquor. She had known for a long time that she got cold sores on her lip after drinking liquor. There must be some significance to this, something about taking liquor into her mouth. Could it relate to kissing? Actually it prevented her from kissing her husband. Maybe that was its purpose.

The analyst remarked that the kiss is often only a disguised bite and that biting was a violent way of taking things.

"You know," she said, "when I was a child my father used to make wine and my mother objected strongly and sometimes would go down in the cellar and pour it all out angrily. Very early in my life I got the idea that alcohol was masculine, that liquor was for men, and perhaps that has something to do with my always getting cold sores when I drink, because naturally semen is also the fluid that belongs to men and as a little girl I thought that women got pregnant by taking semen into their mouths. I spoke to you about taking something into my mouth, didn't I, and a cold sore is a little bag full of liquor, isn't it? Now I must confess to you that until I was married I didn't know for sure that semen was a fluid." (I pointed out that this contradicted what she had just said.) "Well, I know it does, but I thought that all the liquid connected with intercourse was feminine and that the only liquid that men could supply came from their mouths. It isn't clear, but I had some notion about men having a liquid they put in a girl's mouth and it made her pregnant, but I didn't know it came from the penis."

The following day the cold was much better. There was no more coryza, the cold sore had receded (a clinician who read the history pointed out that for a cold sore to heal in one day is very unusual. I can only say that the cold sore as I saw it and the cold as I observed it were quite typical of such affections.)—"But now it is all down in my chest," she said, "and I keep coughing. I believe the chest must represent the uterus and that my cough is something like the cramps a woman has when she menstruates or bears a child. It is just more of what I said yesterday. The analyst is mistaken about my having a penis. I am feminine and my cold is in my chest, I am pregnant.

"Perhaps the cough is rejection of masculinity and perhaps it is a rejection of my feminity also, because I seem to be both a man and a woman. I make myself pregnant by getting my own cold down in my own chest. You know I have often spoken about how masculine I am in so many ways but at heart I am really feminine."

Here she gave me details as to her masculine and feminine tendencies and finally came back to mention of her brother. She wanted to know how her discovery of her castration wishes toward her brother was connected with her cold. I asked her what she thought. She replied by giving details of the last hours of her brother's life. She sat beside him as he hiccuped and belched out bloody fluid which she kept wiping away. Immediately after his death she fainted. She remembered that she was menstruating at the time.

"I believe it means that I had to accept my femininity and be a girl because I had these castration wishes toward my brother, so I have to give up my nose as a penis and get a cold in the chest."

Her cold thus would seem to be a re-enactment of her wish to castrate her brother and acquire his penis, the acquisition of a symbolic penis in the form of a conversion symptom, combined with punishment at the same site and finally the renunciation of this wish in favor of the feminine receptive attitude, masochistically symbolized, the whole drama being transposed from the genital region to the respiratory tract and represented somatically. Most of the symptoms could be traced to childhood experiences. We did not discover why her cold first affected her eyes but one assumption might be that this was related to some sense of guilt about seeing her brother's penis or some parental activities.

I do not mean to suggest that such re-enactments of castration wishes are back of all colds. My purpose is only to show that when the habitual gratifications are disturbed by an analysis, it is possible to see how psychological necessities find what Freud calls "somatic compliance," in such a way that the bodily organs and the sympathetic nervous system carry out what the striated musculature and voluntary nervous system are not permitted to do.

P.S. This case was presented at the Chicago Psychoanalytic Society. Numerous confirmatory reports were contributed by various members. One in particular was contributed by Dr. George Wilson, whose case showed an amazing identity of symptoms and mechanisms, even to the cold sore and the cold in the chest.

Another case, involving a man who was subject to violent fits of coughing, was described in Man Against Himself:

Coughing is a symptom which may or may not indicate organic pathology of the respiratory tract, but which does frequently indicate strong aggressive tendencies. Everyone must have reflected upon this at times when a concert or a speaker is repeatedly interrupted or competed with by an incessant cougher.

That most intuitive and discerning clinician, Georg Groddeck [in *The Unknown Self*], wrote at length about the psychology of the cough, using himself as a case illustration. He happened to be suffering acutely from a cold at the moment of writing but also "chronically all of my life. All my family had the same habit as I have of responding to disagreeable impressions by a fit of coughing."

. . . In a patient whom I studied over a period of several years, my observations confirmed with astonishing correspondence these of Groddeck's. This patient was a lawyer of thirty whose analysis was begun and pursued not on account of physical complaints at all but on account of well-recognized emotional disorders which led to serious conflicts with the family, with business associates and others, to the extent of making it necessary for him to withdraw temporarily from his practice. Very early in the treatment of the case, however, the persistent cough from which he suffered became the subject of much of his discussion. At times this cough would become so violent as to interrupt his conversation for a matter of several minutes or even longer; it had become so severe that according to his own statement he would sleep less than half the night on account of being awakened by it. His family declared they could recognize him in the theater when they sat in different parts of the show by the loud, ringing cough with which they were so familiar. In one apartment building other tenants complained about this family, partly, it was presumed, on account of the incessant, noisy coughing of my patient.

In the psychoanalytic hours he would complain at times most bitterly about the cough, declaring that I ignored it or at least offered no remedy for it, that during these two years of treatment it had gotten no better but that I had still clung to the idea that it must be psychological in origin. My observations about the cough were that it would be absent for as long as two or three months, only to recur when the patient's resistance began to manifest itself again rather strongly. I also noticed that in spite of its loud, spasmodic nature, and the fact that the patient's face and body were contorted and jerked by the coughing, he rarely raised any sputum. But the most pertinent observation was that he would frequently have a period when he would not cough at all until I started to speak, in the course of some interpretations or explanations. Then the cough would immediately appear. In scores of instances my interpretations seemed to be met by a cough in such a way as to leave no doubt that unconsciously the cough was a protest against the explanation, a disguised invective hurled at me so loudly that I could not continue speaking.

The further utility of this cough was made clear by a dream which the patient had, which, though he was exceedingly opposed to recognizing the psychological factors in the cough, he himself acknowledged and interpreted. The dream was that he was in a Kiwanis Club meeting and the members had threatened to drop him from the club. He coughed violently, "a death rattle" as he described it, as if to say to them, "You see, you did this—you caused it," just as he used to do when he wanted to make his mother and father feel sorry by saying to them, "I wish I were dead." The patient himself pointed out that in the psychoanalysis, as in his childhood, he threatened revenge by dying, thus reproaching the physician for his unfeeling attitude. The cough represented to him a demand for attention, a defense against unwelcome interpretations, and a threat of punishment, cloaked by a bid for sympathy.

The patient had gone to no less than twenty doctors seeking explanation and treatment for this cough. Most of them would assure him that they could find nothing, although a few of them so alarmed him by vague or ambiguous comments that he would use these as justifications for going to more and more doctors to get a confirmation or refutation or a more positive diagnosis. Some of the physicians in our clinic examined him upon several occasions and were unable to find evidences of structural diseases . . .

Even such diseases as cancer may have psychosomatic aspects, as suggested by Dr. Karl in the two following Reading Notes:

The title "Emotions as a Cause of Cancer" caught my eye in the *Psychoanalytic Review.* There is a subtitle, "18th and 19th Century Contributions." It cites a very considerable number of observations

and opinions by physicians made during these two centuries seeking
to connect the life situation and the disease process arising out of it.
If they found a constant relationship between the two, it was not unreasonable for them to assume that a cause or connection of some
sort could exist. Out of the whole range of human emotions one
particular emotional state stands out as a precursor of cancer—despair and hopelessness. I should emphasize that this is an emotional
state which they regarded as *preceding* the development of carcinoma.
The author contrasts this attitude with the intensive and minute examinations of the cell and its nucleus which now engage the attention
of most of our research people, but it is quite striking to read case
after case in these old records, such as that of Mrs. Emerson, who "upon
the Death of her Daughter, underwent great Affliction, and perceived
her Breast to swell, which soon after grew painful; at last broke out in
a most inveterate Cancer, which consumed a great Part of it in a
short Time. She had always enjoy'd a perfect state of Health." Most
of the reports are in more sophisticated or technical terms than this,
but that's what they all say. I'll just pick out a few almost at random:
"Case 9 . . . Elizabeth D.; married; eight children. No family history;
no injury; no particularly hard work. About eighteen months ago
lost two children in one week by scarlatina, six months later a stillbirth
and had a bad time, but no instruments. Now carcinoma of the
uterus."

"Case 12 . . . Jessie M.; married; two children. No injury. Some
family history of cancer. About a year ago lost a friend by death;
grieved much about this, and nights were broken; the tumor was noticed a month afterwards." . . .

Again I repeat: one of these days the cancer research people who
have had such enormous financial support and who have worked so
frantically and intensively on the problem for the past thirty years
will wake up to the fact *that psychology has an influence on tissue
cells,* a proposition which they have consistently regarded even until
now as a preposterous heresy.

And, summing up, about psychosomatic illness in general, he said in
Man Against Himself:

The belief that sickness is a punishment decreed by the gods for sins
of the people is centuries old. Perhaps we have gone too far in our
scientific rejection of it as superstition. For we know that every man

creates and obeys his own god or gods, and that every man decrees and executes judgments of punishment upon himself. To say that any organic disease may represent such a self-punishment will probably incur no contradiction, but the general assumption would be that this is only a use to which the suffering is put, i.e., an epinosic evaluation. That such a purpose might have entered into the etiology, the election, or the formation of the illness, would be less likely to obtain credence.

Nevertheless, in studying some organic illnesses one is impressed with the strength and dominance of such a need for punishment in the individual, sometimes apparent even before the outbreak of the illness. One observes how necessary it is for some persons to have their daily stint of punishment and pain, and how—if an accustomed form is taken from them—they seem obliged to replace it promptly. Sometimes an external cross is replaced with an internal one, an organic disease, and sometimes one organic disease is replaced by another.

In Dickens' *Little Dorrit* there is a good illustration of the novelist's intuitive perception of this principle. Mrs. Clennam, who by the misdeeds of her past life had brought about Mr. Dorrit's long confinement in the debtor's prison, is now herself a helpless invalid unable to stir from her room. "A swift thought shot into his [Mr. Dorrit's] mind. In that long imprisonment here, and in her own long confinement to her room, did his mother find a balance to be struck? 'I admit that I was accessory to this man's captivity. I have suffered for it in kind. He has decayed in his prison; I in mine. I have paid the penalty.' "

Such observations lead us to suspect—even though they do not prove—that this need for punishment and this compulsion to punish one's self is unconsciously one of the determining factors back of the appearance of the symptom and even of the organic disease. . . .

CHAPTER SIX

More Dragons

For a man who doesn't like violence, Dr. Karl can be a formidable battler. In addition to his campaigns for prison reform and the aboli- tion of capital punishment, he has championed a host of causes, in- cluding equal rights for minorities, protection of the environment, the preservation of endangered species, and better treatment of the aged, the mentally retarded, and the troubled young as well as animals, both wild and tame. The common denominator in each case has been a compassionate concern for life that mirrors his own profoundly joyful passion for it. And whatever the cause, in public he has been an ar- ticulate advocate, a molder of opinion, and in private, an effective doer. His championship of Negro rights began long ago. The following letter was written on June 8, 1946, to Mr. Edd J. Haas, manager of the Uptown Theater Building, Kansas City, Missouri:

I learned with a great deal of satisfaction [that] you are endeavoring to remove the present objectionable discrimination practiced by the moving picture theaters of Topeka with respect to colored citizens.

I am considerably concerned about this because we have at Winter Hospital a great many veterans, some of them white and some colored, who like to attend the moving picture shows. We have a certain number of shows on the post but we also encourage some of these men to go downtown and see pictures in the local theaters. We also have quite a number of colored employees in whose welfare and happiness I am also interested, and most of our employees are not permitted to see pictures shown on the post by reason of our agreement with the distributing agency for our films.

For the sake of these veterans, both patients and employees, as well as for the sake of other colored citizens of this city, I have been for a long time deeply chagrined [by] the fact that they were not permitted to enter some Topeka theaters [or] were routed to uncomfortable areas in the top gallery. . . . Not only is this illegal, but it is unjust and undemocratic. A similar attitude of discrimination turned against the Jews or other minority groups would, I know, be very disturbing to many of my Jewish friends in the moving picture industry. I am sure that they would concur with me in believing that all such fascistic, dishonorable, discriminatory practices should be abolished in our theaters.

Were it to be generally known that the Topeka theaters were excluding American citizens who come back from combat sick and wounded (for no other reason than that someone doesn't like the color of someone else's skin), I think there would be a considerable upsurge of public conscience, not to say some reproach against the theater management. I am well aware that the theater management thinks it must please the public. Perhaps it is pleasing a certain portion of the public, but there is another portion of that public that has a very different attitude. I believe it is to the advantage of your theaters to consider this other portion, of which I am happy to subscribe myself a member.

I have canvassed a considerable number of the members of my staff and other employees of this hospital (numbering over a thousand) and I can inform you that I am expressing their sentiment as well as my own.

Shortly after this letter was sent, the theater's restrictions were rescinded.

On another occasion, Dr. Karl protested to Dr. Kenneth McFarland, superintendent of schools of Topeka, when a black student-teacher from the local Washburn University was allowed "to observe" in classrooms but not to teach, except in all-black elementary schools. To Dr. Karl's initial protest, the school superintendent replied in part, "We in the Topeka schools are earnestly striving to improve racial relations in Topeka, and to do everything possible to assist every citizen to realize the full measure of the rights that are constitutionally and morally his. If our progress sometimes seems slow, I hope you will recognize that we must necessarily work within the framework of the legal structure under which Kansas schools are currently organized, and that public institutions cannot totally ignore the mores of the people who support them."

This elicited the following from Dr. Karl, dated February 11, 1949:

Thank you so much for taking the pains to write me at such length as you did on February 9th. I am glad to know that you and others in the school system are, as you say, "earnestly striving to improve racial relations in Topeka." I am not personally able to see that improvement taking place very rapidly and it is encouraging to know that you and others are working on it. I think it is a shame that a community which paid in blood and sorrow for the principle of freedom from 1860–1865 should now be guilty of as many Jim Crow practices as you and I know exist here.

I think I would be very discouraged were I a teacher of young people trying to talk about democracy and freedom and other ideals in the face of such a situation. And if I were a superintendent I think I should be very heartsick about the necessity of having to expect my teachers to be either hypocrites or to be silent. Very likely you are often heartsick, and as something of a public administrator myself, I extend you my sympathy and best wishes.

You are achieving a reputation as a great leader and one who inspires and awakens the conscience. I hope you will be successful in using these gifts of yours in the direction of the idealism which your letter indicates.

While trying to build bridges between people, Dr. Karl has spent more than a little time attempting to define the nature of the prejudice that keeps them apart. When asked by the late Dr. Sol. W. Ginsburg, chairman of the Committee on Racial and Economic Problems of the Group for the Advancement of Psychiatry, for his comments on the draft of a proposed report on prejudice titled "Social Responsibility of Psychiatry," Dr. Karl replied on November 14, 1949:

You talk first about "checking" prejudice, a process which eludes me, and then you talk about milder forms of it. I really don't know what these things mean. They got me to thinking about the whole question of what prejudice is, whether what you call prejudice throughout this whole report has the same meaning to a friend of mine who is very prejudiced toward a good many people and groups and things, as it does to me or as it does to you [we who think we aren't prejudiced]. Prejudice is so often only the hostile attitude of the people who don't agree with us. The dairymen are generally prejudiced against oleo-margarine; the Pilgrim fathers were prejudiced against the Church of England; the Crusaders were prejudiced against the Moslems; I have something of a prejudice against cats and against jazz music. Now don't tell me that I don't have a right to use the word prejudice in these connections because these are the connections in which prejudice is being used every day, and I don't believe that your committee has any right to pre-empt the word and say that prejudice means that we don't like the Negroes. I am not at all sure that you can define the word prejudice for the uses of your committee. You may have to coin a new word or else coin a very selective phrase.

Because if you retain the word "prejudice," I think you will constantly be up against the deterring "prejudice" of your relatively non-sympathetic reader who is after all the one whom you want to reach. There is no point in convincing those of us who are already convinced, is there? Yes, I am quite sure that if I were on your committee I would work toward the abolition of the word prejudice from any scientific discussion of the phenomenon. I think what you mean is irrational (but rationalized) hostility, generically directed.

Dr. Karl, as it turned out, was very much in the minority. A committee member, the late Dr. Nathan Ackerman, wrote him to say that his "was the only real 'blast'" among seventy-odd responses to the draft; the final report retained the word "prejudice." Dr. Karl elaborated on his objections to the word "prejudice" after reading an article by Bruno Bettelheim entitled "The Victim's Image of the Anti-Semite," in the April, 1948, issue of Commentary. *Writing to Bettelheim, he said:*

Like your previous article, I found this extremely interesting. It is not only courageous of you to write this but it is psychologically sound, in my opinion, in a way which seems to elude many contributors to the scientific analysis of the problem. I recently told a friend of mine that the barrage of articles against prejudice which seem to imply that the possessor of a prejudice is giving prima facie evidence of his psychopathology in the narrow sense of the word, is making me prejudiced against articles which are so prejudiced against prejudice. I have not seen in any of them the statement made by you that "anti-

Semites are for the most part average people—like Jews. And that is most encouraging." I also like the statement that "there is nothing peculiar about Jews except anti-Semitism . . . and it is even more difficult for Jews to accept the fact that there is nothing peculiar about anti-Semites except anti-Semitism." I think that the truth of this generalization stems from the courageous recognition that broad categorizing involves certain logical conclusions that we don't like to accept but which are inevitable. I mean to say that there is no such thing *as an anti-Semite* whose psychology can be glibly discussed any more than there is such a thing as a Jew whose psychology can be generalized about and you are, therefore, right in saying what you do.

We are having a little trouble right now because of a whispering campaign against this hospital which is running through the community to the effect that Karl Menninger has imported lots of foreigners, Jews and Reds from New York to this previously quiet and peaceful community. Now our doctors by and large are an earnest, idealistic, patriotic, hardworking bunch. They hear these rumors and various of them react to them by justifying them. They proceed to do a lot of arguing, thereby thoroughly convincing the somewhat astonished and somewhat alarmed local citizens that this vociferous stranger is exactly one of those dangerous people he has read about. One of our doctors—a bright, somewhat neurotic fellow who has been here only a few months—got up and explained how he had bought a house and discovered himself surrounded with some very agreeable neighbors, but also discovered that they had very conservative political views. Instead of endearing himself and his family to his neighbors as a human being—as a quiet, lawn-mowing, civic-minded citizen, he proceeds to get into hot political arguments. All his neighbor knows is that this fellow is a Jew (which in itself is somewhat exceptional here), comes from New York (which is also exceptional), seems to have radical politics on the brain (also exceptional). This neighbor will now never have a chance to find out what a nice man this doctor really is. He is already a radical New York Jew. That neighbor is going to whisper his alarm to a dozen people. Charge this off in part to the zeal and bad judgment of youth, if you like, but I charge it off partly to the vicious circle referred to in your article. There is nothing the matter with this neighbor and there is nothing the matter with this young doctor. What is peculiar to both is anti-Semitism. He feels himself different for various reasons and he's got to show how rational one aspect of this differentness is. In the course of doing so he scares his neighbor half to death without realizing it. Consequently, it is just as you say in your article—the only thing peculiar about this Jew is anti-Semitism and then the only thing peculiar about this neighbor is his anti-Semitism. They get together and this getting together generates a conscious and perceptible aroma of anti-Semitism which rises and spreads through the community.

I am stimulated to make many more remarks about your splendid article but perhaps this is enough for the present. . . .

In a more recent, but undated, private paper, Dr. Karl concluded that the phase or aspect of tribalism called prejudice is in today's world simply a sin:

The chorusing protests of black men at the moment against the disadvantages under which they live and labor should remind us also of the unheeded protests of the red man, the brown man, and the yellow man in this country. Our national crimes against all of these are great *and continuing.* To review our dreadful record in California, in the Dakotas, in Oklahoma, Georgia, North Carolina, New England, and New York is to produce a feeling of profound conviction of the power of greed to nourish prejudice until no honor or honesty remains.

Meanwhile, at the same time, a great, amorphous non-black, non-Indian, non-Jewish group of us slyly maintains a quiet, persistent, tacit trickery of discrimination against some of our most cultured and generous neighbors, people traditionally called, and calling themselves, Jews. We keep them out of our private clubs; we keep them out of certain residential areas; we keep them out of certain business deals; we keep them out of political office. Why do we? We don't even *know* why! Nor do they. Are they, indeed, significantly different from the rest of us? They even have white skins—mostly. Their parents were told certain stories and of certain practices by their grandparents, which their grandparents were told by theirs. They were told that they were all in some way related, symbolized by a few simple ceremonials and a high cultural and ethical standard. That is all they know. Someone has called them Jews and by that name they stick together. And is that bad? Don't others? They are outstandingly generous, outstandingly intelligent, and outstandingly merciful. Is that bad? Is that why we surreptitiously mistreat them?

The Germans glorified the cult of anti-Semitism into a national disgrace and followed through on it to the world's terrible and extensive genocide. Today the Jews are streaming out of Poland, that reconstituted, remodeled, reformed, socially democratic, civilized Poland. Too much communism or too little? And the Russian Jews are protesting bitterly that they may not leave Russia.

Surely nobody believes that anti-Semitism is a *symptom*. What is it but a sin, and a sin in which almost everyone, *including some Jews,* must acknowledge a degree of participation.

The sin of prejudice is a stubborn one, because so much of its motivations are unconscious. Its effects, however, are conscious and cruel.

And in Reading Notes:

So long as there remains one particle of hatred of or prejudice against the Jews—and we are reminded nearly every day that more than a little persists—books like *Commandant of Auschwitz* by Rudolf Hoess should be read by all citizens once a year. But perhaps there are no other books just like this [one]; it is the diary of the man responsible for the merciless, pitiless, businesslike destruction of *two million Jewish human beings.* Before he himself was finally executed he recorded in his systematic, compulsive way the horrific record of his performance. It is shocking to read in his autobiography that he was the child of a devout Catholic father whom he seems to have idolized and who inspired him to resolve to become a foreign missionary. He claims now to have been betrayed and disillusioned by a priest who reported a confessional secret. Psychiatrists will find other reasons for his entering first a military, then a criminal career, and finally undertaking the task at which he became a world champion—the torture and execution of political prisoners.

We should not close our eyes to the fact that the American prison system partakes of some of the same principles to which Hoess devoted his life and energies; [particularly] the principle that people that some of us do not like should be put away and kept away and hurt as much as possible, not because anyone thinks it will do any good, but because it has been ordered [by the power structure].

Discrimination against the American Indian is a theme of a great many of Dr. Karl's Reading Notes. He says of his concern about the Indian, "It's not a sentimental interest, nor the feeling, 'Here's a poor, quaint, interesting, pitiful group that needs help.' Nor a sense of guilt because of how we treated the Indian. It's based on the fact that the Indian is part of our heritage. He is the original inhabitant of this country, part of the tradition of the West."

When the Spanish invaded northern Mexico, New Mexico, Arizona, and Texas from 1510 to 1700, they came belligerently and destructively into a peaceful domain and burned, stole, and enslaved until the Indians rose up in the great Southwest rebellion in 1650—only to succumb sadly again after 1700.

Part of this is almost too terrible even to read about. One pueblo was ordered destroyed even though the poor Indians, fleeing from slaughter and slavery, hid in their sacred kivas. Five or six hundred who were dragged out alive were roped together and driven to San Juan, where they were sentenced: Males under twenty-five years of age and women over twelve were given sentences of twenty years of slavery. Males over twenty-five years of age were sentenced to have one foot cut off plus twenty years of "servitude," that is, slavery.

If anyone has any doubts about the cruel and destructive instincts of mankind, this knowledge should settle them.

Our righteous indignation at the terrible crimes of genocide committed by Hitler must have reminded the silent rivers and hills of California of the genocide our forebears committed on the Indians of that state in the middle of the nineteenth century.

Between 1820 and 1850, we infected, starved, burned, hanged, raped, kidnapped and enslaved, and shot or stabbed to death about one hundred thousand relatively inoffensive and certainly undefended, Indians. They were practically exterminated and exterminated with incredible brutality—some of the recorded details of which are too brutal to print.

This is by all odds the worst chapter in the history of our atrocities to the Indians and the worst chapter in California history.

A little east of Topeka is a river named after the most famous of all Algonquin tribes. Do you know about the Delaware Nation? It was that tribe with which William Penn made his famous Treaty of Peace when he founded the City of Love. So long as William Penn lived the treaty was kept.

Then came along some white Pharaohs who knew not Joseph. The Delawares were driven out! They took refuge with the Iroquois. The government forced a treaty upon them, took their land by forced sale against their will, and pushed them further west. They reorganized and settled down on a new location.

But not for long. We pushed them out again.

Then we did it a third time.

We did it a fourth time!

We did it a fifth time!! Yes, really!

Each time all signed a new "treaty," but each treaty was essentially a repudiation of the previous treaty which had said that it would not happen again.

Thinking to escape this successive frustration and heartbreak forever, the Delawares themselves *bought a tract of land* in Kansas, moved out here, fenced their farms, built houses and a church and settled down.

But the Kansans wanted to show that they could be just as mean as the Pennsylvanians and New Yorkers; they forced the Delawares off their land. Of course no white man could ever have been evicted, but these were Indians! With cold-blooded, heartless disregard of law, humanity, and ethics *we Kansans* moved the Delaware Indians for the seventh time, this time to a relatively infertile tract in Oklahoma where a remnant remains. God have mercy on our greedy, cruel, heartless ancestors.

It seems that for over two hundred years it was considered perfectly all right by certain civilized white men to have a little fun in the dull days of winter by hunting down Indians—men, women, and children—shooting them on the run or plugging them as they knelt in supplication. For a documentation of this as a favorite sport in the North Country, take a look at MacLean's for October 10, 1959.

According to this brave but appalling article (*illustrated, too!*), the unarmed human quarry was routed out of tents in the dead of winter and before they could get dressed, were driven naked out of the woods into clearings or onto frozen lakes where they were easier to see, and shoot at! They were shot down like jackrabbits or coyotes in a roundup. This popular amusement went on for over *two centuries* and *no white man was ever prosecuted* for indulging in it. A whole nation of handsome, proud, and peaceful Indians (the Beothucks) was completely extinguished!

Professor Dee Brown of the University of Illinois has been obsessed with the tragedy of the American Indian for many years. He has written ten books about them—all by himself—and three others

with a fellow writer. I never heard of any of these books; I understand none of them had much circulation, but that's about par for
the course. Books about our sins against the Indians usually don't
sell. It has all been said and it is dreary and depressing and makes us
feel guilty and ashamed.

Well, all at once Professor Dee Brown rises up and refutes all of
these generalizations. He writes a great book, a big book, a beautiful
book, a terrible book. *Bury My Heart at Wounded Knee* describes the
successive betrayals and swindles and massacres and robberies committed by us "white," civilized Americans upon the "red" men, women,
and children of a dozen little nations of "primitive, uncivilized savages." Without ever becoming maudlin, but in beautiful economical
prose, Brown describes what we did to the Cheyennes and the Chero-
kees, to the Arapahoes, and the Dakotas, and the Brule Sioux, and
what we did to the Nez Perce and the Utes.

If you think there is no end to it, you are right; it goes on and
on. It simply tells what they did and what we did. It will bring tears
to your eyes, tears of sorrow and tears of shame. But you will read it
up to the very last page—up to the photograph of great-hearted, brave
Chief Big Foot lying in the snow, frozen solid with his eyes open. His
eyes will haunt you for days. So turn to the next picture of Chief Red
Cloud with his eyes closed, and the caption beneath reads, "They made
us many promises, more than I can remember, but they never kept
but one; they promised to take our land, and they took it."

Nor can you ever forget the words of Black Elk: "I did not know
then how much was ended. When I look back now from this high hill
of my old age, I can still see the butchered women and children lying
heaped and scattered along the crooked gulch as plain as when I saw
them with eyes still young. And I can see that something else died there
in the bloody mud, and was buried in the blizzard. A people's dream
died there. It was a beautiful dream . . . the nation's hoop is broken
and scattered. There is no center any longer, and the sacred tree is
dead."

My point isn't that the American Indians are the only victims of
mistreatment by civilized people. One glance at South Africa is enough
to sicken anybody. But even in Australia, as may not be so well
known, there is a small group of Aborigines who live in a most deplorable state, starving and desperate in the main, deliberately poisoned
at times with bags of arsenic, and driven about at the convenience of
whoever wants to use the desert for whatever purposes.

The Australians are ashamed of it, just as we are ashamed of the way we treat our Indians. We blandly pretend that we are trying to improve things, and perhaps we are, but we put this improvement in the hands of incompetents and mediocrities who in the first place don't care much, and in the second place, don't know much.

"Do you know," said a Brazilian visitor in my office recently, "that the government of the country in which I live has systematically exterminated the Indians over large areas with the use of smallpox inoculations, arsenic-dosed candy and direct aerial bombing?"

"Not in 1968!" I exclaimed. "Years ago, yes, but not now!"

"Not for the past six months," he replied. "The government has recently agreed that although this makes the land more attractive for purchase by new settlers, it makes too much ill will and bad repute when other countries learn of it. So, after vigorous efforts on the part of a few of us, these methods have recently been discontinued. But don't shame us. Didn't you Americans find other methods for clearing the land of Indians?"

The book *The New Indians* by Stan Steiner is a poem—a collection of poems in essay form, written by a white man who for twenty years went to and fro among the Indian peoples. He saw the suffering and the frustration and the despair and the neglect and the misery and the starvation and he knew, or learned about, the double-crossing, the heartlessness, the indifference, and, above all, the ignorance of his fellow white men.

But Mr. Steiner also saw a turning of the worm, a new note of hope. There is, he believes, an emergence of young intellectuals, insurgents, *Red Power*. He is encouraged by this and by the steady, persistent support of the National Indian Youth Council and the National Congress of American Indians. . . .

"It isn't important that there are only 500,000 of us Indians," said a young Sioux. "What is important is that we have a superior way of life. We Indians have a more human philosophy of life. We Indians will show this country how to act human. Someday this country will revise its constitution (and) its laws in terms of human beings instead of property. If Red Power is to be a power in this country it is because it is ideological."

In 1947 when Dr. Paul R. Hawley, then chief medical director of the Veterans Administration, asked Dr. Karl for his opinion as a psychiatrist regarding the behavior of General George Armstrong Custer at the battle of the Little Big Horn, Dr. Karl's reply, entitled "A Psychiatrist Looks at Custer," was published in conjunction with an article by Dr. Hawley, "Did Cholera Defeat Custer," in the May, 1947, issue of a medical journal, Surgery, Gynecology, and Obstetrics.

Dr. Hawley has asked me as a psychiatrist to make some comments upon the psychiatric implications of his fascinating account. We are given a portion of the case history of a cavalry officer of about forty-five who was killed in action. We have the following pertinent data. He was a man:

1. Who stood thirty-fourth in his class at West Point.

2. Who was made a major general at the age of twenty-three.

3. Who achieved a certain amount of military distinction in the services of the Union Army where his actions were characterized by aggressiveness.

4. Who was noted for his ostentatious dressing and bad manners. (See J. C. Haskell and other references cited by Douglas Southall Freeman in *Lee's Lieutenants,* New York, Charles Scribner & Sons, 1944, page 734 ff.)

5. Who at the moment of supreme victory (Appomattox, April 9, 1865) violated military etiquette in many ways, loudly demanding surrender from his defeated and inactive enemy (General Longstreet) while General Lee and General Grant were conferring. (Op. cit.)

6. Who "took care of" and refused to return a famous pair of spurs given by General Santa Ana to the father of one of his friends. (Op. cit.)

7. Who in the name of warfare ordered and executed surprise attacks upon communities of men, women, and children and slaughtered the women and children along with the men.

8. Who took his own wife with him to a frontier assignment and later became so worried about her that he was impelled to forget or neglect his military duties.

9. Who deprived wounded soldiers under his own command of medical and surgical attention.

10. Who disregarded the safety and welfare of his troops to the extent of sending them into hostile territory with insufficient military preparation and protection to their almost certain (and quite pointless) death.

11. Who was convicted of one desertion of his own troops and was suspected of others.

12. Who either committed perjury or at least gave incorrect damaging testimony in court to satisfy a personal spite.

13. Who disobeyed specific orders given by the one friend he seems to have retained and the one general that intervened in his behalf.

14. Who presumably planned the sacrifice of the lives of the bulk of his command in order to attempt to achieve a minor piece of personal military glory.

These data describe a personality type only too familiar to psychiatrists, falling into a category of psychopathology typically characterized by excessive vanity, complete disregard for the feelings or safety of others, a lack of loyalty either to cause or to friends, either to the principles of humanity or to the established code of ethics, and a conspicuousness of achievement at times passing for success under circumstances where ruthlessness and boldness are to some advantage.

When this type of personality was encountered among the enlisted men in World War II, it was very apt to come rather promptly to the attention of the psychiatrists and such individuals were "boarded out" on Section VIII or the equivalent. But when a man wears stars on his shoulders, he can "get away with" things for which he would be court-martialed or hospitalized were he a private. This is not to imply that this happened often, but every time it happened it destroyed the morale, if not the lives, of thousands of men committed to the charge of such incompetent leaders.

Three corollary questions come to my mind.

First of all, what is to be said of the act of General Terry—a man whose name and reputation are completely unknown to me—who in spite of Custer's bad record, in spite of the court-martial, in spite of bad behavior in connection with the trial of the secretary of war, and in spite of General Grant's express wishes, insisted on giving a position of leadership and responsibility to a man like Custer?

In the second place, why does the name of Custer still stand in the mind of the average American as that of a great hero?

And thirdly—if by some accident of fate Custer had been successful in his disobedient and ill-planned attempt at coup, what would have been the verdict of history?

The article stirred up quite a controversy when Time, *in a story the following summer about the general's "Last Stand," interviewed Dr. Karl and quoted him as saying, "In World War II, Custer, for all his*

169

dashing aggressiveness, would have been discharged as a 'psycho-neurotic.'" Time *also attributed to Dr. Karl the statement that a "psychoneurotic" with stars on his shoulders could be as dangerous to his own side as to the enemy.*

Whereupon the Hays Daily News *in Hays, Kansas, published a feature disputing Dr. Karl's words, saying, "regardless of how right Dr. Menninger is in finding fault with Custer's psychic character, he is dead wrong in implying that 'Yellow Hair' was not a useful instru-ment in the government's attempts to clear the plains of Indian danger and thus prepare the way for settlement."*

Dr. Karl then wrote Frank Motz, the newspaper's editor and manager, the following letter on September 4, 1947:

I was very much interested in your article in the August 17th issue commenting on *Time* magazine's version of my own comments on Dr. Hawley's article about Custer. The points you make are very interest-ing, and if the end of safety can be used to justify the means, of course Custer has to be given some credit. I still suspect that method is just as important as purpose but I don't feel that his method was one which commends itself to us.

I could very possibly be entirely wrong in my conclusions which are based upon reading *some* of the things which have appeared about General Custer; I certainly have not read all that has been written, and I wasn't there!

By the way, I was incorrectly quoted by *Time* magazine. I did not say that Custer would have been discharged as a psychoneurotic. I don't know whether he was a neurotic or not. That was *Time* magazine's diagnosis, not mine.

Dr. Karl later admitted to being puzzled, however, by reading the ac-count of Custer given in 1885 by his widow, Elizabeth, in Boots and Saddles: Or Life in Dakota with General Custer. *He made his last stand in a* Reading Note:

Last night I read *Boots and Saddles* and I confess I am a trifle con-fused. Let me put it this way: The picture drawn by Mrs. Custer is that of a cheerful, energetic, zealous, considerate, adored man who tried hard to do his duty and trusted his own best judgment. She says noth-ing about his lust for killing Indians, his cowardliness, his abandoning his troops, his phobia of cholera, his gross discourtesy to inferiors, and all the other things I had read about. Now, a brave and loyal widow whose husband died in battle might and *should* scotomatize a few things, but if you have tended to despise Custer and now want to feel just a little bit better about him, read this book.

The delight of the book for me was in the vivid descriptions of the hardships of garrison life. Especially the frightful cold, the lack of fuel, the enveloping blizzards, *and* the mosquitoes! She describes one period when they were so besieged day and night by clouds of mosquitoes that they could do nothing else all the time but fight them. Women wrapped themselves in newspapers (of which they did not have many) under their clothes. Dogs dug holes in creek banks and crawled in like bears. The horses dripped blood and sometimes died; they were extremely difficult to handle and the men who rode them armed themselves as best they could with swathes of mosquito netting.

These pages say nothing of how the Indians must have endured the frostbite, the blizzards, and the mosquitoes from which they had even less defense than the United States Army personnel.

Along with his concern over what men do to each other, Dr. Karl's writings continually emphasize his love for nature. Long before ecology became a popular byword, he was writing of the dangers of mankind's reckless destruction of the planet's wildlife and natural resources. But he didn't always feel this way. He explains: "Like many others, I thought there was enough of everything for everybody—even including the hunters, and the real estate developers, and the air-polluters. But now we know there isn't, not even enough for the present population, to say nothing of the increase. Yet we keep on wasting and spoiling and destroying."

To illustrate, he cites the following which appeared in Reading Notes. *"This was written in 1950," he says. "It is now 1973. Still no bear protection to speak of. Bear hunts from airplanes are still 'big sport' in Alaska—for the rich killers."*

If you think the atomic bomb threat and the Chinese rumblings and the hysteria on the right and the financial problems of the United Nations and the silliness of preparing to go underground are somewhat monotonous as things to worry about, turn your eyes to the January issue of *Reader's Digest* and read the article on the polar bear. Here is a magnificent creature, extremely important to large groups of people and highly interesting, like whales and giraffes, to the rest of us. But like the whales, he is being exploited and exterminated. Canada and the Soviet Union prohibit shooting polar bears, whereas Norway and the United States almost encourage it. Recently it is all the rage for certain brave he-men to rush to the Arctic and blow lead into a polar bear just as the heroes of the last century went to Africa and blew dynamite through elephants.

As of this writing, says the author, there is a strong and concerted action to pass a Marine Mammals Act to protect the fabulous white bear. If there is a little of the bear totem in any reader, let him drop a line to the Department of the Interior and give it his blessing. I did.

And again on "sport":

Nature magazine for November [1954] contains an account of the campaign to save the mourning dove in Illinois. Legislation is sought to remove it from the game list and put it on the songbird list. The same is due in Kansas this year. It has already passed in twenty-four states, but farm boys in Kansas and Illinois are still shooting mourning doves off the telephone wires and they are diminishing in numbers.

. . . Shooting turtle doves off the telephone wires may be lots of fun for country school boys and blasting away at them in flight may be lots of fun for the town boys and the big brave men. It is less fun for the mourning dove which is decreasing in numbers over the country in spite of what the sports magazines and ammunition advertisers say.

In 1959 twenty million doves were brought in by hunters, six million more were wounded and killed but not brought in. The estimated number of nests of eggs left with one parent is seven million. It is these orphaned young which are especially apt to die of . . . infection. . . . To psychiatrists, the most interesting point . . . is the psychological disturbance the wholesale hunting causes the doves. It disturbs their routine programs of feeding, drinking, nesting, and migrating.

Doves are particularly susceptible to a parasite *Trichomonas gallinae*—a relative of the species we doctors know about. Chickens are immune to it but doves and pigeons are highly susceptible. Hence, some hunters justify their slaughter by saying they might as well shoot turtle doves as let the germs get them.

I happen to like mourning doves. I like to hear them and I like to see them; and as for eating, I prefer chicken and turkey, but in matters of taste there is no argument and some may still want to pick away at a dove wing. The rest of us should know, however, that we are paying for this fun for the few. Someday will come a showdown on this question of whether fragments of wildlife belong to the guy that can knock them down, or to all of us, or to none.

Hunters who may have gotten to feeling a little too guilty by now will get some arguments on their side from the Ohio Division of Wild Life which disputes us in eight pages of argument—sincere, no doubt.

Did you ever hear of Dr. Herbert R. Mills, a pathologist, of Tampa and St. Petersburg, Florida? His name will go down in history because of his almost single-handed rescue of the egrets, herons, ibexes, and other birds of the Florida keys through persuading the State of Florida and personal friends to establish bird refuges there.

Intelligent people know that most hawks are immensely beneficial birds. This is quite aside from their beauty, sitting or sailing gracefully through the sky in the evening. Thousands have been autopsied and their stomachs contain 95 percent rodents, beetles, and such things. Nevertheless they are persistently slaughtered by a few ignorant farmers who are convinced that they kill chickens and even label them all "chicken hawks." There is no such thing as a chicken hawk. They are also killed occasionally by teen-agers and other trigger-happy gunmen. They are killed in a few places, directly contrary to law, by the owners of game farms who set up traps on top of tall poles to which hawks are attracted by the flutter of the young quail and pheasants in the pens.

But the most incredible thing is the slaughter of thousands of hawks made from blinds in the brush on certain ridges in the Pennsylvania mountains along which the hawks are known to migrate. Hawk-shooting is an organized sport there and has been going on for at least seventy years. The state once unfortunately offered a bounty for the scalp of the goshawk, which is indeed a destructive bird but which is comparatively infrequent. The hawks are lured by tied pigeons and are shot at left and right. Many are left crippled, broken-winged, and dead all over the ground. There are only a few "hunters" who violate the laws by digging into this bloody sport, but there are over three hundred shooting sites along the Blue Mountain, furthered of course by local "businessmen" (beer taverns, sporting goods stores, etc.) in spite of such efforts as the Pennsylvania Game Wardens have exerted. See the article by Maurice Broun, "Pennsylvania's Bloody Ridges," in *Nature* magazine for June–July [1956].

MORE DRAGONS

Dr. Karl has made a plea to save almost every animal so threatened from extinction, even ("especially," he says) the coyote. He wrote Larry McGhee, of the WIBW Farm Department, author of an article published in Midway *on February 20, 1966, which extolled the sport of hunting coyotes:*

Everyone has a right to his opinion . . . Personally, I prefer coyotes to rats and gophers, which coyotes destroy, and to the coyote poisoners who destroy coyotes—and other things.

And in Reading Notes *the following year:*

First prize for the ugliest article of the season goes this spring to the June, 1967, issue of the usually impeccable *American Forests* for a description of "The Strychnine Caper." It is written with complete cool about the way the federal government, egged on by a small group of western sheep raisers, has developed an army of professional wolf poisoners who go about sprinkling millions of strychnine tablets in the proper places for one of the most gallant wild animals known to man to eat unsuspectingly, and after writhing in convulsions and agony for about six hours, die.

Because I have seen one or two human beings die of strychnine poisoning and a few rats, I could not be a party to giving strychnine to the most dangerous animal in the world, let alone giving it to hundreds of thousands of useful, nondangerous coyotes. I consider this federal program an immorality.

For another article which has the merit of the cold truth with no euphoric disguise of its ugliness, read again Montana Senator Arnold Rieder's denunciation of this heartlessness in "The Coyote's Last Stand" (*Defenders of Wildlife*, April, 1964). Senator Rieder is chairman of the Montana State Commission on Stockgrowing and Grazing and he, himself, is a ranch owner and operator of long experience.

And on pollution:

If the *Bulletin of the Menninger Clinic* doesn't say something about the national evil of pollution, it will be the only journal in the United States which hasn't mentioned it.

It is a curious attitude we take toward it—all of us—a kind of hysterical mass denial. Smog, we say, is something they have in Los Angeles and filthy rivers are something they have in Eastern industrial centers. Tourists' litter is something the ignorant leave in the national parks. Sewage contamination is what one of the towns upstream is doing or what the Eastern Seaboard does to the oyster beds.

No pollution here, we say. Oh, no—"there ain't no flies on me." Take a ride down the highways and watch the trucks darken the atmosphere with an oily stench. Look at the litter on the roadways; and while you are looking, look at the billboard pollution of the natural beauty of the countryside.

Does no one stop to think how the billions of little wild creatures, who live unobtrusively in the corner of the land which we have not yet paved, like the stinking poison of the atmosphere? What is the psychology of this broadside smearing of the universe (because we are actually sending debris into outer space, thereby doing a little polluting out there)?

Pollution of the air does more harm to farming in the state of New York than does bad weather or insects, says the A.A.A.S. [American Association for the Advancement of Science]. Air pollution costs California farmers 100 million dollars per year in crop damage. It costs farmers in six states, including the great forest states of the Northwest, more than all the havoc wrought by wind and cold and ice.

The missionaries and Indian Bureau officials used to go into a rage at the Sioux Indian children because they took it for granted that they might use the great outdoors, most anywhere, for the discharge of natural functions. The early European city dwellers thought it was appropriate to just drop anything they didn't want about the house into the street. Well, we haven't gotten much beyond the early Indians and the Londoners, have we?

But why does everyone pretend not to notice it? Is this a situation calling for discreet looking the other way?

Some readers are probably weary of my preoccupation in these pages with the horrible evils of air pollution, water pollution, soil wastage, and the cruel destruction of our natural resources. Nevertheless, I have to tell it like it is, and these are things that really worry me. I am not alone, but sometimes noting the preoccupation of many of my friends, I am a bit lonely. Then I pick up an extraordinary magazine like the September–October 1968 issue of *Audubon* and I feel reassured that there are intelligent reporters making faithful and startling reports to an audience that must include many intelligent readers. The article on "The Infernal Smog Machine" tells us nothing new but tells it vividly. The reprise of the breathtaking tragedy of the passenger pigeon destruction is a good prelude to the beautifully illustrated Eliot Porter portfolio of the Kentucky valley which is about to be destroyed.

But the climax article of this issue is the report by George Laycock of the bloody, grizzly, brutal, illegal, and immoral business of alligator slaughter—for the sake of a commercial product. The Florida alligator is given three or four more years before total extinction—a victim, let us say, of the world of fashion, women who want alligator purses or men who want alligator shoes. He is the victim of a thousand professional poachers in Florida who scoff at the laws protecting the alligator and sell a million dollars' worth of alligator hides per year.

While we are talking about disappearance of old friends, let's mention the black walnut tree. The slogan "Save the Redwoods" is almost sure of a partial victory, but as yet no one has shouted very loud, "Save the Walnuts!" Maybe someone should. Walnut wood has become so scarce and valuable that few farmers can resist the fabulous prices offered for even average sized trees. There are walnut tree thieves abroad, also; in one night they can lift $10,000 worth of lumber out of a farmer's wood lot.

Is anybody doing anything? Yes, people are always doing things, but not fast enough—not effectively enough. Walnut is scarce and walnut is desirable and money talks. Kansas, incidentally, has one of the few remaining sources of supply.

Updating the above commentary, Dr. Karl adds: "And the state has encouraged replanting because the seedlings grow rapidly. The farmers are doing it. And so am I."

Dr. Karl welcomes others to the cause. Commenting on a Wall Street Journal *story of January 2, 1970, he said in a* Reading Note:

All at once the press and the President add their voices to those of the lonely minority which has been shouting huskily, "Help! Help!" for fifty years. "Help" for poor old nature, for ravished nature, for disregarded nature, for insulted nature, for smeared nature. And the *Wall Street Journal*, which has a keen eye for important issues, has finally had the courage to do what, to my knowledge, none of the other papers or journals ever did.

From Stuart, Florida, Tom Herman of the *Wall Street Journal* told how that beautiful area was ravished and nearly ruined by the absurd, pretentious, and expensive project of lake drainage forced upon the citizens of Florida by the U.S. Army Corps of Engineers.

Supreme Court Justice [William O.] Douglas once called the Corps "Public Enemy No. 1" and Senator [William] Proxmire of Wisconsin "an oversized goose that lays thousands of golden pork barrel eggs a year."

My brother Edwin and my then father-in-law, Henry N. Gaines, were among the few who fought against the destructive drainage canals, especially the one through Stuart. The objectors were brushed off like flies. Tom Herman quotes the Army Engineers regarding them: "Those silly butterfly chasers and self-serving politicians can't stand in the way of progress. . . . Those ignorant, misguided, conceited fools! They know not what they say. We are the nation's leading conservationist group because we have conserved the earth by molding it to suit man."

Take a look at the once beautiful St. Lucie river inlet at Stuart, now black with mud—the fish gone, the oysters, clams, pelicans, ospreys, and wild ducks almost gone. The Corps has the grace to admit that they are largely to blame. And I remember too what the Corps of Engineers did to the Seneca Indians at Warren, Pennsylvania, where the bitterness it caused will burn for years. And much more of this bitterness will occur if some of the projects which the *Wall Street Journal* article lists are carried through in the neighborhood of Fredericksburg (Virginia), Gaysville (Vermont), the Ohio River towns, and other places.

I had written all this before I ran across that spirited *J'Accuse* book *America the Raped* by Gene Marine (1969). In three hundred pages the author slashes and scorches and flogs the Army Corps of Engineers until I almost felt sorry for them! (Not very.) Nor for them alone, either, for people who think like they do and plan like they do and effect so much terrible damage in their efforts to be constructive. This infection is so widespread and imminent and socially relevant, it involves and threatens every one of us. One or another of Marine's fourteen chapters is about *you* and *yours*. Read it and see.

And on the brighter side:

I like books that describe the realization of a dream. *A Thousand Ages* by Nancy D. Sachse (1965) is about an arboretum at the University of Wisconsin, which I made a special trip to see because I had heard what a wonderful thing it had become.

In 1853 one man of vision urged the university to obtain specimens of the trees and shrubs characteristic of the state and said he would "venture to predict that the university or college that shall first surround itself with such an 'Arboretum' will first secure the patronage and good opinion of the people, and will outstrip those institutions that show a lack of taste and refinement by omitting to plant trees."

Well, the university was a long time getting around to accepting this suggestion. The Arboretum was again urged by a landscape artist in 1907; this stirred up "enormous enthusiasm. Enough of the older generation remained to recall the wilderness paradise and demand action." During the years I was attending the university, the president tried to get funds for the proper land acquisitions but failed. Then in the late 1920s a man named Michael B. Olbrich began to speak out for an Arboretum and the preservation of wildness. One member of the famous Dr. Jackson family, the son of the pioneer doctor, Joseph W. Jackson, listened. (One of his descendants is now a Fellow in the Menninger School of Psychiatry.)

In 1929 came the financial crash and the sudden death of Mr. Olbrich. The Arboretum idea seemed lost. The Indian mounds were being destroyed by vandals. But twenty-eight acres of unmolested wilderness, containing some mounds and an Indian trail to a spring where an Indian still lived, aroused the special interest of the Dr. Jackson, aforementioned, who had never forgotten Olbrich. He gave a dinner in 1931 to revive the project.

Then ensued "an extraordinary period . . . during which the regents and the administration of the university maintained an attitude of greatest caution." (!!!) But, under the leadership of Dr. Jackson, the Arboretum finally got going and a committee was formed on which many agencies were represented. I will skip the ups and downs thereafter—the tremendous difficulties they had getting started, the many men who were disappointed, the hopes and failures of their efforts. With the greatest difficulties, little piece of land after little piece were acquired until finally a wonderful collection of trees and plantings, springs and mounds, wildlife habitats, ponds and hills, were put together in one of the best arboretums in the nation.

I am proud that a member of our profession helped push it over the peak of the resistance. And what is the lesson of this for us in regard to *our* arboretum (feebly begun in 1933) and other projects?

CHAPTER SEVEN

Man's Proper Study

Dr. Karl has long been a chief exponent of psychiatry to the world at large. Speaking in many forums and to many groups—doctors, lawyers, senators, college students, to name just a few—he has sought continually to improve the public understanding of the aims and processes of his profession. One of his best explanations came in the second of a series of three Alden-Tuthill Lectures that he was invited to deliver at the Chicago Theological Seminary in 1951. In this talk, besides discussing the things psychiatrists do, and distinguishing their work from that of the ministry, he emphasized some of the things psychiatrists don't do, pausing particularly to puncture the "common, but vicious" assumption that they favor sexual promiscuity. The lectures, given January 23, 24, and 25, under the general title "The Relation of Religion to Psychiatry," were published the following March in the Chicago Theological Seminary Register. *Here is the second lecture:*

Like most other human beings, psychiatrists are busy with their daily work, giving too little time, perhaps, to reflections regarding the name and nature of God or the proper form of worship. The adjuration of Alexander Pope is quite generally our guiding motto:

> Know then thyself, presume not God to scan;
> The proper study of Mankind is Man.

As individuals, we psychiatrists grew up in various religious traditions, and we tend to continue in them, reared by parents of differing origins, who taught us *their* forms of acknowledging the great mysteries as well as they could—as well as they could repeat and restate and perhaps extend the instructions they had received from *their* parents, and so on back. Thus we carry on in various forms of worship the acknowledgment of our reverence. The forms vary greatly, as we all know; and for some this very variance is distressing and improper; they conceive of a standard and universal form, "the one true church." For others, this idea itself is absurd and unsatisfying. I am often reminded of a remark made to me by a devout Catholic colleague as we were listening to a patient singing at a recital in the wards of a psychiatric hospital. "In how *many* different ways people pray!" he remarked, quietly, as we walked back to my office.

Prayer might be defined as the issuance of communication directed to God. If one believes in the existence of God, the question of communication between Him and His creations, or between them and Him, becomes an issue. The existence of a God does not imply the existence of such communications, but it seems to be assumed in most formalized beliefs. But if I were asked, for example, as a sample scientist and psychiatrist, whether or not I believe in prayer, I could not make a conscientious answer without stipulating that the question be resolved into various parts. If I were asked, "Do you believe that prayer exists?" I could answer easily, "Yes"—for me, and for many others. If I were then asked, "Do you believe that the prayers of men are heard by God?" I could answer in the affirmative because my conception of God is such that *everything* reaches Him. If I were asked, "Do you believe that God answers prayers?" I could answer affirmatively, but my affirmative answer would not necessarily mean that I agree with what is in the mind of the questioner.

The effect of prayer upon God is scarcely subject to investigation, but the effect of prayer upon those who offer it could well be made a matter of scientific research. A psychiatrist, Samuel W. Hartwell, suggested that prayer may be a very hygienic and even therapeutic experience, because it enables people to verbalize certain introspective reflections and half-conscious wishes under circumstances of intimacy and trust which rarely prevail in interpersonal relationships.

I once asked Chaplain Robert Preston of our Winter VA Hospital to tell me, from his long observation of hundreds of psychiatrists at work, what he could conclude in general terms about our religiousness. "What do psychiatrists believe?" I asked him. "We don't come to your services very often; you don't hear our devotions. What do our lives seem to you to indicate?"

He thought about it for a while and then wrote me this:

You psychiatrists seem to believe that some people can be understood and, by understanding, be helped. Behind this belief there seems to be a belief that many people need help. The facts seem to justify these beliefs. Furthermore, you seem to believe that in re-examining your efforts constantly in the light of the results obtained you can discover and affirm a principle of workability. You seem to have concluded that long-term results are more important than immediate results. This brings you into the field of social relationships, which I shall mention further in a moment.

You seem to have a belief in the importance and the dignity of the individual human being. It is an assumption, of course, which you seem to make with a dedicated faith, that every individual is worth helping. You seem to believe that each individual has capacities for being destructive and capacities for being constructive and creative. You seem to feel that it is possible for another human being like yourselves, granted an understanding of the particular problems and mechanisms of this individual, to guide him in the direction of constructiveness and away from destructiveness. You have demonstrated that it is possible to regain strength from the beneficial positive factors in the case of severe conflict and to restore people to an inner equilibrium. This requires a disciplined honesty in seeking the real sources of trouble and implies that health demands truthfulness within the self.

Concerning society you seem to believe that human beings are interdependent more deeply and crucially than most people realize. The measure of an individual's health is linked in your concept with his level of usefulness in carrying out his own responsibilities and contributing to the welfare of others. Hence, you contend, tendencies which are harmful to others are a mark of disorder within the person and arouse your feeling of responsibility for the use and techniques of modification.

You are more keenly aware than most people of the influence of groups upon the individual because you see in the mental hospital the persons who have been broken by, or at least not helped by, social institutions—domestic, economic, educational, and religious. Sometimes you observe that the teaching of religion has affected individuals in ways which were not intended by the teacher or by the religious leader. Surrounded by the extremes of tragedy, dwelling with the victims of disillusionment and self-destructiveness, you are constantly impressed with the deceptiveness of superficial explanations. It leads you to a feeling that there may be praise with the lips while the heart is far away and, hence, that if "faith is the substance of things hoped for, the evidence of things not seen," it must be made as substantial as possible.

In this beautiful and I trust truthful appraisal of the work of the psychiatrist, you will note that Chaplain Preston says "you *seem to believe.*" He means that psychiatrists *act* in certain ways which imply (to him) that they possess such beliefs. "By their fruits ye shall know them."

Such behavior could be considered, in two categories: behavior with reference to fellow creatures, which involves "morals," and behavior with reference to God, which is subsumed under "worship."

Worship may be private or public, or both. Perhaps we should agree that it must be consciously and thoughtfully done to be considered worship, whether public or private. There are certainly psychiatrists who do not formally worship in any way. There are others who feel that their attitude toward their God, in whatever form they envisage Him, is a matter for private and intimate contemplation only. Still others—and here I include myself—see value in group assemblage and some kind of formal ritual. As a Presbyterian I am not a genuflector but I respect genuflection as one of several simple maneuvers which have the same meaning of reverence, enhanced for any particular individual by the conditioning of childhood training and the example of loved ones, companions, and friends. The mutual stimulation, reinforcement, and encouragement that the individuals of a group receive from one another are well known to psychology, and the effect of a common relationship to a leader—pastor, rabbi, or priest —has been carefully examined by many scientists, including Freud.

Alfred B. Haas, professor of practical theology at Drew University, has contributed a valuable comment on the therapeutic value of hymns. In it he points out that, because of their emotional associations, hymns reduce anxiety, alleviate a sense of guilt, strengthen inner resolves, bring comfort, and divert self-preoccupation. Of course, not all hymns do this. Nor would I minimize the value of other forms of church music in arousing religious sentiments.

Going to church is not equivalent to religion—perhaps not even essential—but it is a form of religious activity which comforts, encourages, and supports those for whom its forms and its fellowship are acceptable. It, too, arouses the religious feeling. In this sense it appeals to many psychiatrists as a prescription for patients, if not for themselves. No one need be reminded of its abuses, but it is characteristic of this world that any good thing may be turned into evil.

If we take literally the words of Jesus, "If ye do it unto one of the least of these my brethren, ye do it unto me," we do not leave the question of behavior toward God when we turn to consider more specifically behavior toward our fellow men. And, for the psychiatrist, fellow men are chiefly patients. In what ways and in what spirit does the psychiatrist minister to his patients?

"Psychiatrists are wicked men," we are told. "They persuade their patients to a godless, immoral philosophy. They repudiate the conscience; they advocate irresponsible self-expression to the disregard of moral law. They attempt to thwart the design of the Creator, whom they deny while they themselves play God. They order and reorder human life and arrogate to themselves the molding of the conscience."

This misunderstanding stems from the fact that mental illness has long been a mystery. It is enormously prevalent—more abundant than all other forms of illness put together. It exists in myriad forms. Every priest, pastor, and rabbi spends a considerable amount of his time, I am sure, listening to parishioners who are in distress because of recognized or unrecognized mental illness. Clergymen more than most people are aware of the vast extent of misery and suffering in the world. They and the psychiatrists are together on this. Like the psychiatrist, the minister feels impelled to do something to diminish this suffering, not only by advice to the individual, but by proclamation of principles of living. In their sermons they endeavor—most of them—to hold out hope, comfort, encouragement, and reassurance to congregations in which there are many who need this help. Meanwhile, the psychiatrists are spending *their* days listening, comforting, correcting, and reassuring.

For the mystery of mental illness has begun to yield to science. It began with Freud's discovery that most psychological processes are not conscious ones—that there is a vast organization of mental functioning of which our conscious experiences are only a small part. This is actually no more novel than the discovery made many centuries ago that there were internal organs and internal physiological processes not visible in the intact human body. But just as the dissecting scalpel, the microscope, the X-ray, the sphygmomanometer, the electroencephalogram, and many other technical devices have now enabled us to look behind the bloodshot eye, the pallid skin, and the wasting flesh to determine what preserves or destroys these structures from within, so we now have methods for looking behind the surface of conscious thinking and overt behavior, there to see undreamed-of intricacies, forces, functions, and processes. And these methods of looking have provided us with methods of changing the patterns.

The study of personality on this grander and more inclusive scale is really the basic content of modern psychoanalysis and modern psychiatry. It is the basis of our therapeutic program. This function of the psychiatrists understandably alarms some clergymen, for it seems to put too much responsibility for personality-molding in the hands of the psychiatrists. We have long since accustomed ourselves to relinquishing the personality-molding of our children to underpaid, poorly trained grade-school teachers; we have no doubts about qualifications for surgeons to whom we resign ourselves for modifications of the structural aspects of our personalities. But psychiatrists remain suspect. This is particularly true in the case of psychoanalytic therapy used by the psychiatrists, but is the one which is based on the principle that full self-knowledge permits better self-realization. "Ye shall know the truth and the truth shall make you free." Some clergymen, some theologies, view such individual freedom, such greater knowledge, as dangerous.

The technique of psychoanalysis is highly specialized, and it is no wonder many people misunderstand it. Some seem morbidly anxious to misunderstand it and to turn a penny publishing their ignorant defamations.

In the contrary direction I commend a most excellent article by Lois Perry Jones in a little magazine called *Life Today* (December, 1950). Mrs. Jones accurately points out "what a psychoanalyst *doesn't* do!" Thus:

1. He doesn't use bristling Freudian terms in talking to his patient.
2. He doesn't dispense sympathy in the form of sympathizing.
3. He doesn't insist on changes in the patient's environment or habits; indeed, he does insist that until the analysis is completed no radical changes be made.
4. He doesn't make decisions for his patient.
5. He doesn't remove his patient's conflicts.
6. He doesn't make his patients perfect.
7. He doesn't make his patients happy.
8. Indeed, strictly speaking, the analyst doesn't cure his patients; he helps them to cure themselves.

What he does do is this: By helping his patients to understand the truth about themselves and their environment, he enables them to choose more wisely and hence more nearly determine their own destiny, to decide what they really most desire, and hence what their life shall be like—within limits—achieving through love and work and play a desired goal.

I should like to illustrate some of the pronouncements which seem to impugn psychiatry but which actually serve rather to demonstrate the speaker's ignorance. One is quoted as saying, for example, that psychoanalysis is a form of escapism. This is a correct statement, if the verb *is* be changed to *may be*. Some patients undoubtedly seek psycho-analytic treatment to escape from realities, or even unrealities, which they cannot bear or which they think they cannot bear, and it is the duty, the custom, and the proper procedure for the psychoanalyst to point this out to the patient, at the right time. In this way he can be helped to cease "escaping." But many persons find their own neces-sary and quite satisfactory escapes. Playing golf may be escapism; like-wise taking a vacation or going to sleep. Escapism in itself is not an evil; it is a phenomenon. It may be useful; it may be harmful. Of course it is true that from certain things there is no escape, but a good psychoanalyst is going to point that out to his patient with just as much honesty and deftness and clarity as the priest or the minister will.

Another quoted charge against psychoanalysis is that it "fails to relieve the unresolved sense of guilt of sin." As it stands, this statement doesn't add up to any charge at all. I see no reason why psychoanalysis or surgery or cosmetology should relieve anybody from feeling guilty about a sin.

If *just the opposite charge* had been made—namely, that the psychoanalysts *did* undertake to resolve a sense of guilt for sin, it would have been a stronger point. Some patients (and others) get the im-pression that some psychoanalysts have taken upon themselves the responsibility for absolving people from a sense of guilt and that this is against public policy, against theological concept, and against moral principles in general—that it is the business either of the state or of the church to do something about guilt, and certainly not the function of a physician.

But such pat assignments fail to distinguish between *guilt* and a *sense of guilt,* and between a sense of guilt related to *actual* offenses and a sense of guilt related to *imaginary* offenses.

To approach the matter immediately from a clinical standpoint, I would remind you that every psychiatrist sees patients every day who feel extremely guilty *about something they have not done.* If such in-dividuals were to go to a judge and ask to be sentenced for this sin, the judges would be astonished; if they were to go to a priest, he would no doubt assure them that they had never done anything and therefore had no guiltiness and therefore *should* not have any *sense* of guilt. But if they insist on having a sense of guilt even when they have no actual guilt, there is nothing the priest can do about it except to send them to a psychiatrist! For, on the other hand, there *is* something that a psychiatrist can do about it. A psychiatrist can, with the scientific tools now at his disposal, ascertain the unconscious, invisible reason for the false sense of guilt attached to a nonexistent sinful or criminal act. This is not the place to go into an extended discussion of the psychological mechanics of forming or relieving a sense of guilt attached to non-existent crimes. It is a very, very common clinical symptom with which every skillful psychiatrist is constantly faced. One could go so far as to say that in almost every mental illness or nervous illness there is a very strong component of this. For such a symptom, psychoanalysis offers relief, and the church does not offer any relief. If a man has horse-whipped his children, I am sure that no psychoanalyst would want to see him absolved or relieved from a sense of guilt about it in any other way than that prescribed by law and concurred in by the church. On the other hand, if a man imagines that he has caused the death of someone in China through remote control, or if someone feels guilty to the point of suicide because he feels that he wasted too much water washing his face in the morning or because he stepped over the threshold on the right foot instead of the left foot, then I think there would not be any doubt as to whether he should be offered relief by a priest or a psychoanalyst.

There is a common assumption that psychoanalysts favor sexual promiscuity and that they encourage people not to have any sense of guilt about it. This assumption is false, and its reiteration is a lie, a slander, a canard, and a misrepresentation of facts. Freud refuted this charge nearly fifty years ago, and no honest, intelligent, informed person can allege it. Psychoanalysts do not favor promiscuity, do not encourage it, do not attempt to relieve any patient's guilt about it, and, in short, are no more to be considered immoral exciters to crime than anyone else who is doing his best to diminish the errors of mankind. Quite the reverse, most of them spend hours and hours attempting to relieve patients from the compulsive feeling of need for these very "immoralities."

One might ask, "What keeps alive this common, but vicious, misconception?" I think it is very easy to say. Parents necessarily constantly restrict the sexual life of their children and sometimes in most crude and harmful ways. Sooner or later the instincts of the growing child bring him into conflict with the code of society, and he reacts to his parental experience in one of several ways. One way is by complete inhibition of his sexuality, which, if continued throughout life, means that he develops an abnormal personality. Neuroticism, impotence, homosexual propensities, and other sexual irregularities may be substituted for normal sexual adjustment. Many people come to psychiatrists because of a certain degree of inhibition in their sexual life which results from a feeling that any kind of sexual activity is wrong, including normal sexual relations with the spouse. Now it is not sufficient to *tell* such individuals that this is incorrect; they have been told so in a thousand ways, but they cannot believe it. In psychoanalysis they *do* lose an inappropriate and abnormal sense of guilt which had attached itself to sex in general; they discover that sex is not the evil thing which they have considered it to be but a purposive life function. In their sudden joy in such a discovery, such individuals by word of mouth or even sometimes by deed try to indicate that they no longer have the crippling inhibitions that have ruined their lives. But the errors of such individuals no more indicate the sinfulness of psychoanalysis than do the sins of certain Catholics indicate the wickedness of Catholicism or the offenses of certain Protestants the failure of Christianity.

I have made use of some of these recent accusations as to the immorality of psychiatry and psychiatrists to indicate how some of the charges against our "works" are made in ignorance. For I do think that psychiatry has a morality, and I do think that beliefs which must in the last analysis be described as religious are implicit in the theory and practice of psychiatry.

Consider, for a moment, what the daily work of the psychiatrist is. Consider his ministry of care to the most miserable, the most unloved, the most pitiable, and at times the most offensive and even dangerous of human beings. Consider the psychiatrist's role, properly conceived, as that of the friend, the guide, the protector, the helper, the lover of these unhappy people. "Passing through the valley of weeping, they make it a place of springs" (Psalm 84).

Consider what *you* call his tolerance, his forbearance, his patience with stubbornness, anger, spitefulness, silliness, sulkiness, belligerency, desperateness, unreasonableness, maliciousness—all the manifestations of hate. These he meets, if he is a good psychiatrist, with an attitude he is not ashamed to call love. We can live, he tells them, if we can love.

"You can be angry with me, if you must," the psychiatrist tells his patients (by his behavior); "I know you have had good cause to be angry at someone, so angry you became afraid of it. But you need not be afraid here—not afraid of me, not afraid of your own anger, or of your own self-punishing conscience. You needn't be afraid that your anger will arouse my anger and bring you pain again, and make you feel wronged and disappointed and rejected and desperate and driven mad once more! For I'm not angry, and I won't get angry, and after a while you won't be angry, either. These people all about you whom you can't look at now—you will find that they are your friends. We are all your friends. We all love you, in spite of the unlovableness you feel. Presently you will begin to realize that, and relax a little, and then more and more. And as you come to understand us better, and we you, the warmth of love will begin to replace your present anguish, and you will find yourself helping us and getting well!"

This is what the psychiatrist must say in every gesture, every act, every order, every word. This, in modified forms, is what he must say to every patient. Does it sound ungodly?

The psychiatrist dedicates his life to the furtherance of the welfare, the life-betterment of those whose capacities for adjustment have been overtaxed. So, of course, in a specific way do the shoemaker and the dentist. But the overtaxing that brings patients to the psychiatrist reveals itself in pain, in queerness, in isolation, in discouragement, in ineffectiveness, in disagreeableness, in idleness and isolation, in despoliation and defilement. These are unlovely pictures, and it is the goal of the psychiatrist to inspire and guide and effect their change. By the grace of God he is *usually* rewarded with success—not *his* success, but the patients'! *Most* psychiatric patients get well. Hence it is that the chief prayer of every psychiatrist should be: "Keep back thy servant also from presumptuous sins; let them not have dominion over me."

Concern with the crucial distinction between such terms as "guilt" and "sense of guilt" is typical of Dr. Karl. He has always shown a fine sensitivity to nuances of meaning and, by the same token, an antipathy toward the use of jargon—what he calls "the mumbo jumbo" of the profession. Jargon, he believes, is not only misleading but downright dangerous for patient and psychiatrist alike. He gave some of his reasons for this belief in the "Speaking Out" column of the Saturday Evening Post, *April 25, 1964, under the heading "Psychiatrists Use Dangerous Words."*

Every profession has its own jargon, and we psychiatrists have ours. But while the strange terms a lawyer or an archaeologist uses are harmless enough—the worst they do is mystify outsiders—the terms psychiatrists use can hurt people and sometimes do. Instead of helping to comfort and counsel and heal people—which is the goal of psychiatry—the terms often cause despair.

Words like "schizophrenia" and "manic-depressive" and "psychotic," for example, frighten patients and worry their anxious relatives and friends. The use of these alarming terms also affect us psychiatrists. They lead us back into the pessimism and helplessness of the days when mental illness was thought to be made up of many specific "diseases," and when each "disease" bore a formidable label and a gloomy prognosis. . . .

"What would you substitute?" I am sometimes asked. "What do you want us to call these people—or these conditions?" Such questioners obviously have not caught my point. I wouldn't *call* them anything. I want us to emerge from the name-calling stage. Psychiatry should repudiate it. Some angry people don't call their opponents liars or skunks any more; they call them psychiatric names like "psychotics" or "psychopaths." Why? Because these technical words have become pejorative. They no longer mean merely psychiatric illnesses; they mean something despised. . . .

Why is this so hard for the public to see? Why is the public so willing to retain its pessimism and cling to the ancient superstition that mental illness is incurable? For the mentally ill *can* be saved, most of them. They can be cured, but they need help. Their symptoms are a cry for help. We cannot plead ignorance to excuse our neglect, for we know what to do. It is not our helplessness that has deterred us so long but our hopelessness—and perhaps, in part, our dreadful vocabulary.

Dr. Karl's concern about the ways in which specific labels are attached to general conditions led him to raise a strong objection to a new nosological list proposed by the Committee on Nomenclature and Statistics of the American Psychiatric Association. In a letter on May 3, 1967, to Dr. Ernest M. Gruenberg, the committee chairman, Dr. Karl said:

I have a letter from you dated March 2, enclosing a preliminary draft for the printing of the second edition of the APA's *Diagnostic and Statistical Manual*. You say "the committee is eager to have any comments and reactions you may wish to send us."

I have looked over the membership of the committee and wish to express my deep respect for the professional abilities of the several members with whom I am acquainted. Indeed, my admiration and affection for them have deterred me thus long from replying to your letter. . . .

I wish I could commend the committee's achievement. . . .

Unfortunately . . . I think it is not an improvement on the first edition in style, in content, or in basic theory. . . . I find it more static, rigid, and ontological in concept than the much earlier edition. . . .

While in places I do not agree with the new definitions or do not understand what is meant by them, my chief objection is not to these particulars but to the assumption that these many dreadful "things" exist and can be [hunted for, found,] identified, labeled, indexed, and sent to the statistical machine. Mind you, this may be true, as you assume. You may be entirely right. But for many colleagues, this is *not* true; and to pretend that it is a matter of common or universal acceptance in order to bolster a punch card for so-called statistical "needs" is to betray our professional convictions. Statistics should be our servants, not our masters. Over and over I hear residents say, "I don't believe this appellation is appropriate, but we are obliged to put down a number or the record librarian sends it back." What statistics!

Human beings sometimes act in ways and in patterns which can be described by adjectives, not nouns; human beings are not possessed by devils with binomial Greek and Latin appellations.

I realize that the committee has been trying to cooperate with colleagues in other countries. I commend this. But psychiatry has been notably underdeveloped in many of these countries and it is they who should make the big changes rather than for us to regress to the thinking of forty years ago. We American psychiatrists should not sacrifice the advances we have made in theory and practice by adopting languages and designations which discourage therapeutic efforts by implying incurability.

We have fought hard and long for these gains in America and I hope we will not return to neatly boxed-off "disease names," either for the sake of collaborating with foreign colleagues or for the purpose of assisting the computers and statisticians.

No changes were made in the APA definitions, but Dr. Karl has continued to argue his point of view. In an interview with Mary Harring-

ton Hall that appeared in the February, 1969, Psychology Today, *he said:*

We label mental diseases the way little girls name their dolls. And one little girl's *Helen* is not like another little girl's *Helen.* In the same way Dr. A's "schizophrenia" is different from Dr. B's "schizophrenia." And as long as we think of mental illness as a horrible monster with a name like schizophrenia, we won't be able to prevent it.

We must see mental illness as simply a considerable degree of disorganization in a particular person. And we must discover ways to improve his organization.

And again, with almost religious fervor, Dr. Karl attacked the "schizophrenia" label during a Menninger Foundation symposium on that "disease," which was reprinted in the July, 1969, issue of Group Practice, *the journal of the American Association of Medical Clinics:*

My thought is that the assumption that we know so definitely that a disease, not a condition, by the name of schizophrenia with a capital S exists implies more certainty than any of us possesses. I think nobody denies the existence of a schizophrenic syndrome. To say that this disease picture is a reified thing may be correct if you are the author of the definition of the disease. But if you take the word disease in its commonly accepted sense, then the reification of schizophrenia, it seems to me, is unsupported by any consistent description.

In spite of all that has been said, it implies a hopelessness which has a derogatory effect on the patient, which is an important consideration because this is a psychological disease.

In a psychological disease the individual is affected by the knowledge; consequently, the self-defeating, the tendency toward the establishment of a self-defeating prophecy, develops.

It seems to me that we saw a demonstration on a grand scale in the old state hospital situation where nobody expected the patients to get well. This fact was soon communicated to relatives, and it was also communicated to the patients.

As soon as the expectations changed, the prognosis began to change. Doctors began to be interested in the possibilities of the case, more doctors appeared on the scene, more personnel began to work with the patients, and more recoveries occurred. I don't think this was because later doctors were any better than earlier doctors. You later doctors certainly had a very much more positive and expectant attitude toward the possible courses of the schizophrenic syndrome than we earlier doctors did. But more than that, it seems to me that the diagnosis of schizophrenia has importantly become a pejorative and declassifying diagnosis. . . .

I don't agree that this syndrome should be given the designation of [being] a disease as if it were a thing, a fixed thing, a thing which only a few unfortunate, stupid, or otherwise unlucky individuals happen to get. This, I think, is immediately to distort the fact of that kind of diagnostic distinction. It hurts the individual. The individual so labeled is no longer a troubled individual. He's no longer just a sick man or a patient. He is regarded now as belonging to a special class of people to be treated, perhaps to be feared, to be scorned, to be pitied, to be avoided—always to be degraded, always to be suspect in regard to his predictability, in regard to his adaptability, and in regard to his competence. Objectively and subjectively he is stigmatized even if he ceases to have any of the symptoms upon which the original labeling was established.

It's like those indelible marks they stamp on your wrist when you go into Expo and other places. Once that's stamped on your wrist, then that's what you are. You come and go when you like, but you're always stamped for that day. It seems to me that that's what we tend to do. I think that this is not right. I make it a matter of morals. I make it a matter of ethics. I'll make it a matter of scientific idealism if you like. I think it is not right for any of us to do this to any of us. Certainly not those of us who have had the wonderful privilege of learning something about the troubles of mankind from the standpoint that we doctors have. I think most of all, it is *we* who want to help people who should avoid anything that, as Hippocrates says, instead of helping, harms the individual who has come to us for help. Now this is why I feel so strongly about this—why I think that I can endure any amount of ridicule for it.

From Reading Notes, *on the question of making diagnoses:*

Lieutenant Commander Jack V. Wallinga of the navy examined the diagnoses of 804 psychiatric admissions over a period of ten months. Two thirds (65%) of those admitted from other hospitals had more than one psychiatric diagnosis attached to them, and 47% of those admitted directly to his own hospital had accumulated more than one diagnosis. Four hundred and seventy of the 804 patients had their diagnoses changed during the course of their illness. The author modestly suggests that from the impressions gained in this study "the clinical handling of acute psychiatric patients might be simplified . . . by the initial use of a more tentative, descriptive, and less specifically psychiatric label . . . emphasizing the degree of emotional disturbance, the duration of the illness, the self-destructive and aggressive tendencies." *Thank you, Dr. Wallinga. (United States Armed Forces Medical Journal, 1956).*

Dr. Martin Hoffman of Syracuse in the American Journal of Psychiatry for September, 1960, takes a good square look at the word "health," and the expression "mental health," and concludes that they can only be defined as referring to a state of affairs approved by someone, especially "the people." What one profession or political party or specialized community thinks is healthy, others regard as unhealthy. This applies to technicians like ourselves. Consequently, Hoffman gets around to the precise position that we have frequently announced, namely that the important thing is not the labeling, but the question of how to deal with the people whom we were formerly content to merely label.

He also gratifies this reader highly by saying that not only mental health but also mental illness, normality, abnormality, neurosis, psychosis, perversion, psychopathic, and sociopathic are words that *cannot be defined.*

A lighter comment on labeling, from Reading Notes:

In the course of my work with the governor, I had occasion to study the biennial reports of the Board of Penal Institutions.

I am particularly interested in the State Industrial Farm for Women, which is the euphemistic designation for the women's section of the penitentiary. Each year, apparently, the record clerk submits a batch of statistics to the superintendent who forwards them to the Board of Penal Institutions by whom they are incorporated in the biennial reports. These include sixteen tables showing such things as the number of prisoners in the various age brackets, the counties from which they come, the offenses committed, and so on.

But hear this! Hear this!

One table lists the *"habits* of prisoners received during the biennial period just ending." Liquor was the habit ascribed to 4 prisoners;

liquor and tobacco to 61; tobacco alone to 12, and those having "no habits" numbered 16! Another table lists the religion of these women. Six had no religion, 15 were described as Catholic, 66 as Protestant and (hold everything!) 6 of them were Baptists! That's all!

And now a few quotations from Table 11, "showing cause of downfall of women received during the biennial period ending June 1954." As might be expected, liquor leads the list of causes with 27 cases. Four were the victim of circumstances. *"Foolishness" was listed as the cause of the downfall of 4, and "men" the cause of the downfall of 6.*

I was so interested in this conception of the reasons for human downfall that I looked up the earlier records. Two years previously there were about the same number of prisoners but "foolishness" was still the cause of 6 downfalls, and "men" the cause of 5. In 1950 it was about the same, but in 1946 there were more than three times as many prisoners and of these men were the cause of the downfall of 104! Temptation was the cause of the downfall of 13; circumstances (that evil thing) was the cause of the downfall of 4 and 10 ascribed their downfall to the need of treatment.

In 1944 there were over 500 prisoners. Self-defense was the cause of the downfall of 27 of these, and the need of treatment the cause of the downfall of 22, but men led the list with 58. Only 11 women bravely and wistfully announced the cause of their downfall to be "Myself."

The failures of psychiatrists are not written up as often as their successes. After reading In a Darkness *by James A. Wechsler, editorial page editor of the New York* Post, *who told how years of treatment had failed to save his son from committing suicide, Dr. Karl wrote this moving letter to Mr. Wechsler on April 6, 1972:*

I have read your book *In a Darkness* in an almost reverential frame of mind. I don't know anything quite like it. I have usually seen this tragedy, as you can understand, from the doctor's position.

But you give us a picture of the original parental bewilderment, then the uncertain groping for therapists with no realization of what you were getting into, then the conflict with professional ethics and other such complications, then the contradictory doctors, then the accidents, and the hospitals, and the new experiments, and the new doctors.

As you went along from episode to episode, I kept thinking of the agony of suspense that you and his mother went through and the patience and forbearance it must have taken. You had to control your exasperation and your grief and your worry and it's a wonder to me that you have any tolerance left for doctors at all (or any money). With much dignity you refrained from saying how vastly expensive this all was to you and what problems this must have brought to the family.

I read in some review that your book told the heroic struggles of a troubled man. I think the book shows the outstandingly brave and heroic struggles of a father and mother.

The temptation to blame one or another of the doctors is strong, but upon finishing the book, I reflected that each one of them had really done the best he could. Each of them had probably used his particular method on other patients and been successful, sometimes. Your son's problem was too strong for any of them. They all tried, and how could you possibly know which one would have been best for your son at the beginning or at any particular time? And the mix-up about Phil's warning is so typical, and so tragically understandable. Phil did the right thing, of course. Dr. Eighth betrayed you, but that's understandable, too. He was on the spot and didn't know how to get out.

I don't know whether or not you have followed psychiatric writings enough to know of my theory that the suicidal impulse, which Freud said was in us all, constantly demands tribute—or "hush money." People pay in various ways to avert the necessity of the ultimate step, and many of the ways *they* choose are actually thinly disguised but attenuated forms of self-destruction such as alcoholism, fast driving, even smoking, to say nothing of some neuroses. I would say that, in your son's case, his reserves for fighting against [or buying off] the suicidal impulses failed him, played out for no reason that you know or could possibly know. He tried, and you surely tried to help him. But the inevitable happened.

You were a very brave man to sit down and write this book, to dwell on each of the details that must have grieved you so deeply. It's a brave book, and I think it will be a helpful book. You are not alone, you know, and this book can be of immense comfort to others who, on a darkling plain have groped their way through the same agony.

P.S.
Your publisher, who sent me the book, asked for a comment. You could tell him that this is my comment. I doubt if it will be of any use to him in promotion, but I hope it is. I know you don't want your

book promoted in the ordinary sense; but want it distributed where it will help. My colleagues all ought to know about the book; I shall mention it in my column.

Dr. Karl also recommended to his colleagues in a Reading Note *a book about how to choose a therapist.*

Daniel Wiener is a clinical psychologist for the Veterans Administration in Minneapolis and an associate professor at the university there. He sat himself down to write exactly what the title of his book says it is, *A Practical Guide to Psychotherapy* (1968). Psychotherapy is what everybody—well, almost everybody—is doing to and for everybody else—or rather for those others who complain. (There are many silent sufferers, and many who need relief other than psychological.) But there ought to be a *model* of psychotherapy, he thinks, for all of us to follow or refer to—not necessarily a medical or psychological model but definitely a scientific one. "As a healing science, psychotherapy is a failure," he declares; as an art it is questionable. We should think of it as a "skill."

Doctor Wiener then goes about setting up "guidelines" for psychotherapy and quite sensibly, too. There are instructions on choosing a psychotherapist and a preferred method of therapy, and what to expect of the initial interview. Finally, some verbatim samples of different kinds of psychotherapy sessions—psychoanalytic, nondirective, eclectic, and "behavior-change"—and that's the book.

Well, we started it, we psychiatrists—this peculiar business of talking down to another human being one or more times a week for many weeks and charging for it by the hour. A rather presumptuous promise is implied: "I can help you if you'll come clean," we say, "so it's up to you." It's all in the favor of this book that it is written as a manual of information for the *customer*, not as instructions about technique for the operator. Some of the young operatives could certainly use it to advantage, however, and I hope they will read it.

But one cannot help wondering where we will be in this fifteen years from now. I heard of a situation recently (no doubt fictitious) where a chap was being treated by a psychotherapist who himself was in psychotherapy with a psychiatric resident physician who is receiving psychoanalytic therapy as a "control case" by a candidate in the Institute for Psychoanalysis! Four in a row, each one passing on the magic. I leave out the details of the additional network involved—the wife of one and the child of another also being treated. Are we becoming either a "drug culture" or a "psychotherapy culture" people?

What role should psychiatry play in shaping public policy by advising government officials? When a woman in Scarsdale, New York, moved by Dr. Karl's books, suggested he replace Harry Hopkins as advisor to President Roosevelt, Dr. Karl wrote:

Thank you for suggesting that I replace Harry Hopkins. I deeply appreciate the compliment indeed, and I think the effects of having a psychiatrist in the White House milieu might be salutary, but so far I have not been sent for!

Questioned about how he felt about the "Eagleton affair," in which Senator George McGovern, the Democratic nominee for President, asked his vice-presidential running mate, Senator Thomas Eagleton, to withdraw from the race in August, 1972, following the disclosure that Senator Eagleton had received electroshock treatments for depression on three occasions, Dr. Karl said:

"I personally would have voted for Senator Eagleton. But as a politician, I never would have advised that he be put up for the general public to vote for (or against). One can be even healthier than before after recovery from mental illness. But the public hasn't found this out yet. Thousands of people would have voted against Senator Eagleton. After he was "martyred," as they thought, many came out for him who wouldn't have voted for him before.

It was characteristic of the condition ascribed to the Senator that on the one hand he had to be more alert, lively and productive than the average person *and* to underestimate the effect of his moods, when they were out of the ordinary, on his environment. He did not think through the effects his disclosures would have on strangers who knew only the bare facts. He went through the nightmare of being ill, and having rather unpleasant treatment, and getting over his illness. To him this seemed to be the end of the story. Such individuals do not realize that in the public mind there is a strong tendency to believe, in vulgar terms, that once "insane," always "insane." Unfair it is, unjust it is, untrue it is.

However, I don't think it's fair to use a national election to prove a point. If Eagleton had really thought things through, he would have said, "The best way for me to demonstrate my recovery is not to over-play my hand." To go from electroshock to being vice-president of the United States is a terrific leap. However, even if Eagleton had been elected and then had had another attack of depression, I don't think that would be the end of the world.

Although I think electroshock administered for depression has occasional value, it isn't my choice of treatment. My colleagues and I have never used it much. I don't know whether Eagleton was the exceptional case or whether it is the regular treatment at the institutions to which he went. It is not at the Menninger Clinic.

CHAPTER EIGHT

Sex, Love, and Aggression

The "sexual revolution" is anything but new, and Dr. Karl's comments on it some fifty years ago have a very modern ring. For the column "Books and Things" in The New Republic *on July 5, 1922, he wrote:*

Is there anybody on this planet, now, at the end of the first half of 1922, who sees the problem of sex in relation to all our other problems? Most likely not. Even if he existed, and were to speak the truth that is in him, the rest of us would most likely band ourselves together and tell him he did not know what he was talking about. This would probably be the mildest of our welcomes to such a prophet.

But that sex is a problem, that the problem is difficult, that nothing but harm is done by denying this—those among us who believe these assertions, and whose belief expresses itself, whether by reluctant acknowledgment or by loudest house-top trumpetings, we are increasing in number day by day. . . . Years hence, centuries hence, historians will mention the early part of the twentieth century as one of the times when mankind began to take a new attitude toward sex.

Let us hope they will call our attitude a sign not only of change, but of change for the better. Let us hope they will call our beginnings, whether shy or vociferous, a beginning of enlightenment. At least they will admit that we are less silent than our immediate forerunners.

Even contemporary we, who have learned to be tentative in our self-appraisals, have reason to think we are not mistaken in saying that silence about sex is at this moment on the wane.

Our task was twofold. First we had to break that silence, which had done so much evil in the world. Secondly, we had to substitute for silence something else more useful and healthier. We are doing the first half of our task, for which nothing is essential but will, somewhat better than the second half, for which wisdom also is necessary.

Lately I have been reading two books about sex, one by Miss Maude Royden, *Sex and Common-Sense* . . . the other by Mr. Havelock Ellis, *Little Essays of Love and Virtue*. . . . They are noble books. They will do a great deal of good in helping parents and teachers to realize what a crime it is to treat sex as either a vile topic or an unapproachable mystery. That reader must be a dirty dog indeed who can even skim these books and not perceive their high-mindedness, the ardor of their longing for beauty and truth in sexual relations, their faith in the attainability of these good things.

Except at these points, and at one other, to be mentioned in a moment, the two authors are quite unlike. Miss Royden is a Christian, and a believer that renunciation, even lifelong renunciation, is often necessary and may be rich, human, full of love, creation, and power. Mr. Havelock Ellis has more learning and curiosity, more indulgence and mysticism. His windows open upon a wider prospect, a more varied world of sex, which he observes to my taste too intently. . . .

The only grave defect I notice in these two books is the one other trait they have in common. I am afraid that they will do harm by being a little too holy, by leading young people to look for a finer spirituality in sexual relations than most people are capable of finding in any relation whatever. In *Little Essays of Love and Virtue* I find this passage: "From our modern standpoint we may say, with James Hinton, that the sexual embrace, worthily understood, can only be compared with music and prayer." Why compare it with anything but itself? Why ought all mankind to understand it in the same way? Why not leave every decent person free to understand it in different ways at different times, free to call none of these ways unworthy? Happy are any two persons who can quite naturally think of their bodies as altars, and who can as naturally think of the fire descending upon those altars as divine. But for most of the human race this mental attitude is not natural, this experience is rare. An animal gladness shared with an intimate friend—it is not comparable with prayer or music—but on the other hand to call it unworthy seems to me illiberal and a priori.

One of the modes of spoiling sexual relations is to seek in them more than nature and nurture have given us an aptitude for finding.

I could wish for, though I cannot distinctly imagine, a book which would make me envy, more keenly than either Miss Royden or Mr. Ellis has made me envy, men who are more spiritually minded than I, which would make me wish I were eligible to their company. In both Miss Royden and Mr. Ellis there is an exaltation which does not put me at my ease.

And so far as possible I should like to be at ease about sex. I should like to have been told, when I was a young man, that for the average young man sex, of all the important objects of emotion and thought, is the one most likely to receive attention in excess, that it is possible to think of sex cleanly, to think of it unselfishly, and yet to think of it too much. I should like to have been told that the right amount of attention, which is not the same for all men, is for each man terribly difficult to measure. I should like to have been told that my preoccupation, which I took to be shameful and unique, was the common lot.

Perhaps no one has done more to collect data about man's sexual behavior than Dr. Alfred Kinsey. However, to many psychiatrists, it seemed that Kinsey erred in his studies of sexual behavior by over-emphasizing the physical while virtually ignoring the psychological— that, in effect, Kinsey was "telling all" about sex, but nothing about love. Dr. Karl took him severely to task for this in a review of Kinsey's second book, Sexual Behavior in the Human Female.

Looking back on this review, Dr. Karl comments: "I'm rather proud of myself for the following review. Kinsey was a big name in those days and it was rather brash of me to go for him so hard, but I still think I was exactly right in my estimate of him. I respected him as a scientist trained in laboratory techniques, but he was a very naïve man about sexual research. He discovered that if you asked people about their sexual activities, they generally tell you. He made a business of asking anyone who would talk. His scientific training deserted him. His samples were not scientific."

Dr. Karl's critique appeared under the title "What the Girls Told" in the Saturday Review of Literature, *September 26, 1953:*

As everyone now knows, some years ago a distinguished entomologist, intrigued by students in his classes at Indiana University, was moved to seek answers to those questions by asking a considerable number of cooperative fellow creatures to tell him frankly what their own personal experiences had been. This inquiry he and three associates gradually extended to more than sixteen thousand men and women, selecting his total "sample" more and more carefully in the direction of advice from students of statistical science. Influenced by his professional experience in studying insects, in which the significance of a fact is reinforced by its frequency of repetition, Professor Alfred C. Kinsey then tabulated the incidence and timing of atomistic sections of the behavior and sensations reported by his communicants.

From this he arrived at various totals, split into subtotals by reference to such extraneous criteria as the economic and educational "level" of the subject interviewed, the existence or nonexistence of a marriage license, the number of *years* lived, and the relative devoutness of religious conviction—to select only a few.

The first results of this study, conscientiously pursued over a period of ten years, appeared in 1948 as *Sexual Behavior in the Human Male*; the second report, *Sexual Behavior in the Human Female,* has just been published. Together they clearly demonstrate the existence of various phenomena long familiar to psychiatrists, which apparently neither Kinsey and his colleagues nor some members of the general public had previously been quite able to bring themselves to believe. They document with figures precisely what Freud submitted years ago in his famous book *Civilization and Its Discontents*—that civilized man has inhibitions which cost him something in the interest of the total welfare of society. Coming, as this does, from a scientist skilled in collecting numerical data without contamination by the prejudices of psychiatric experience, the Kinsey material is all the more impressive.

Another man whom Professor Kinsey resembles is Havelock Ellis, who also persisted earnestly in the proposition that sexuality was noble and beautiful and not shameful and wicked. But Ellis was a social philosopher, and Freud was a discoverer, clinician, and theoretician. Kinsey is not a theoretician, not a clinician, and not actually a discoverer, but a taxonomist. He had curiosity, the mainspring of scientific research, and he had a ingenious idea; with earnestness, persistence, patience, and courage he listened to, recorded, and tabulated what many people told him of their experiences. Thus he has produced a set of statistics which, criticize them as we may, do have a certain scientific validity and a prodigious interest for the general public.

It is difficult for a fellow scientist affiliated with a branch of the science for which Professor Kinsey appears to have a somewhat hysterical antipathy to appraise his new volume with complete objectivity. The real difficulty a psychiatrist has in reviewing the book arises from the sharp difference in our viewpoints regarding the science of man.

After the appearance of the volume on males five years ago I went on record as believing that this might prove to be one of the most important scientific studies published in our lifetime. Together with many other psychiatrists and social scientists, I admired the intrepidity, persistence, and earnest purpose of the authors. I heartily concurred in their apparent convictions that individual variation deserves respect and not intolerant condemnation. We all rejoiced in the Kinsey group's success in crashing the iron curtain of social hypocrisy and submitting convincing data in a way that Freud, Havelock Ellis, Krafft-Ebing, W. F. Robey, Margaret Sanger, Victor Robinson, G. V. Hamilton, R. L. Dickinson, K. Davis, and hundreds of psychiatrists whose names I have no room to list, had failed to do.

But, along with many of my colleagues, I was aware of serious flaws in the first volume. These were carefully pointed out by thoughtful, sympathetic fellow scientists, and I had every hope and expectation that Kinsey and his associates would make use of their suggestions and improve the research before the appearance of a second volume.

In this I was to be greatly disappointed. So far as I can ascertain, Kinsey appears to have heeded scarcely a word of the scholarly analyses and wise counsel of such penetrating critics as Dr. Robert P. Knight, Dr. Lawrence Kubie, Lionel Trilling, and numerous others. Kinsey's compulsion to force human sexual behavior into a zoological frame of reference leads him to repudiate or neglect human psychology and to see normality as that which is natural in the sense that it is what is practiced by animals. Kinsey entered the field of sexuality from entomology and Freud from neurology; but Kinsey has never outgrown his original viewpoint that sexuality is just something that occurs in animals. Freud discovered that in the field of human relations one must recognize the functions of love and hate as scientific realities interrelated with reproduction. Kinsey did not; the word "love" rarely appears in his book.

Kinsey repudiates the concept of normality as beneath scientific contempt, but by implication he substitutes for it the use of two other concepts, that of naturalness and that of prevalence (*i.e.*, high relative incidence). Homosexuality is to be regarded, he says, as a natural form of sexuality, like any other, because it is common in human beings and because animals also practice it. Now this may reflect, as Trilling suggested, "a generous impulse for tolerance, acceptance, liberation, a broad and generous desire for fellow men not to be harshly judged," but it puts the authors in the untenable position of establishing inappropriate norms and setting up the worship of the factuality of the fact, its material physicality and its numerical strength. To use these as his criteria "has the effect, ironic in a work that is so clearly directed to democratic values, of removing the human subject from its human implications. (It also) has the effect, equally ironic in a democratic and instrumental document, of preventing the consideration of the consequences of certain forms of human conduct . . . suggesting a most ineffectual standard of social behavior—that is, social behavior as it exists."

Professor Kinsey's conception of sex as something to be let out (he refers to the "total outlet") is a somewhat scatological concept, and leads logically to two of his most egregious errors. The first is the inference that the more of this "sex" that can be let out the better; the second is that the orgasm is the total goal and ultimate criterion of sexual satisfaction. No one would seriously hold that since eating is a good thing and a pleasant thing, the more one can eat the better. The fact that many people would feel inclined to agree with it is likewise no proof. The starving inhabitants of a desert island might easily subscribe to the notion that the more food they could obtain the better, but any dietitian could refute this. And, furthermore, Kinsey clearly demonstrates that there is no considerable amount of sexual starvation in America.

As for an orgasm being the chief criterion of sexuality, everyone knows that one orgasm can differ from another as widely as do kisses. A kiss by Judas is one thing, a kiss by Venus is another, and a kiss by a loving mother still a third. The orgasm of a terrified soldier in battle, that of a loving husband in the arms of his wife, that of a desperate homosexual trying to prove his masculinity, and that of a violent and sadistic brute raping a child are not the same phenomena. The muscles and nerves and secretions may be the same but the orgasms are not the same, and the sexuality is not the same. They may add up to the same numbers on an adding machine, but they don't add up to significant totals in human life.

Indeed, the psycho-physical separation which the Kinsey associates decry at the beginning of Chapter 16 is precisely what has victimized them throughout their study. They would seem to be under the impression that it is possible to describe the mechanics of human behavior in purely physical and chemical terms without reference to the mystic vagaries (as they conceive of them) of psychology. This point of view, one must concede, is by no means limited to the Kinsey group. It is the chief *casus belli* between the biological and the psychological scientists, and the reviewer is definitely with the latter.

It isn't that sex cannot be separated from love; we all know to our sorrow that it can. But we psychiatrists take the position that this separation itself represents an abnormal state of affairs in the human being, and hence statistics about sex based upon an assumption that the presence or absence of love, to put it simply, is unimportant, are vastly disturbing to us.

These very points have been made with startling clarity by Maurice Zolotow, a feature writer, in a newspaper article distributed by the Spadea Syndicate, the whole of which Dr. Kinsey should take to heart. Among other things, Zolotow wrote: "I believe that both Kinsey reports . . . with their graphs and statistics, may bestow an aura of scientific approval on a delusion that has misled all too many people in the past twenty-five years. I refer to the delusion that sex is an indoor sport and, like contract bridge or Scrabble or canasta, it can be mastered by studying technique and practicing as often as possible with as many partners as one can induce to play . . . Unless the movement toward sexual integration is an expression of love for the other person there can be no sexual ecstasy . . . Love is an intense awareness of the other person, a feeling of respect for him or her as a human being and as an instinctive attitude that the needs of the other person are as important to you as your own needs . . . Sexual promiscuity or experimentation or athleticizing . . . without feelings of tenderness and affection—is . . . destructive."

When the first volume of the Kinsey study appeared, Dr. Martin Gumpert commented that one highly gratifying effect of the book would seem to be that it appeared to lift the feelings of guilt from hundreds of thousands of readers. "People work with touching eagerness through the appalling mass of boring charts and statistics in order to discover with relief that they are not outcasts, not psychopaths, not criminals when they masturbate or enjoy other 'abnormal' sexual outlets. They learn that they are as 'normal' or as 'vicious' as anybody they meet on the streets of their hometown."

Unfortunately, this guilt lifting is an equivocal blessing. I, for one, think that some guilt feelings are better *not* removed—they belong. Certainly, the rightness or wrongness of an act can scarcely be justifiably determined by the frequency of its occurrence. If human welfare be considered a criterion of rightness, the fact that nearly every person in the United States regularly ran past stoplights or exceeded the speed limit would still not make it right to do so. Dr. Kinsey and his associates point to the influence of religious training as inhibiting the violation of laws and customs regarding sexuality, such as marital fidelity. If one believes in the principle that maximum sexual expression is the most desirable goal, then, of course, it is encouraging for one to learn that he is not the only sinner against religion, which holds that certain other principles are more important than sexual "freedom" and that more abundant life is not necessarily implied by more abundant sex. And in this instance, surprising as it may be to some, most psychiatrists and psychoanalysts will be definitely on the side of religion.

To be freed from the torturing delusion that one is a monster, a lone and isolated exception among human beings, is indeed a comfort and a salutary benefit if derivable from such statistical announcements. But it is by no means certain that if one learns that other people have temptations, and sometimes yield to them, he will have a happier marriage, better sexual adjustment, and all the other bright results spoken of in the newspaper and magazine reports. Indeed, if one followed Kinsey in his (I believe incorrect) assumption that sexual behavior is entirely a matter of sexual equipment, conditioning experience, and chance, there is no reason to assume or hope that the publication of his findings will in any way change things.

If human beings *were* only animals, if they were "free" from the restraints and social considerations of civilization, if they could once more be simple savages, perhaps their sexuality could likewise be more free, more independent of emotions, more susceptible to statistical evaluation. It would be—in one sense of the word—more "natural," more "normal." But, unfortunately for this hypothetical simplification, human beings are possessed of love as well as hate, and willy-nilly, for better or for worse, civilization has gotten a foothold!

That the unrestrained expression of "sexuality" becomes impaired thereby is, as Freud pointed out in *Civilization and Its Discontents,* inevitable. This Kinsey and his associates have proved statistically. Is it to weep or to rejoice? Freud himself would not say. But he did say:

> Men have brought their powers of subduing the forces of nature to such a pitch that by using them they could now very easily exterminate one another to the last man. They know this— hence arises a great part of their current unrest, their dejection, their mood of apprehension. And now it may be expected that the other of the two "heavenly forces," eternal Eros, will put forth his

strength so as to maintain himself alongside of his equally immortal adversary.

By the "eternal Eros" Freud meant the development of the capacity for loving one another, a relationship which far transcends the achievement of frequent orgasm.

Dr. Karl also has been an active critic within the profession. For example, he severely criticized a proposed report on homosexuality by the Group for the Advancement of Psychiatry (GAP) that was sent to him in 1950—when Senator Joseph McCarthy was looking for security risks in the State Department. The report, entitled "Homosexuality with Particular Emphasis on This Problem in Governmental Agencies," stated that homosexuality was primarily psychological, that many homosexuals served their country with honor and distinction, and that each case had to be considered on an individual basis. Dr. Karl commented on the report in the following memo, dated May 29, 1950:

I have tried and tried to restate this homosexuality business, and I come to the conclusion that it is impossible to make a "statement" without knowing to what end the statement is to be used.

I very much object to the statement that you submitted on May 25th, first because in certain places it is literally not true, and secondly because its inference is not true (I mean the inference that only ignorant laymen think homosexuality means genital stimulation; as a matter of fact, we all think that), and third because I don't think it adds up to any clear, definite point. This is partly because we are not sure just what point someone wants us to make.

In the fourth place, I think unexplained oracular pronouncement of this kind infuriates a lot of psychiatrists who will say that GAP has no right to speak for American psychiatry. It is true that your first paragraph is modest and cautious, but its weakness consists in the second sentence. You say that because the public is interested in it, GAP has formulated a statement. Now I don't think GAP can or should formulate a statement about everything the public is interested in. I think that is presumptuous in a high degree and in fact a little silly. If you can say that a question has been asked of you by a responsible public agency, then you have a legitimate reason for making an answer which can be given to the public if that agency requests. As it is, however, it sounds as if you had suddenly had an inspiration to educate the public just because the public is curious. I think this is undignified and improper.

In the fifth place, assuming that what the State Department wants to know is whether or not homosexuality predisposes to blackmail, I think you could say in theory yes; in clinical experience rarely. If what they want to know is whether homosexuality is a definite condition, I think you could say yes and no; it is a universal tendency which in some individuals becomes excessive to the point of disease. If what they want to know is whether or not its overt form can be unerringly detected, I think you could say no. But until we know just what their questions are, I don't see how you can make a statement within the limits of five hundred words that will contribute anything to anybody's understanding or do anything to change anybody's attitude. You must have something to attack. You mildly attack the proposition here that homosexuality is a rare, easily detectable, freakish piece of psychopathic criminal behavior. You don't anywhere say that this is just what it is, and you don't anywhere make clear what I think you are trying to say which is that this like all other extreme behavior reflects universal human tendency.

Conclusion: I urgently counsel that GAP not make any statement on this subject except in the form of specific answers to specific questions. The only exception to this would be, in case the questions were of a certain type, that GAP might make a general statement that homosexuality in all its manifestations is primarily a clinical and only secondarily a legal matter, and hence not a proper subject for congressional investigation.

Today, talking about homosexuality, Dr. Karl says:

The "worm" has turned. Homosexuals have been treated very unkindly and inconsiderately. They are asking to be considered no different from other men. The homosexual is a man who lacks the sexual urge to jump on women and penetrate them. Homosexuals want to pet other men, love them tenderly. All men have this wish to some extent, but the urge of homosexuals is stronger.

We lump together all men who prefer men into one group. But homosexuals differ. Some like to hurt other men, degrade them, whereas some like to exalt other men, admire them, idolize them. Some want intellectual companionship, believing that chattering women are not intellectual and that they must seek out another spirit like themselves. You see them walking hand in hand, sharing the same dreams.

Homosexuals want the rest of us to love them. But in a way, they've already turned us down. They don't want to give love to women or society. Yet they want us to tolerate some of the aggressive things they do. And they do some very aggressive things.

Amplifying this thought in Reading Notes:

If you haven't been a teacher you may not have thought how difficult it is to explain to people what sexuality is. We might begin with saying it has something to do with the fact that for many biological species, including our own, there seem to be two kinds of similar but slightly different models. In human beings the chief external additions of one kind are on the chest and of the other kind in the groin. Well, now, is this anatomical fact the basis of "sexuality" or does this word relate to the mutual interests of these two different kinds in one another? In the latter case what do we think about those who are not interested in the alternate model but in the same model as they themselves are? And what do we think about those that are not interested in either one? The word homosexuality is of course sheerly descriptive. In matter of taste there should be no dispute, but there is a great deal of dispute as to what this curious preference means. Not how really exceptional or how widely prevalent it is, or whether it is in an advanced stage of development or a retarded one, or whether it represents a peculiarity of genes or a mistaken kind of bringing up.

Once upon a time we thought we knew all about it. It was a sin, a crime, a disease, and/or an anomaly. Well, suddenly nobody seems to know anything about it. It ceases to be quite so taboo, and yet not quite kosher. Individuals may now confess to it without being thrown out of the room or out of college. There are clubs and fraternities and "fronts" and political organizations made up of professed homosexual individuals.

The homosexual (frequently) does not consider himself a freak or a cripple or an anomaly or a sick man. He considers himself one of four million or more Americans with this different personal preference value system. Most psychiatrists regard it as a disease or an anomaly. There is a great deal of difference between these two propositions, but there is no difference in the minds and feelings of many—if not most —homosexual individuals. They don't want to be considered either one.

All this should be borne in mind when we notice—as all do—that in the theater and in numerous novels bitter reprisals and reproaches are directed by the authors and playwrights against the heterosexual establishment. The audience gets it full in the face and usually doesn't know what hit them or why. After the show, at the cast party, there is often great hilarity over the unpleasant shock effect they had been able to inflict. Some of the critics know and bravely retaliate; others are in on the game.

Over the years, Dr. Karl has said on a number of occasions that he thought many homosexuals, who wished to be, could be successfully treated and recover or change. And now he adds:

There definitely is a new understanding, I believe, of homosexuality. Dr. Judd Marmor, a vice-president of the American Psychiatric Association, charged at a recent meeting that the persistence of cruelty, dishonesty, and simple lack of humanity among us psychiatrists prejudiced against homosexual people is a disgrace to the profession. This was at a panel on this theme. I agree with him fully. The rest of society is prejudiced, it is true, but we should not be. We should realize that.

I was picketed at one of the universities recently, where I addressed the student body on prison reform. A group of homosexuals arose, one after the other, to tell me I ought to repent! They had listened patiently to me, so I listened patiently to them. They said I had spoken derogatorily and prejudicially about "homosexuals" as if they were all alike and all bad, or sick or evil. I told them that I thought they had a point, that the book from which they quoted was written many years ago and ought to have been amended, in this respect, long since, but had not been. I added that I doubted whether they advanced their cause by aggression and belligerency, however that might score a knockout here and there; in the long run, homosexually inclined people don't want to be distinguished for their occasional knockouts any more than heterosexual people of the right stripe do. Homosexuals don't want to be pitied and they don't want to be scorned, and they don't want to be feared or disliked for their disagreeableness, as they sometimes are.

We must work persistently for new attitudes toward congenital deviation of sexual interest patterns. I knew a man once who was addicted to the chewing up of lead pencils, of which he consumed a dozen or more daily. Now, most of us would consider that different from anything that seems attractive to us, but we don't get angry at such an individual. We don't call him names. We don't say he has a disease—or do we? I don't think we should. There's no disputing about taste. There are too many factors that enter into people's preferences for satisfactions to permit us to be arbitrary or dogmatic about

controlling them. It is understandable, I think, that people with homosexual inclinations should resent the mistreatment society has given
them. They should be careful, however, not to retaliate in kind, because counteraggression never solves problems of aggression.

*Years previously, he had discussed more fully whether homosexuals
could be helped by psychiatrists in answer to a letter from the late
Dr. Ira S. Wile, who had written on December 24, 1940, to ask about
Dr. Karl's experience with sexual offenders and what forms of treatment he found most successful:*

. . . We have had from time to time quite a number of cases of
exhibitionism, active homosexuality, passive homosexuality, peeping,
seduction, and rape. The exhibitionists, as you know, are relatively
easily cured by psychotherapy. Active and passive homosexuality is
something else. I think a great deal depends upon what type of homosexuality one is dealing with and I don't believe that "active" and
"passive" is sufficient differentiation. I could go into a lot of detail
about this but let me simply say that our experience in the main has
been that an individual who has established himself in a homosexual
adjustment without any heterosexual activities usually does not want
to change, and it is very difficult even with legal pressure and all the
rest of it to get him to want to take any treatment. There is an exception to this; namely, the relatively less experienced partner in a female
homosexual liaison who often welcomes the assistance of the psychiatrist in getting her out of the situation.

Peeping and assaults on women (either actually to have intercourse
with them or to tear off their clothes so as to look at their genitals,
etc.) we have encountered quite a number of times. The curious thing
is that in several instances these individuals have turned out to be ad-
mirable characters in other respects.

I seem to be in a reminiscent mood and I recall at this particular
moment a prominent businessman who had married a banker's
daughter and was considered quite well-to-do. He had some real
estate, besides his wife's property. He became involved in what some
people considered a technical charge and was put in the penitentiary
for the misuse of the mails and served a sentence there. Everyone was
quite sorry for him and for his wife and his lovely children. The
children were kept in ignorance of his whereabouts. He returned to
his home and lived with his family and it was then that people were
especially sorry for them. His children went to high school and even

211

to college and only the older one, apparently, even suspected where their father had been. But wait a minute, I'm getting ahead of my story.

After he had been out some six or eight years he was arrested on the charge of running a "vice ring." He was supposed to take his agents and other boys, white and colored, with him on trips and to seduce them into homosexuality. He was charged with it, it was in the newspapers, and the day before the trial his lawyer called me and asked if I would see him and I said, "Certainly." He came out to see me and with all this evidence staring him in the face, he sat there and told me he had not the slightest idea what all these charges meant, what they were all about. I said, "Come, come now, you don't know what buggery is?" He insisted he did not. He didn't even know the meaning of these "terrible" words and these "terrible" charges they had brought against him.

I telephoned his lawyer that had he told me the truth and expressed himself as wanting help for a condition that he realized was ruining his life I might have been able to do something for him as the lawyer had proposed. I am not telling this story very well but the point was that he not only got himself into this scrape, but when he had a chance to get out of it by getting my testimony, he came out and lied to me in such an obvious and determined way that there wasn't anything I could do about it either to help him personally or to help him out at the trial, and off to jail he went.

Well, just to show you how things go—his wife again concealed the affair from his children and even told some of her friends that it was all her fault that he got into homosexuality because she had perhaps not always been cooperative heterosexually and had been sick so much. This is just gossip, of course, but it is quite typical of the wife's attitude. He got out of jail and straightway got entangled *again* in a homosexual affair and went back to prison for a third time and there he is now.

I went into all this detail to illustrate a type of homosexual aggressiveness which I think is a trait in which more than mere homosexuality is represented. The aggressive factors which I have discussed in my book *Man Against Himself* are very strongly present.

I think of another illustration of this which we ran into from two sides, from the top and from the bottom. The executive of a large store would take various male employees home with him as his guest to dinner and then after dinner he would tell them it was too late to go back into town and they could plan to stay all night. He would continue to be very "nice" to them and get them in bed with him and attempt to have sexual relations. If they protested, he would threaten to fire them. In this way more or less he enslaved quite a number of the employees.

I seem to have run off into the viciousness and incurability of a certain type of homosexuality and to have understressed the fact that I think that some types can be cured with the aid of psychoanalysis or with the aid of milieu treatment, either in the properly conducted psychiatric hospital. I certainly do not believe that mere custody, no matter how splendid the appointments or how luxurious the service, nor, on the other hand, no matter how painful and restrictive the custody, accomplished anything for such people. I am trying to say that state hospitals and private sanitariums which do not employ personal treatment techniques such as psychotherapy and psychoanalysis and our prisons and penitentiaries, all fail to correct homosexuality. As a matter of fact, I think the jails frequently make the tendency toward sexual abnormalities much greater, as for example in the case I cited above.

Should sex offenders ever be put in jail? Can rapists, exhibitionists, and aggressive homosexuals control themselves? Should they be treated differently than people who commit other sorts of crimes? Do psychiatrists tend to sin against society by adopting too tolerant an attitude toward the individual sex offender? Dr. Karl addressed himself to these important questions in a lecture at the Winter Veterans Hospital in Topeka. Here again, he finds the distinction between the drive to achieve physical gratification—what he terms "the search for the greater orgasm"—and the total sexual instinct to be crucial.

It was in Atlantic City, of all places, at an annual meeting of the American Psychiatric Association on May 10, 1952. A kindly elderly colleague from Vienna, now long in the United States, was presenting a paper on the psychodynamics and therapy of sexual perversions. In a thoughtful, scholarly way he recited his concept of these deplorable conditions and his success in treating them. As I listened to him describing the vicissitudes of childhood which later lead some individuals to use their procreative organs in such strange antisocial ways, I thought how different the attitude of the psychiatrist was from that of the general public. Here was a man deeply sympathetic with the unhappiness of certain persons who, to the outside world, appear in blackest colors. The mother of an eight-year-old girl who has been coaxed into a cellarway by one of these victims of circumstances or who has been raped in a park or slashed with a knife; the father of a boy who has been seduced in a toilet to submit to strange and unnatural practices, or of the high school girl who has been startled and embarrassed by the exhibitions of one of these fellows—these parents, these laymen, do not share that apparently sad sympathy or the scientific detachment with which the psychiatrist calmly describes "the obstacle which stands in the way of mature heterosexual gratification."

Just a few hours before I had listened in another fashion to a description of the difficulties some individuals have in attaining a sexual orgasm in the normal way. I had heard a handsome and intelligent mother describe the reactions of her nine-year-old daughter, and of her family, to an assault made upon the daughter by a man who had eluded the police on a dozen similar occasions. The mother had been told by the county attorney that, in his opinion, the only proper punishment for such a villain was castration, which, as she told me, she realized would only add to his frustrations and increase his obvious hatred of society. On the other hand, she had been told by her attorney that the maximum detention that could be expected for such an offender was eighteen months, after which he would be free to continue his search for the only kind of sexual gratification his perverted nature could enjoy.

What is wrong with this picture? The law, it would seem, considers such indecencies a minor affair unless murder or proven rape are involved. The lasting imprint of horror and fright and disgust which such experiences leave on the lives of children apparently are of no concern to the law. This is not tangible damage. But we psychiatrists know how great this damage is and as I listened to that kindly doctor describe the inner sufferings of these villains—not the victims—and describe his own patient efforts, sometimes successful, to return them to a normal mode of living, I wondered if it might be that we psychiatrists too often seem, to the public, to be aligning ourselves against one kind of patient in favor of another kind.

Certainly we should not fail to scrutinize the mind of a murderer, the mind of a rapist, the mind of an exhibitionist, the mind of a homosexual, any more than we would shrink from examining the mind of a man who is depressed or deluded or obsessed. Perhaps we have leaned over backward to do our duty in this respect not so much because of the indifference of the law as because of the virulence of the public reaction. We have thought we understood the latter attitude as related to guilty wishes and fantasies of the common man, provoked and punished in the casual violator. We have seen such guilty fantasies in the lives of so many normal people, or at least law-abiding people, that we are not so horrified at the behavior of the "pervert." And we felt a certain loyalty and protective responsibility for our unfairly judged subjects.

But in leaning over backward it certainly seems as if we neglect to consider the reality aspects of the behavior of the offender. For there is no doubt about the fact that aberrant ones create and disseminate more evil and more harm than is realized. In a certain way the public is justified in getting so excited over the occasional shocking example. It may not know the extent of the evil, but it knows evil when it sees it, and if the public exaggerates in such instances, that may be in part because it correctly suspects what it doesn't actually know.

It is also indisputable that a so-called sexual pervert of this kind is a social menace so long as he is driven constantly to corrupt, to defile, to seduce, and to injure. To lapse into the vernacular, these individuals raise all kinds of hell and produce hellish consequences. They try to do so as surreptitiously as possible and the existing legal and social structures offer little determent to their devious modes of satisfaction.

As one listens—and I speak now as a psychiatrist and as a psychoanalyst—to scientific discussions of how it comes about that some individuals behave this way and how, in some instances—too few, alas—they can be induced to act in a different way, I wonder if we psychiatrists have not stood in our own light. Formally we recognize that it is undesirable behavior of which we are speaking. But can we justifiably maintain it is undesirable behavior in the same sense a convulsion is undesirable behavior? Or that the violent assaultiveness of a maniacal or delirious individual is socially undesirable? I wonder if we psychiatrists have been sufficiently explicit in our distinction between these two kinds of symptoms? Of the one kind we say the man is bereft of reason, that he doesn't know how to control his actions and must therefore be confined until he is safe for himself and society. The other we do not describe as bereft of reason. We assume that he can control his behavior and we wink at the fact that whether he can or not, he doesn't.

Is there a difference between the criminal and the mentally ill? Is the criminal truly unable to control himself? If so, let us then treat him as we treat those whom we call insane and confine him until he can control himself. And as for the sexual pervert, is he able to control himself or not? If so, why should such self-control not be a prime requisite for any kind of extramural treatment? If not, why should he not be confined during treatment?

Sexual abstinence has never killed anyone. It has not impaired the health of millions of individuals who practice it. If the only alternative to sexual abstinence is behavior of an essentially criminal type, why should not abstinence be strictly required of anyone who seriously wishes to be a decent citizen and if one does not wish to be a decent citizen, why should he become the object of psychiatric treatment as an outpatient merely because he has the money with which to pay for it?

I believe, indeed from experience I know, that there are many individuals afflicted with impulses in the direction of sexual aberrancy who can and do refrain from indulging in the expression of these impulses during the course of intensive, often successful treatment. But it is my impression that many of my colleagues take too tolerant a view of a compromising situation in which the patient's antisocial activities are overlooked as incidental "trivia" or unavoidable complications occurring in the course of his reformation.

In addition to the practical side, on the theoretical side, it seems to me we psychiatrists are taking the wrong position. It was this that particularly impressed me as I listened to the presentation of my colleague in Atlantic City. His thesis was simply that those who practice sexual perversions are doing the best they can to obtain sexual gratification, having been inhibited or diverted from normal modes of accomplishing this as a result of childhood experiences. Several colleagues reminded him there was considerable evidence that certain biological factors enter the picture. Some individuals would appear to be born with a greater susceptibility to find abnormal methods for sexual gratification. This does not mean they are condemned inevitably to such behavior but it does mean that some of their frustrations are other than psychological. But even on the psychological side, I find it wholly unpalatable to be treating a patient whose sole objective is fulfilling his sexual needs in the narrow sense of that word.

There was a time fifty years ago when the correction of sexual difficulties was neglected by the medical profession, and the whole subject viewed with hypocritical pseudohorror. Freud, Krafft-Ebing, and Havelock Ellis among others bravely challenged this prudish attitude. The sexual life is worth studying, they said, because it is a function of the human being, no more to be ashamed of than the function of vision. They made careful explorations of sexual life of many individuals, normal and abnormal. Freud in particular uncovered the details of the psychosexual development of the child and wrote the natural history of the sexual instinct. The fact that nearly everyone has some kind of sexual frustration and sexual inhibition and, in a theoretical way, even some kind of sexual perversion, became a matter of common knowledge. Kinsey attempted to document this statistically in our culture. No psychiatrist has any doubt but that a greater fulfillment of the sexual instinct is a desideratum for every patient, perhaps for every human being.

But what Freud was careful to say is apt to be forgotten. The sexual sensation, the sexual orgasm, is a small part, he said, of the total sexual life and of the yield of the sexual instinct. The important factor in sex is neither the excitation nor the discharge, but the tendency toward the union of human beings. Sexual sensation is centered in the sexual organs but the sexual instinct is expressed by the total organism.

Thus Freud should be clearly credited, among other things, with a repudiation of the search for genital pleasure only. I have called this search the philosophy of "the search for the greater orgasm." This point of view in psychoanalysis has no scientific backing whatever. It is directly contrary to Freud's concepts. There is infinitely more in life than achieving an orgasm, and every thoughtful person, the sexually excited adolescent excepted, knows this.

A onetime follower of Freud, Wilhelm Reich, set the paradigm for this point of view. He developed the thesis that the sexual orgasm was the chief aim of life and that the criterion of health was the degree to which one satisfactorily accomplished this orgasm. Reich is no longer taken seriously by psychoanalysts or psychiatrists, and yet this doctrine of "search for an orgasm" lurks here and there in some psychoanalytic teaching and psychoanalytic practice.

What the proponents of such a philosophy ignore as they champion a demeaning concept of human life and human personality, indulging in a pitiable narrowing of the objective of treatment, is one of the main points of Freudian theory and the most significant element in the perversion—the fact, as shown in clinical practice, that every sexually perverse act, and every sexually perverse impulse, is motivated less by sex than by aggression.

To consider the exhibitionist, the rapist, and the aggressive homosexual as pathetic, frustrated persons who cannot achieve natural orgasm and are forced by fate to find a devious, destructive contact is to romanticize the facts and cloud the clinical picture. Such persons have entered upon a peculiar and vicious marriage of their destructive impulses and their sexual urges.

The aggressive sexual pervert weds his aggressive impulses to his feeble sexual drives and the consequences are tragic, both for his victim and himself.

Therefore, the treatment of sexual perversion by psychiatrists, to be successful, must lead to helping a man face this destructive drive, and a repudiation of his hypocritical, violent gestures toward human contact through the physical act of sex. It is the destructive impulses in his aggression that require treatment by the psychiatrist. This will necessarily involve intense frustration, for only someone very frustrated would be so violent, though the frustration should not be seen in the naïve, narrow, misleading light in which it is often presented. It must be understood in its broader aspect as one more example of a poorly and inadequately controlled death instinct.

This is what Freud realized in the latter third of his life when he added to his theory of the libido concept by introducing his "dual" instinct theory. Evil exists in this world whether psychoanalysts want to face it or not. Evil exists in the motives of every human being, and destructive tendencies do not disappear simply by being ignored.

Control the aggressive drive and the sexual drive will take care of itself. The reverse does not work.

CHAPTER NINE

The Crime of Punishment

I am still helping the Veterans Administration as much as I can. . . . But my chief emphasis now is on improving the correctional system beginning with the terrible jails.

This statement is from a letter that Dr. Karl wrote to General Omar N. Bradley on April 14, 1972; it was in reply to a letter of congratulations that he had received from the general on the occasion of the naming of the medical library at the Topeka Veterans Administration Hospital the Karl A. Menninger Library. Though now occupying more of his time, Dr. Karl's efforts to reform the nation's correctional system are by no means of recent origin. In 1930, for instance, in the August issue of Plain Talk, *he posed some hard questions about the philosophy of punishment—questions that unfortunately are still timely today.*

The fundamental idea back of the American methods for handling criminals is punishment. Ask the average man the purpose of prisons and he will reply, representatively and correctly, "punishment, of course." What does penitentiary mean but a place to be sorry and what does the word penology come from but a root meaning pain.

Punishment has had able defenders from Plato to Thomas Aquinas and Kant. And it has had other apologists. But does it do any good? It is supposed to reform the prisoner, to detain him, and to deter others. Let us analyze these briefly.

How is it supposed to reform him? He is supposed to "learn a lesson" and resolve never to do it again. The great mockery of all this is the fact that in practically every prison where statistics have been carefully gathered, the considerable majority of all the prisoners are there for the second, third, or even the twentieth time.

Most of them are not detained for long. In the state of Kansas, for example, a life sentence means on the average about twelve years of servitude. Very few prisoners serve their sentences out. I do not mean to imply that I think they should; I merely mean to point out that the prison does not keep them from being a menace to society as it is supposed to do.

As to the spectacle of punishment's deterring other prisoners from committing crime, all we can say is that there is no proof of this. There is a good deal of proof to the contrary; it is an old story that in crowds gathered to watch the hanging of pickpockets in England many had their pockets picked while they watched. Those of us familiar with criminals have not much hope that the type of person who becomes a criminal will be deterred from crime by the punishment inflicted upon others.

Punishment does none of the things it is supposed to do. But it does accomplish something else. Psychiatrists feel that it is this something else which explains its persistence in spite of the general knowledge among all serious students of the subject that it is inadequate and unscientific. What is this something else that it does?

The one thing that the punishment of criminals does and does satisfactorily, although very expensively, is to gratify our passion for revenge. It gratifies, it comforts, it gives pleasure and satisfaction and even delight to the general public. It does this regardless of its futility, its expensiveness, and the fact that it permits such things as prison riots, crime waves, and gang wars. . . .

Prison riots express the intolerableness of a solution of the crime problem which expensively gratifies unconscious feelings of guilt on the part of a society which consciously believes it wants protection. It is defended by rationalizations about "exemplary deterrence" and prattle about concepts of "justice" and "responsibility" which no one understands. What is needed is a coldly calculated system for segregating and detaining the socially impossible in such a way that riots are not provoked nor money wasted, nor sadists gratified, nor the public endangered, nor parole boards expected to do miracles.

THE CRIME OF PUNISHMENT

Today, according to Dr. Karl, there are 4,051 jails in the country where people are detained, awaiting sentencing, and these jails should all be done away with. After a 1972 visit to one of them—the Tombs in New York City—he said it was "tragic," adding, "every jail is a tragedy." The state and federal prisons are subject to certain standards under the law. But village, town, and city jails are locally controlled and, in his words, "they are dreadful," full of people "who don't belong there."

The heart of the matter is the sentencing procedure, he believes. "The whole business of sentencing should be changed," he says. "Offenders should be sentenced to a diagnostic center and studied. Those who can be treated should be given treatment. Those who cannot be treated and are dangerous to society should be put where they cannot do any more harm—nor be harmed."

In a Reading Note, *he exclaims:*

Stop and think about it a minute: In America we have a system of controlling crime into which additional millions of dollars are being poured upon preceding investments of billions. About ten in every one hundred offenders are arrested along with numerous non-offenders, and some of the ten are chucked into jail—the poor ones. Sooner or later, if they don't get tired of the sweaty, noisy waiting and plead guilty, they will be tried; half of them may be found guilty.

In the long run about two out of every one hundred offenders is ground through the horrible institution known as a jail and on into a prison, to remain God knows how long. Few people realize how miserable, tawdry, noisy, confusing, inept, and unjust the criminal courts are—populated, as one author said, by "the stagnant backwater of the country's legal profession."

Trials are usually two to five minute hearings dominated by a sketchy police testimony. Drunks and various other cases are run past the judge at a rate of fifty to one hundred an hour. An attorney may be trying to make the judge hear over the din without himself being aware of his client's name.

The judge, beholding the miserable, sick, vomitus-smeared drunk thrown in the "tank" the night before, may make a cynical crack about the benefit of a few weeks in the jail, and the case is over. Next!

The inadequacies of the present penal system were reviewed by Dr. Karl in some detail on June 3, 1971, at the request of Robert W. Kastenmeier, chairman of Subcommittee No. 3 of the Committee on

THE CRIME OF PUNISHMENT

the Judiciary, United States House of Representatives. Here are key sections of his testimony:

Mr. Kastenmeier, it might serve as an appropriate introduction if I say how it is that I, a doctor, a psychiatrist, should be as concerned as I confess I am with the correctional dilemma in this country.

My profession, as you know, is concerned with seeing patients, examining and treating people who have some distress of mind. Like many of my colleagues, I used to testify in court regarding the mental state of some accused individuals who had enough money to employ me. Those who didn't have enough money, by far the majority, I did not get to see so often. One has to be dismayed by this obviously unfair situation. I was also dismayed by the fact that so few people who came before the court got any kind of examination, and by the fact that when I was on the stand I was never asked the right questions, it seemed to me.

I was asked what I regard as rather silly questions: Whether a man knew left from right, whether he knew right from wrong, whether he knew where he was, and that sort of thing. I was never asked: "What went wrong in this man's life that he is here instead of out on the road? How is it that he is in trouble with his people, his city, and his government? What is different about him from the rest of us? What do we do about his present predicament—and ours?" I was never asked questions that had anything to do with changing the erring individual but only some technical questions regarding his so-called responsibility.

I began to go to the jail where these people were [held] and to the prisons where they were [committed]. I began to realize that the judges who sent them there never saw them again, never saw these jails and prisons to which they sent these men to be "changed." Nor did they really know what was happening to the men they had sent there. It distressed me very much to realize that I had contributed to it by testifying in court for the rights of some rich patients instead of tackling the problem as a general social problem affecting people of all incomes, of all colors, in all states of mind.

In the course of time I became consultant to the prison commissioner of the State of New York. I visited many jails and prisons there. Besides that, I was and am still a consultant in the Federal Prison System, and have visited Federal prisons and consulted frequently with Mr. Bennett, Mr. Alexander, Mr. Carlson, and others in regard to the national program.

More and more my concern was not with the mental state of the prisoners on [whom] I was asked to pass judgment but with the mental state of the people taking care of these prisoners. Everywhere I went I found weary and discouraged wardens, and confused and resentful guards, and even uncertain and somewhat bewildered police officers. . . .

I sometimes feel as if I would like to scream out to the American public that they are squirting gasoline on the fire. The prison system is now manufacturing offenders, it is increasing the amount of transgression, it is multiplying crimes, it is compounding evil. How do you tell people that? They think it is a figure of speech. Gentlemen, it is more than a figure of speech. Mr. Ramsey Clark, in his book, makes the same point. Numerous other people also have. And if something that is supposed to control a situation actually aggravates it, I think it deserves our attention.

In considering this dilemma of correction, I was reminded of experiences thirty years ago relating to the revolution in our state hospitals. Our mental hospitals were getting fuller and fuller and fuller, with long waiting lists, and people resentful that they could not get in, and resentful at how they were treated when they did get in.

There existed widespread the whole snakepit situation you all know about. Patients were being mistreated, abused, hurt, and even killed. Some were kept from being sent home. In fact, it was a pretty sure thing that if you had a friend or relative who had to go to a state hospital, he or she would never come home. If they didn't die, they would remain there in chronicity.

A little investigation showed that instead of helping the mentally ill as state hospitals were created to do, they were aggravating mental illness and increasing the problem in the country.

In 1948 we had a revolution. (By the way there was a previous revolution of the same sort in 1840 in Massachusetts, but unfortunately it died out.) In 1946, 1947, and 1948 we began to take a different, revolutionary position about mental illness. We said: These are not hopeless cases. The public should not be allowed to think that they come here only to be kept and kept in asylum until they die. Our hospitals should be treatment places. We should try to change these patients and send them home. They belong on the farm, or wherever they were; they do not belong here in the back wards of this hospital.

So we set about to change it. We changed the way patients were handled from admission to discharge. We increased the number of doctors several hundred percent; we increased the number of nurses; we put in therapy programs. We enlisted the help of volunteers. All across the nation we changed the state hospitals from snakepits to reputable places of treatment and healing.

There are still a few backward states where the state hospitals are deplorable, but only a few. In the city in which I live the state hospital in 1948 had 1,850 patients, with only 1,500 beds. Many regularly slept on the floor. Since that time we have built no new buildings anywhere in the state and the population has increased as it has everywhere else. But the present population of that hospital is now less than 900, half of what it used to be twenty-five years ago. There are empty beds in every good state hospital today for the simple reason we have realized that most mentally ill patients recover and go home in a few months if they are treated right. If they are wrongly treated they stay in the hospital for life—a loss to everyone.

Now the prison system has never quite caught on to that idea. They seem to think some way or other they must force chronicity on the prisoner, they must force these people to continue in the way they have been going instead of helping them to change their way of life, get in line with the rest of us. Of course, the prisoner's stay is determined before the treatment begins, which to a doctor seems absurd.

The big city courts are terrible—a nightmare. You've read about it. But from them, one or less in a hundred offenders comes to be put through the machine. For what purpose?

Is he put there really merely to comply with some formalities? Is this simply a kind of official public private torture? It used to be public, you know. It was in 1789 that some Pennsylvanians led the nation in saying, "We don't want this public torture anymore. Let's cover it up and let them reflect and repent."

The whippings, the cutting, the dunkings, the stocks, and all the rest of it went out, except for imprisonment and idleness and lonely hours.

The State of Maine created a series of dungeons, as you know, in order that each prisoner could be completely isolated; prisoners were lowered into these dungeons with ropes and they stayed there for the period of their sentence.

On the other hand, we must remember that in those days sentences were for a month or few months—not, as now, for years and years. However, Maine had so many cases of men being driven mad by even short terms that it was altered, and today Maine is quite progressive.

How many judges think, as they are looking at the man before them: "The cheapest and best thing for this community is to get this man back in circulation as quickly as is safely possible? How do I do it?"

Judge, you can't do it by sentencing him to five or ten years in prison. You know that then he will never come back. Nobody ever really comes back after that long a period. No one is rehabilitated in those long stretches. Rehabilitation means to be put back where he was. Most of the people we are talking about should be put back somewhere else, where the social situation is not too much for them. If it is going to continue to be too much for them, they should stay in prison the rest of their lives. If it is not too much for them, for heaven's sake, why not get the business over with as rapidly as possible?

Why charge the State of Delaware, the State of Pennsylvania, or the State of Kansas, x dollars per day for years to keep a man just for the sake of keeping him? In what way will the man be cured of his propensity for check forging after he has had six years of confinement rather than six weeks? Six years is not going to change anybody's propensity for check forging. . . . I don't think any lawyer, any judge, or any warden really thinks that anybody is cured of a propensity for bad check writing by being kept in an iron cage with a lot of other people for six years or sixty years.

At this point Mr. Kastenmeier asked if Dr. Karl thought a man "might be deterred from writing bad checks." The reply:

Not in the least. Not in the least. Deterrence, you know, is one of those trick questions. Deter whom? Deter him, or deter other people from doing what he does? "Oh, look what they did to Jake. Jake forged some checks and they put him in prison and they kept him there six years, poor devil, and he has gone to pieces there. So we had better not forge any checks." Nonsense. Nobody thinks that way, really. No intelligent person believes any such sophistry as that.

Because for every fellow serving time for check forging there are, as we all know, fifty others who are forging checks but who are not caught, or not tried, or at least not imprisoned. The chances are nearly 100 to 1 that what happened to Jake will not happen to you—so why be deterred?

What it really means is that we continue into the twentieth century this old medieval morality play put on for the villagers where somebody does something bad and is discovered and punished and lives happily ever afterward. These morality plays were acted in small towns in England and Germany and France for a couple of centuries to show what happens to the bad fellows who disturb the king's peace. They were a device for public education and public morals which worked two hundred or three hundred years ago. But morality plays don't work in the twentieth century. Nobody believes that stuff, because it is not true.

Mr. Kastenmeier then asked, "What does work then?" Dr. Karl replied:

Remember that before a man gets to prison he is thoroughly mistreated, abused, and dehumanized in the local jail. At the present time the wretched, abominable local jails in this country prevent the few good prisons we have from accomplishing any good. The local jails are so bad that they make what the prisons attempt useless.

There are some very fine prison wardens in this country; there are some improving prisons; there are programs such as those my associate, Harry Woodward [director of correctional programs for the W. Clement and Jessie V. Stone Foundation, who accompanied Dr. Karl to this subcommittee hearing], and Mr. W. Clement Stone are achieving in prisons. And there are educational programs and work release and others. But most of these fellows have already been ruined for life in the local jails before they go to prison. If a child or grandchild of mine were in trouble and had the choice between a six months' sentence in a local jail or a two- or three-year sentence in prison, I would urge that he take the latter, quickly! Don't let a child go through the corrupting, ruinous experience of spending any time in a local jail. . . . These awful places have the same ruinous effect on our citizens as the concentration camps maintained by the Germans for the Jews and others.

A person who goes in these places never comes out a whole man again. Homosexuality is forced upon him. Degradation is forced upon him. I don't think this point can be made too strongly because so many judges still say or think, "Thirty days in our little jail will help you straighten up, maybe." Or, "Well, we will have to teach you a thing or two about obedience to the law." It certainly will. It will teach a person how it feels to be raped. It will teach him a vocabulary he never heard before in his life. It will teach him never to commit a [mere] misdemeanor again—if a crime is necessary.

I know whereof I speak. I have been in many of the local jails. The public really has no idea of what they are like, thinking, "Unpleasant no doubt, maybe a few bedbugs and lice, but then those kids should not have misbehaved, they should not have let themselves in for a jail stay."

Right. They should not have. But the fact that they did does not entitle the state, county, city, or anybody else to inflict a dehumanizing, degrading, injurious, destructive experience on a child of sixteen, or on a man of sixty, or of any other age. . . .

I return to the theme with which I started: the sense of discouragement and desperation which commissioners of correction and wardens have about the wretchedness of the system, the futility of the various changes they pretend to put into effect, the hypocrisy of those who talk glibly of "teaching an offender a lesson" or "locking him up for good." This discouragement needs to be lifted by ·public leaders and statesmen like yourselves.

Mr. Kastenmeier then asked if the nation should continue to have jails and prisons and, if so, in what form, and if not, what else society might do with offenders rather than incarcerate them in prison. Dr. Karl answered:

You know, many of the people sitting in local jails today have not been convicted of any crime. We know this. You know this is a constant problem for the jailer, too. He has people in jail whom he has to keep. They feel it is unjust treatment; the jailer often feels it is unjust. This totally unnecessary situation prevails in six states. In the other forty-four, it is a minor problem. In most instances, the Federal Government has no authority over these local jails except indirectly. Local jails must, I think, in their present form be eliminated. You don't need them. There are other ways to handle people who are not as yet convicted of a crime.

Half the time of the police on duty is taken up bringing in drunks. In my opinion, no drunken person belongs in a jail unless he has committed a crime. Drunkenness is not a crime in the sense that the offender has injured anybody. If any of you were found drunk out in the street, you would not be taken to jail. You are wearing nice clothes, you are white, you have a friend somewhere. You would be taken home, or to a hospital, or to a detoxification center. This alone reduces the problem of the average local jail by 50 per cent.

Then there are many other ways to handle it. Temporary emergency lockup, for example. I happen to be a consultant to two communities of under 100,000. They are both rebuilding their city hall complex without jails. There will be no jail in these communities. Furthermore, there will not be any more transfer of felons out of the county to the state. People convicted of felonies will not be sent to the state prison but detained in a dormitory within the community and employed in that community under surveillance. They will not be dumped onto the state and held there uselessly for years while the local community struggles with their relatives. The minute a worker fails his assignment, he becomes a different type of problem and there will be another program for handling him. The expectation is that there will be only about 10 per cent who fail. . . .

Some need psychiatric treatment, but not in any great numbers. Someone mentioned that retarded people are not necessarily in trouble; they rarely need treatment. Mentally retarded people cannot be cured by psychiatrists. Certainly there are mentally retarded people in prisons; they are easy to catch. They make it easier for a policeman to fill his quota of arrests; they can usually be picked up without much difficulty.

Also, a mentally retarded prisoner is not a big problem in the prison whereas the mentally disturbed individual is. In my opinion the mentally retarded one should never be put into prison. When judges have the diagnostic center resources I think they should have, the mentally retarded will not be sent to prison. A diagnostic service would immediately detect and deflect those people. They would be sent to a place where they could be treated.

The questions a diagnostic center would ask are: (1) Is the man dangerous? (2) Is he treatable? (3) Is he deterrable? (Some people are deterrable without being treatable.) (4) Is he educable? (5) Is he employable? Nearly every warden to whom I have talked said that between 75 and 90 per cent of those in his institution would be better outside the institution than in. . . .

A lot of the people who get themselves into a fix permanently are really incompetent people. I have a list of some of the queer, strange things they do to get themselves into the hands of the law, almost as if they wanted somebody to take care of them. Many of these people need just simple, ordinary counseling or a little friendliness. . . . The loneliness of prisoners is only equaled by the loneliness of prison employees. They feel that they are working with deserted people, with no understanding from the public, in a job they are sure to fail at.

Asked what he would do if he were running a prison, Dr. Karl replied:

I might let many of the men stay in prison one day a week and work outside the other six days, living with their wives and families. I would want these men to be back in society, be human beings, not puppets. I don't want to make them into worse monsters than they were when they went in. Which is what I think our system does.

And, in Reading Notes, *he added:*

I have repeatedly proposed that it would be helpful if prisons were looked upon as educational institutions. Here are some people who are badly in need of learning something they don't seem to know. Not that we believe intelligence is sufficient to guarantee probity and virtue, but the men in prison are men who have done something that we do not want done, and which it has been to their disadvantage to have done, and which they should try to learn to avoid doing. Nobody disputes this. The question is, what are the best methods of instruction? The present methods are so different from what we ordinarily call teaching that people are always a little startled at first by the very word. But reflect upon it. Why should we not say that with somewhat different admission requirements and somewhat different curriculum, prisons really do intend to instruct, to correct, to realign, to redirect? I think the day will certainly come when there will be nothing startling about this proposal and we shall expect prisoners to emerge from prisons far better equipped than they entered—better taught, and more learned, in the right way. They will not be called prisoners nor will the emphasis be given to their detention and imprisonment, compulsory though the course may be.

"Our Dreadful Jails" is a recurrent theme and title of Dr. Karl's talks. One, delivered at a symposium, "The Purposes of Corrections—Directions for Improvement," was published October, 1971, in the University of San Francisco Law Review:

Some people—and I am proud to be numbered among them—are so deeply and continuously disturbed by the knowledge of the great American jail atrocities that we cannot keep still about it. We write letters, we make speeches, we harangue our friends. Over and over we say the same thing, but the same thing goes on and on. Yesterday a local newspaper told of a ten-year-old child sentenced to jail for stealing a cupcake; last week a nine-year-old was arraigned for possessing and using armed weapons (he had found and displayed an old gun). An eighteen-year-old sentenced to sit in jail for a year to reflect on the sin of having had some marijuana in his pocket. One long, lonely, ruinous, tedious, hideous year!

This great horrible cruelty is being practiced in semi-secret in over four thousand places! One hundred and fifty thousand human beings, mostly young ones, are locked up in cages and dungeons in the name of "justice" and mercy by agents of the very people who are being wronged. This expensive, futile, absurd, cruel business does not rehabilitate anyone; it does not reform anyone; it does not change anyone for the better. It only enrages and stupefies and crushes already unstable, misdirected, and confused people. It ruins them for life under the guise of a light disciplinary slap on the wrist. After a jail sentence, the best of prisons cannot accomplish much. . . .

We have to provide for the temporary detention of some violently disorganized and dangerous individuals. . . . But let it be remembered that only a small per cent of all criminals and crimes are "violent." It is most difficult to get across to the public that these are a *small minority* of our penal "customers." It is in the interests of some —prosecuting attorneys, sensational newspapers, and others—to give the impression that prisoners are a great seething mass of coarse, fierce, and violent men. Nothing would be of greater help to the cause than to find a way to let the public see and talk with the people we are taking care of for them—wistful, mildly disorganized, a little confused, poorly directed, and sometimes clearly mentally defective but rarely fierce or frightening.

Everybody knows our jail system is wrong. Everyone knows it is not rehabilitation, it is not correction, it is not prevention, it is not deterrence. It is punishment, cruel degrading punishment done at the order of judges who are not fools, not monsters, not heartless autocrats. It is done at the order of judges who follow the routine of the system in which they are caught, and mouth formulas of mismanagement ordained by legislators long dead. The judges can only live with themselves by avoiding any comprehension of what it is they are doing. Every honest judge who submits himself for twenty-four hours to the ordeal he prescribes for others comes out of it a shaken man. They say such things as, "I simply had no idea of what I was doing these past twenty years."

Until we stop it, the shame of our jail system will hang about our necks like an albatross along with the shame of our slaughter of the American Indians and our century of the unspeakable slave traffic. . . .

We hear from some of our friends the bitter reproach that we sentimentalists like only bad people and do not care about the good people who are being murdered, raped, and robbed. "You are so sorry about those vicious kids that are locked up in jails and those dangerous criminals that are being punished in prisons where they belong, but you never say a word about their victims! Think of all the poor people who have been raped and murdered and beaten up and frightened nearly to death. Yes, and the people who have had their cars stolen and their purses snatched and their names forged on checks. But you don't care about them!"

Oh, yes I do! I care a great deal about them, and I sympathize with them; indeed am one of them! I have been a victim myself several times. It's for the sake of the victims that I try to portray—as vividly as I can—the futility, the failure (as well as the expensiveness) of our present system. It just isn't working. It's working in reverse. It is constantly making more of the trouble it is intended to cure. It is as if some way or other the gears of a car had been mixed up so that when started up, instead of going forward, the car leaps into reverse and crushes pedestrians. The jails crush their victims and these victims return and victimize us.

The innocent victims of crimes are going to continue to increase in number just because of the stupid expensive methods now being used to control the danger that we want protection from.

I tried to say all this in *The Crime of Punishment,* and I've tried to say it again in other articles and addresses. I keep seeking for a more forceful way to state the case, to catch the attention of the victimized public, because until the public realizes that in the long run it pays the bills, and suffers the consequences, the present stupid routine will continue.

I was startled after my book had appeared to learn that the title which my wife suggested, and of which I was very proud, was exactly the title used by another author long before. In 1931 Margaret Wilson, the wife of a British prison warden, published an excellent volume with just that title. . . .

George Bernard Shaw antedated both Mrs. Wilson and me with his powerful little tract entitled *The Crime of Imprisonment.* And, as I became increasingly involved in my commitment to changing our system, and as I learn more of the internal operations of penology and corrections and judicial operations generally, I come increasingly to believe that G. B. S. had a more nearly correct title than Mrs. Wilson's and mine. He hit the nail right on the head. Imprisonment is intolerable.

It is the ostensible purpose of the law to impose a bearable burden as a penalty, not an unbearable torture. Some people believe that physical confinement and the degradation and horror incident to it is not punishment because there is no physical pain and a little sitting around and feeling sorry won't hurt anybody.

The word "punishment" means different things to different people; if punishment is taken as identical with penalty, a fine for running against a red light is punishment. That isn't my notion of it. I distinguish punishment as that excess of penalty which causes "backlash" instead of correction. A slap on the wrist might be called punishment and a pilfering child might be corrected by it, but a blow with a steel bar or a slash across the wrist with a sharp knife is a different kind of "penalty," a kind—or degree—which I call punishment.

To me this is hideous sophistry. No one just loafs around in jail. One is caged. One is locked in, one is fenced in. One is pilloried. I wish now that I had entitled my book, like Shaw, *The* (or *Our*) *Crime of Imprisonment*. For I think it *is* a crime to cage people or animals— a crime and a heinous one.

Shaw said imprisonment seems to those who have not experienced it to be more merciful than cutting, branding, flogging, burning, or half-drowning people. We used to do all those things and more. Then we substituted the cage. This *apparent* mercifulness of imprisonment is a part of the evil: it sounds as if it might be somewhat boring and wearisome but surely it is easier to bear than torture. Shaw spoke with despair of getting people to realize that having one's liberty completely annulled and being chained and caged and penned like an animal was the most horrible and painful punishment possible. Aside from the physical discomfort—hard beds, vermin, dirt, narrow and ugly quarters—imprisonment causes agony and the destruction of the feeling of self-direction. It may cause frenzy, mania, delirium.

Over all, it produces despair. It destroys self-respect and hope, without which none of us can really live. The months drag into years, and the years into a century. It is slow, drawn out, cruel torture, and no physical improvements of jails or prisons can ever change this entirely.

We have to provide, of course, for the temporary detention of some violently disorganized and dangerous individuals. But there are civilized ways to do this. We psychiatrists used to keep disturbed people shut up like rabid dogs. Many times I have stood at a reception door of the state hospital and helped to carry in poor wretches whose relatives, with or without the aid of the sheriff, had trussed him up with ropes, straps, and handcuffs and loaded him in the spring wagon to be hauled to the asylum, presumably there to be placed into the violent ward or "the padded cell." And sad to say, in the old days that's where they went—and that's where they stayed, often for years. Heartless, we'd say today. Needless. Primitive. For there are kind and wise ways to control such people and assist them back to sanity. . . .

I don't want to hurt the feelings of some of my friends in prison who might read this. Some of them like to be thought of in terms of their great potential wickedness and dangerousness. Some of them swear great oaths and vow horrible revenge. But even as they do it, I think to myself, "Poor devils, these hot fires of your vengeance will gradually die down. You don't know it, but you are not going anywhere. You are being denatured right now. They've got you. They will release you in a few years but you will be right back in here. You have already been hamstrung and emotionally castrated. You have already had a life sentence. In a way, you have already been given capital punishment." . . .

Recently I visited a magnificent new civic center with a beautiful and impressive courthouse directly across from the city library and adjoining a public concert hall. Extending into the basement of the courthouse is the city jail, a mass of concrete and iron put together like a gigantic, medieval fortress. Its outside walls are gleaming white, its corridors are spotless, but dark, very dark. Two of the three floors are below ground and over the windows of the third floor, the only one which has windows, paint has been smeared irregularly to keep out the hot rays (and the light) of the sun. The temperature the day before I visited was recorded at 105 degrees. The prisoners had picked up some marijuana or absented themselves from school or driven a car they didn't own or snitched some goods from the supermarket with less skill than their mothers and aunts. Here are the bad boys and especially the poor boys, the black boys, the Mexican boys, and the Indian boys. Here are those bad lower-class, friendless boys in dirty clothes from across the tracks who must be punished for something. They must be taught a lesson. They must be rehabilitated. And so here they linger, slowly decaying, festering, brooding, sinking down in this magnificent brand-new marble monument to civilization's primary tool of justice—an attempt to control crime. . . .

There is no recreation area. There is no exercise area. Once a week a prisoner may peer through a glass pane at a visiting friend or loved one, trying to communicate through the use of a cheap battery telephone which does not work well. After fifteen minutes of frustration, he is returned to his cell, and the visitor leaves. The prisoner relapses into his state of ruminative rehabilitation.

One of the prisoners walked back and forth in front of us groaning. He had several times cut his wrist in an attempt at suicide. The jailer explained his present agony by saying that his trial (he had not yet been convicted of any crime) had once more been postponed, this time for two months. Two witnesses, police officers, had found it inconvenient to be present at the hearing held this morning to which he had so long looked forward for a definite decision regarding his fate.

Into the jaws of this great iron beast, boys are cast day after day for periods of six months, twelve months, eighteen months, and two years. Many are only awaiting trial to see if they are "guilty" of some crime. Others have committed petty crimes—else they would have been transferred to state or federal prisons which are far more humane institutions. . . .

How does one go about improving "our miserable crime control system"? Dr. Karl has taken the unusual approach of actually asking the people who are in a position to know best—the prisoners. His first letter "To Men in Prison" brought requests for reprints from many prison newspapers throughout the nation. The earliest manuscript version was dated 1952 and is on file in The Menninger Foundation Archives under "Letter to the Editor, Undertow." *It later appeared in the* Menninger Quarterly, *Winter, 1955:*

Three groups of people know that the modern prison system is an utter failure. The wardens and law enforcement people know it, psychiatrists know it, and prisoners know it. These three groups of people, strangely assorted though they may sound, would all agree, I believe on the following points:

1. There is evil in the hearts of all men, and life is a constant struggle to control it.

2. For various reasons certain individuals fail to control it—too often, too consistently, or too extremely.

3. Some of these individuals go off the deep end so far that they are regarded as crazy. Others are not any more crazy than the average person, and not any less. And when they go too far they get caught in a system, the theory of operation of which is that man must be shut away from the rest of the people for awhile in order to show them that crime does not pay and to keep them out of other people's hair.

4. But the result of the system is that they learn that if they are smart enough crime does pay; "look at so-and-so and so-and-so, in high places and low places." Furthermore, those particular fellows who have done the most damage, such as little-girl molesters and a few others who ought to stay in jail a long time, generally get out in a few years and go back to their old tricks. So the jail that is supposed to protect society doesn't do it, and the jail that is supposed to reform the offender merely embitters him and teaches him some new tricks, ruins his chances to get a job, and costs the state a lot of money.

Now, as I say, some of us well know these facts, but we don't know what to do about changing the system. What is the intelligent, constructive, sensible thing to do with offenders? What could be done that will really protect society from those that can't be reformed and which will accomplish some kind of reformation for those who can be? I'm asking you.

In the long run prisoners know more about this than anyone else, and ought to come up with the best ideas. The law enforcement people all know the present system isn't working, but they don't know what to do. Furthermore, they are hounded by a public that doesn't realize their problems or the prisoners' problems, but expects the traditional practices to continue, chiefly out of fear.

We psychiatrists are overwhelmed with our clinical problems, because there are far more mentally sick people out of prison than there are in the prison system, but to tell the truth, we can't put our minds to it. We haven't the time. Nor do we really know enough about it, because most of the people we study are obviously sicker than most prisoners. Incidentally, the improvement in the human care and treatment of the mentally ill and the change in public attitude toward it sprang very largely from the suggestions, recommendations, and reports of former patients, such as Clifford Beers, Harold Maine, and Mary Ward.

So I come to the point that progressive ideas about the control of social offenses and the wisest handling of offenders for their own good and society's protection are likely to spring from the constructive thinking of some who have had personal, bitter experience, and who are able to rise above that experience and devote themselves to the solution of a magnificent life expression for some of those who have suffered.

One newspaper that reprinted the letter was The Clock, *of the Idaho State Prison in Boise. Following publication of Dr. Karl's letter, the editor, a man who signed himself "Saguaro," offered "A Reply to Dr. Karl."*

Saguaro suggested that when a prisoner first arrived he be sub- jected, over and over, to a "shocking amount" of "down-to-earth per- suasion aimed at blasting the mind—which for years has been bent toward larceny or other illicit objectives—into new, legitimate chan- nels of thought" such as "you can't win by breaking the law." He maintained this would be an effective way of changing the thinking habits of men who had broken the law, that there was no more potent force than "propaganda," made up of one or a few simple ideas re- peated again and again. After the first week of this "shocking" treat- ment, there could be a follow-up program over the prison's closed radio circuit presenting the same sort of thinking "along constructive lines," he added.

He concluded his article: "Well, Doctor, I have done my best to come up with what you asked for—a progressive idea. . . . Whether or not this method strikes you as having merit, I believe you will agree that the right therapy sensibly applied to the prisoner's mind will do more good for him and society than all the steel bars and stone walls ever built. Inside the unruly, uncaged mind, that's where the trouble lies, not in the shackled body."

To this, Dr. Menninger replied:

You may be right, that for some offenders a certain amount of "shock" treatment has a beneficial effect. Upon others I am sure that it would have (and *does* have) a bad effect, and it is just the diagnostic discrim- ination as between those that need "shock" treatment and those that need treatment *for* shock, as it were, that I am most interested. Sup- pose we assume, to begin with, that every one is doing the best he can; then we must discover why the best some people can do is so poor. How has this fellow or that one been crippled, or hurt, or discouraged, or made desperate? How can he act so "dumb"? Who has been "kid- ding" him? How can we get this fellow headed in a different ("better") direction? You know a good many of these men and you know how often their views of themselves are incorrect. How many of them need to be shaken out of it, so to speak, and how many need to have their confidence in their own potentials reinstated? I don't think this can be done by shock.

Dr. Karl wrote "Another Letter to Men in Prison" for the first issue in January, 1972, of "Correctional Programs News," published by the

THE CRIME OF PUNISHMENT

W. Clement and Jessie V. Stone Foundation for the inmates of the nation's prisons.

I wrote "a letter to men in prisons" some years ago. I said you could help greatly in improving prisons because you knew so well what was wrong with them. And that is happening! I know how miserable prison life is and how little that is friendly or encouraging occurs in your daily lives. This knowledge grieves me and worries me, and this puzzles some of my friends. They think prisoners are all alike, a bunch of tough, hard guys who don't need sympathy—just "punishment." I don't agree with that, you know. I know you are not all alike, by any means, and I think you've already had too much punishment. What many of you need is a new goal and a new hope and some new friends. That's no small order, but it isn't impossible.

You and I both know that there are some really desperate people around who will have to be kept somewhere a long time. But most of you in prison are not that tough. I know you. Not all that vicious and dangerous; not so mean and not so tough; just sad, and bored and lonely and frustrated at the futility of idly waiting, waiting, waiting— locked up in a cage like a zoo animal.

But take hope. There's a new spirit coming on, including a new crop of young lawyers, some of whom are determined to change the system. High up people in the government publicly acknowledge that our present system is wretched, wasteful, costly, inadequate.

A new attitude toward prisoners is growing, so don't make the same mistake about outsiders that they do about you; don't assume that they are all alike. People are not all alike, inside or out. There are many conscientious, concerned people in the world—a great many of them. There are helpful and intelligent people, some of them right in the penal system. Trying hard to change things.

Mr. W. Clement Stone of the W. Clement and Jessie V. Stone Foundation of Chicago works through Mr. Harry H. Woodward as director of Correctional Programs to help offer a better life for convicts and ex-convicts. The John Howard Association of Chicago works to improve the prisons and assist former inmates to get jobs. The Fortune Society, 1545 Broadway in New York City, is composed of ex-prisoners who are trying to help themselves and other former inmates in various ways. The (reorganized) Seventh Step Foundation operates in various cities. These are just a few of many others.

No one knows the evils of jails and prisons better than the wardens, although they sometimes get upset when other people point them out. By and large, the wardens are our friends. They often have to put up with a lot of double-crossing from their assistants and public criticism from politicians who want publicity, just when they (the wardens) are trying especially hard to improve things. Remember, the wardens do not make the laws. Or build the prisons.

We have to get to the lawmakers, and lawmakers are hard to reach. The old ones who wrote the laws are dead, and the young ones aren't always interested. But when we reach them they correctly tell us that they must listen to the voice of the people who elect them. And how do we educate people? You can help do that. But you can't educate the public by fighting it or stealing from it or defying its laws. You may feel like kicking it in the teeth, but don't. A wrong for a wrong for a wrong doesn't get anywhere. Make up your mind now that when you get out, you will help those of us who are trying to educate the people and their political leaders about better ways, cheaper ways, more successful ways, more humane ways.

Well, there's something to think about and plan about, constructively. Think it over, because one of the points emerging from a recent Williamsburg National Conference on Corrections is that there is a new attitude, everywhere, toward offenders. You have rights and responsibilities. The philosophy of corrections is really turning away from punishment—toward the notion of being helpful. Not all prison employees have heard about this yet, but they will. So lift up your heads.

And get started on a reading course; get into a discussion group; try a bit of writing or painting. Whatever else, keep your hope alive. I realize that's a tough order but where there's hope, there's life! So keep alive.

To prison wardens, in an article in The Correctional Trainer, *Winter Edition, 1970–71, he said in part:*

. . . One demoralizing feeling that many prisoners have is that their plight is unknown, that they are really luckless, forgotten people of whose existence and suffering no one is aware except guards and possibly some officials of the prison. This seems to me to be a very widespread sentiment. Prison newspapers do something to combat this, I presume, because there is some exchange among them, I believe, and this is increasing. Furthermore, the Fortune Society and some of the newspapers have published letters from prisoners which I think do tell the public things they don't know and reassure the prisoners that the public is not altogether comfortable in its mind about the situation.

I wonder if it would not be a good thing if every prisoner could see copies of such publications as *The Correctional Trainer*. No secrets are being revealed. What could be better for prisoners than to know that other people—even wardens!—have troubles and that the problems of crime and corrections are being studied and discussed? What could be better for them than to know what an extraordinary leader we have in our state commissioner Mr. Bensinger [Peter Bensinger, Commissioner of Correction for Illinois] and how earnestly he is trying to improve procedures and conditions? What wardens would not favor letting prisoners read this material which cannot help but improve morale?

And if this is too extreme a suggestion, how about seeing that all guards and other prison personnel get copies? Surely there could be no objection to their knowing of these efforts and opportunities to improve things.

Here's another suggestion that I would like to try out on you. Why are prisoners kept in "cells"? There is nothing in the law that says sentenced offenders should be caged. Confined, yes, but how did we ever get started on the iron cages and the cell blocks? Some recent experiments have shown that where prisoners were put in ordinary rooms with no bars, there were no more runaways and escapes than when everything was locked up. But even if we locked the doors, I think architects ought to be ashamed to supply blueprints for any more of the old-fashioned cell blocks and cages. There are civilized ways of detaining people in groups, and if a man is unfortunate enough to be an offender (and it is indeed a deplorable misfortune) he may need detention—some undoubtedly do. But he ought to be detained in a way that does not dehumanize him, lower his self-respect, humiliate him in the eyes of his children, or destroy his hope of ultimate social living. He is not a parrot or a monkey or a lemur; he is a man; and I think he should be housed as a man, and detained as a man—not as a beast. Indeed, the humane societies would not permit animals to be kept in some of the dark, dank dirty jails that I have seen. . . .

To help the police understand more about their own and their prisoners' behavior, Dr. Karl wrote an article for the Kansas State Police Officer's Magazine, *December, 1950, the essence of which he has given numerous times in lectures:*

It should not be very hard to persuade a policeman to agree that his job expects him to have the ability of a superman. As a matter of fact, in choosing his profession he has elected to be a *Super man*. What he has said is that he wishes to announce himself ready to act more forcefully, more wisely, more calmly, more bravely, and more law abidingly than the average man.

But can he? He isn't really a superman; how can he act like one?

He can prove it sometimes by physical tests. Furthermore, a study conducted at the Menninger Clinic a few years ago showed that our Kansas police officers, at least, are also well above average in intelligence.

But intelligence and physique are not the only factors to be considered in the selection of competent police officials. Motives and emotions are important as well as brains and muscles. Why does an applicant want to be a police officer in the first place? What concept has he of the profession he is about to join? What ideals does he have and what sacrifices is he willing to make in order to fill his uniform with competence and pride? Does the young candidate aspire to his job because he wants to look important? Because he wants to bully people? Because he wants to have an excuse to get away from his wife a little more often? Sometimes these secret motives are the real ones.

The man who has secret inferiority feelings, the man with an over-strong, vengeful conscience, the man who lacks self-respect, the man with burning resentment against authority of any kind—such a man will become a bad police officer. He is not a superman, except in authority—and he promotes public danger rather than public safety. Such individuals, given the authority of the law, become the destroyer of the law. They think that to insure respect they must inspire fear.

Policemen have destructive tendencies just like everyone else. And they must learn to master them in themselves before they can efficiently master them in others. In this respect, if in no other, a competent policeman would deserve the title of "superman."

A police officer is a personification of conscience. This may either be a conscience of ideals or a conscience of vengeance. The police officer has many temptations, and one of them is to use his power and authority vengefully and hence destructively instead of constructively. The possession of authority is a great burden. Few can bear it and still fewer can be trusted to employ it constructively.

To be a policeman takes intelligence, understanding, warmth, kindness, patience, tact, and an immeasurable amount of self-control. It takes, in fact, the abilities of a "superman." Are these qualities appreciated by the public? Most certainly not. But let me ask you, too, if they are appreciated by the policemen themselves? When police officers come to have a higher opinion of themselves, to recognize that they are leaders in the community (the conscience of the community, as it were), umpires in the great game of semi-domesticated human beings trying to live peaceably with one another in a complicated world, they will inspire similar respect, support, and admiration from the public at large.

In the final analysis, the responsibility for our correctional system rests with the general public, which supports prisons in their present form —and whose backing is essential if meaningful changes are to be made. And not just "the general public" in the anonymous mass, but one by one, as individual, concerned citizens, who are willing to make the effort to make the necessary changes. Individual efforts do count, as is shown in the following 1967 Reading Notes:

Most of the letters I have received in regard to *The Crime of Punishment* have been very kind. They have been as complimentary, on the whole, as have the reviews. Now and then someone speaks his mind and tells me I am all wet or that I neglected an important illustration or exception. One or two have pointed out real self-contradictions and inconsistencies, which I shall try to correct in later editions. A few reproach me gently for being so pessimistic about prisons. Don't I realize that the police have reformed and the prisons along with them? The mistreatment of helpless prisoners is a fiction of the sensational newspaper writers—prisoners don't get beaten up any more, handcuffed people are not slugged—men forced to lie flat on the cement floor are not jumped upon by guards wearing boots—men are not put in a bullpen anymore, or kept as long as eight hours with no toilet, no urinal, no drinking fountain—men with severe back injuries and joint conditions are not purposely struck in the back and twisted about—men are not shoved to the floor and forced to eat their food on a tray on the floor. And if any such goings on occur occasionally, it isn't common practice and only involves vicious criminals.

Well, if you are one of these Pollyannas, cast your eyes upon the report of a Catholic priest and a prison physician cited in a secret survey, portions of which have reached the pages of the *Nation* for September 15. And these brutalities occurred to some of the nine hundred prisoners confined mostly for misdemeanors (not felonies) in a place built for four hundred.

THE CRIME OF PUNISHMENT

It may be something of an antidote for this bad news to read Joseph Whitehill's lecture to the School of Communications of the University of Pennsylvania published in the *American Scholar* and then later in the *National Observer*. He got summoned to serve on the Grand Jury which had to do a little inspecting of the dog pound, the air raid shelter, and the city jail. His experience in the latter was so shocking that he got hooked. He decided to see what he could do in order to know what he should do. He began visiting the jail two evenings a week and prisoners were allowed to talk to him. Before long he was hooked in a big way. He found out about a side of life he hadn't known before. He began to see all sorts of things that someone ought to do and he just up and did them. He probably saved one man from the gas chamber. He got another fellow who was indicted for second degree murder started on the way to become, as of the present time, coordinator of a recording for the blind project. He helped with a Great Books class. But I won't go on with this.

He did what every citizen might do, but very few of us do do, and he developed a strong conviction that I have, that the *lex talionis* is just wrong. "We know," he says, "that the longer a man spends in prison, the less likely is he to rejoin what for some of us is a highly interesting and various society; he rejoins a highly interesting and various contrasociety—and ends up back in the joint." "We know, too, that every sentence, for whatever crime, must be indeterminate; those who can go back quickly ought to be got out as quickly as possible; those whose offenses may be minor but who show the pathology of danger to themselves or others must be detained indefinitely."

"Our new President said more than he meant to when he said that government cannot do it all. Truthfully, government cannot do anything at all important. It can make war and defend special interests . . . but it cannot love, and it cannot care."

Last year I distributed to a few of my friends a pamphlet we had received in the mail bearing the startling title *"Have you been in jail lately?"*

This is a Quaker publication which refers to the visitation of prisoners—an injunction by Jesus which is rarely followed by good Christians these days. This pamphlet contains suggestions for occasional visits. It has in mind less the comfort of the prisoners than the education of the visitors regarding the conditions of the prisons to which our judges mechanically direct offenders day after day. It suggests the visitors look into the general atmosphere, the overcrowding, the ventilation, the cleanliness, the vermin, the separation of juveniles and first offenders from old-timers, attention given the ill—including the mentally ill—the "character of the staff," the way in which the prisoners are permitted or expected to spend their time, the amount of exercise permitted, the availability of personal counseling, the availability of medical examinations, the concern for the religious life of the prisoners, the methods of discipline used, the sort of preparations made for release, especially the questions of friends and jobs.

". . . especially the questions of friends and jobs." The prospect faced by the typical prisoner upon his release from confinement was vividly described by Dr. Karl in "The Tasks of Penology: A Symposium on Prisons and Correctional Law," published in the Nebraska Law Review *in 1966:*

The ex-prisoner . . . re-enters a world no longer like the one he left some years before, and certainly nothing like the one he has been living in. In the new world, aside from a few uneasy relatives and uncertain friends, the prisoner is surrounded by hostility, suspicion, distrust, and dislike. Complex social and economic situations which were already too much for him have grown no simpler. The unequal tussle with smarter, "nicer," and more successful people begins again. The ex-prisoner, proscribed from employment by many concerns and usually unable to find new friends and ways of living, is forced to survive without any further help except an occasional warning from a watchful parole officer.

His chief occupation for awhile is the search for an occupation, accompanied by innumerable rebuffs, suspicious glances, discouragements, hostile encounters, and, of course, inevitably, temptations. Aside from that of his parole officer, toward whom he may not always feel kindly, the first friendly face that such an individual is likely to see is that of some crony of the old days who has been waiting for a little help to do a little job.

Remember, we are talking about a human being, a handicapped one at that, one who needs all the things the rest of us do—something to do, something to eat, someone to talk to, and a little bit more! You and I can get along without committing crimes (most of the time). But obviously the criminal cannot or at least does not. The fellow who has been in jail not only has in him what made him commit the crime, but he has what the jail did to him. Like the rest of us he is inevitably attracted to other people, but it is a lot harder for him after discharge to get to those other people, and the people he is finally able to get to are often poorly equipped to help him, to love him, or even to like him.

Do the churches reach out to take him in? Do business firms recruit him? Do the unions quickly take him in and find him a job? Does the country club give him a locker? Does any but the lowest class restaurant or rooming house welcome so unprepossessing, shabbily dressed, and often ill favored individual?

Does anyone know or care if he is depressed, desperate, deluded, hallucinated, delirious, suffused with ideas that he is being persecuted or convinced that he is an avenging angel who must slay the enemies of white supremacy? Does anyone ask whether he might still be dangerous? Does anyone ask what useful things this man might do, what values he might render to society in exchange for the offenses he perpetrated upon it? Does anyone ask what might have been done to deter him from continuing as he was obviously going? Does anyone ask what might be done to redirect him?

No, certainly not. That is not in the book. Criminals are not to be "helped." Criminals are to be *held,* and hurt, threatened and warned, pushed and punished, released and paroled. But "helped"— for heaven's sake! Softheaded sentimentalism, liberalism, egghead stuff, practically communistic. These men are toughs; they are dangerous; they are vicious; they are enemies of society. Do not pity them; pity their poor victims. They owe a debt to society. They should pay for their crimes. And keep paying.

If there were ten times as many parole officers as there are, and if they were all as good as a few of our palole officers are, and if they could carry ten times the load these men and women are now carrying —which is already too great—and if these parole officers could have just a little more training and occasionally a little encouragement from the judges, a little assistance from psychiatric clinics or other behavioral scientists, above all if they could have a little more appreciation from the public for what they do—well, this is one of the biggest combinations of "ifs" imaginable. But if all these "ifs" could be, these indefatigable but inconspicuous friends and guides of former prisoners might turn the tide. But at the present time they are swamped and often weary and perfunctory and discouraged with their sometimes seemingly hopeless task.

The acting out of the impulse to hate is sometimes sanctioned by society in the name of law as "punishment" for crimes. The most extreme form is capital punishment. The following very eloquent short speech,

THE CRIME OF PUNISHMENT

"Why We Kill," was presented thirty-three years ago, April 26, 1940, at the annual conference of the American League to Abolish Capital Punishment:

At a time when people are beginning to recognize the importance of psychology and of psychiatry in medicine, in business, in politics, in industry, in sociology, and elsewhere, it is appropriate that we also consider the psychological factor in law. Unfortunately, however, this is, for the most part, an unexplored field.

I have been asked to speak on *why we kill*. This topic leaves me free to compare the motives of the criminal who kills someone he does not like with the motives of society, which also kills someone it does not like.

If we were to ask one who could interpret the law to us what distinction there is between the murder of a victim by a criminal, and the murder of a criminal by the state, we would be told that this is an arbitrary distinction, based on the assumption that what the state decides to do can never be wrong, and that what the individual decides to do is right or wrong according to the decisions of the state.

The state long ago decided that it was right to kill people who had killed others. I shall not review the legal philosophy justifying that decision. You are familiar with the several arguments which are customarily adduced to support it. You are also familiar with the refutations of these various arguments which have been offered repeatedly by criminal lawyers, judges of criminal courts, scientific criminologists, and sociologists.

In psychiatry, when a patient gives reasons for doing something—reasons which may appear to be logical, but which, upon analysis, prove to be false and untrue or, at least, insufficient—we are apt to conclude one of two things: either that his judgment and thinking processes are seriously faulty, or else that he is unconsciously fooling himself. In the latter case, we describe his tendency to find reasons which imperfectly explain his act as "rationalizations."

The kindest thing that can be said about the arguments offered for the continuation of the death penalty as a social and legal necessity is that they are rationalizations. It is a little kinder to say this than to say that they are due to defective judgment, and it is probably more accurate. I am inclined to think that the advocates of the death penalty are neither stupid nor insincere, but I think that most judicial, scientific investigators of the facts would say that they are mistaken.

If we can agree that these are rationalizations, or if we assume that they are rationalizations, we have yet to elucidate what the real motive, the unrecognized motive, the unconscious motive may be in the mind of the individual and, as the result of collective attitudes, in the minds of the public generally. This brings us to the crux of the question, *why do we kill?*

Prior to Sigmund Freud, it was customary in psychology to assume that the wish to kill was pathological. This, to be sure, is still the popular view of the matter. A person with murderous intent, murderous purposes, is regarded as abnormal. But Freud fearlessly explored the unconscious layers of the personality, and disclosed the fact that it is no more abnormal for a human being to want to kill than it is for a cat to want to kill a mouse or a fox to kill a rabbit.

It is true that not all animals kill, but a great many of them do, and the unconscious of human beings shows them to be allied psychologically to the carnivora. Freud showed that we think of it as being abnormal to kill only because society has become accustomed to a self-imposed, arbitrary prohibition against killing. There are various reasons why this is a good prohibition, but they do not contradict the fact that, instinctively, we want to kill.

Most of us are able to control these instincts. We may get very angry, we may even destroy a friend's happiness or his reputation, but most of us do not actually take his life. Civilization has greatly reduced the occasions upon which one may exercise this instinct to destroy. It may still be done in self-defense and in war. It may be done vicariously by killing wild animals, although many people can no longer do this with a good conscience. It is sometimes very clear how definitely the wild animals and birds, which some men hunt so assiduously, represent human beings whom they unconsciously hate. Sometimes this is obvious to everybody but the hunter himself.

Such a phenomenon is called displacement. We say that such individuals displace their wish to kill from the original object to a substitute object. This is certainly one of the mechanisms which leads so many people to find satisfaction in the official killing of criminals. We should not forget that the killing of criminals was formerly done in public as a form of popular pleasure. People loved to see criminals executed either by being thrown to the lions or by being chopped up by gladiators or by being burned at the stake. They made no attempt to conceal the fact that they enjoyed seeing this killing done by others, since they were themselves prohibited from doing it. They could escape any sense of guilt for this by reminding themselves that these victims were bad fellows who ought to be killed. Therefore, they might as well all join in the pleasure of seeing it done.

The same spirit of vicarious pleasure in killing continues to dominate the public mind, and explains why the abolition of capital punishment meets with such strange, silent, but stubborn opposition. The abolition of capital punishment is too civilized for the acceptance of a great many people, who must retain some opportunity to express vicariously their wish to kill. One often hears from such people that the abolition of capital punishment means that there will be more murders committed. Statistical facts contradict this statement, but the idea persists.

Why does it persist? It persists because such individuals are unconsciously afraid of their own murderous impulses. I do not mean that there is any likelihood that they would themselves commit murder, but I mean that they are unconsciously aware that something in their psychology is disturbed if the opportunity for vicarious murder is removed from them.

Nevertheless, the trend of civilization is very definitely in the direction of still further reducing the opportunity for killing. Some psychologists believe that this is the reason that war seems so inevitable. We take away all the opportunities for killing and get people nicely civilized only to have them blow up and begin to kill each other in the name of patriotism.

This is a very pessimistic conclusion, and one which might be used by the opponents of our program to justify the continuation of capital punishment. If there were a choice between capital punishment and war, I think we would all choose capital punishment, but I do not believe that any such alternate exists. As a matter of fact, except in symbolic exceptions, capital punishment is already largely abandoned. The great majority of murderers in the United States are not executed. I doubt if the majority of those convicted of murder are executed.

What this Association is really combatting, I believe, is the hypocrisy of the resulting judicial inefficiencies of threatening a punishment, and inflicting it upon a few, while citing technical excuses for not inflicting it upon others. The whole process considerably impairs the logical action of jurisprudence.

Be that as it may, I would not like to leave the impression that I thought that by abolishing capital punishment completely, we would be encouraging war. There are a vast number of substitute forms of aggressiveness which do not involve the actual murder of anybody or anything. It is the program of preventive psychiatry, or what is sometimes called mental hygiene, to encourage a social order in which these opportunities are multiplied in order to absorb the aggressive energy that is now invested in the medieval and futile practice of the official murder of a few scapegoats.

Some twenty years later, Dr. Karl expressed himself even more vehemently in a heretofore unpublished manuscript:

Were it not for persistent recalcitrancy of a stubborn minority, it would seem ridiculous for a scientist to discuss the inappropriateness of capital punishment in a civilized society. In his magnificent but futile statement to the California State Legislature, Governor [Edmund "Pat"] Brown put it well when he said the naked simple fact is that the death penalty has been a gross failure. "Beyond its horror and incivility, it has neither protected the innocent nor deterred the wicked. The recurrent spectacle of publicly sanctioned killing has cheapened human life and dignity without the redeeming grace which comes from justice meted out swiftly, evenly, humanely . . . in actual practice . . . it is primarily inflicted upon the weak, the poor, the ignorant and [the members of] racial minorities . . . the overwhelming majority [being] psychotic or near-psychotic, alcoholic, mentally defective, or otherwise demonstrably mentally unstable."

I have been a member of the American League to Abolish Capital Punishment for nearly a quarter of a century. During that period I have seen the number of executions diminish almost to the vanishing point. The Navy, of course, has not executed anyone since 1843, and even in the Army there are fewer and fewer instances. By 1948, executions in other prisons had dropped to a little over one hundred for the entire country and by 1958, to less than fifty. We still carry out ritualistic official murder about once a week in this country. For everyone executed, there are about two hundred eligibles who are not executed. The chief function of the ritual is perhaps a symbolic satisfying of the revenge lust of a minority of our less educated citizens and perhaps headline lust for some of our sensational newspapers.

With the decline of executions there has been a corresponding increase in the interest of psychiatrists in human misbehavior. Until they are no longer exploited as pawns in a game between lawyers regarding the treatment of a particularly sensational individual, psychiatrists will not take an interest in criminology and penology. We conceive of our role as constructive. We are not interested in proving a man to be in the pink of condition and therefore fat and ripe for the executioner.

If anyone thinks it will help those timid governors and legislatures who have not yet made the obvious, civilized move, as has Delaware and many others, let us add our voices officially to the chorus which is swelling every day and demand that our country take one more logical, intelligent, and civilized step.

Dr. Karl himself has not hesitated to speak out. For example, on behalf of Caryl Chessman, convicted of rape and murder, he wrote Christian A. Herter, secretary of state, on April 27, 1960:

A committee of individuals, none of whom I know, has petitioned me to write you urging a commutation of the death sentence on Caryl Chessman to life imprisonment. . . . I am complying with this opportunity because I believe in its principle. I am opposed to any capital punishment. I think it lowers us to the [moral] level of the offender. I think it militates against the prevention of crime.

As a physician, it would be my impression that some of the [public] emotions in this case center about mysterious deviations in the sexual conduct of the accused. Most members of the public do not realize, of course, that perverse sexuality is an expression of an inhibited, distorted, and weak sexual urge rather than the reverse. We doctors are probably guilty of not having furthered public education to the extent that there would not be such a clamor for the execution of a man thus driven to desperate and repugnant antisocial acts.

I do urge commutation of the death sentence for Caryl Chessman if this is within your province. . . .

And in another letter, this time on November 19, 1962, to the then governor of Kansas about a young college student Dr. Karl had examined:

I think you would take a great step forward for penology in Kansas and for humane government and for intelligent leadership if you would up and commute this fellow's sentence. I mean this clumsy, queer . . . boy who shot his parents and sister. Nothing is going to be gained by executing a man as sick as this. It won't do him any good and it won't do anyone else any good. Mental illness is not prevented by the public execution of any of its victims.

There will be a few bloodhounds in the state who will criticize you for it, but I think there are more intelligent, humane-minded people than there are bully boys. However, even if it would hurt you politically—which I don't think it would—I do advise you to do it.

Despite Dr. Karl's plea, the execution was carried out. On November 30, 1962, Dr. Karl again wrote to the then governor:

According to the newspapers it took eighteen minutes for the state to strangle the . . . boy yesterday. That's a long time. If we have to go on killing people up in Lansing, I think it would be more humane to shoot them.

I wrote you recently urging clemency, because as a physician, I oppose all killing and certainly the killing of sick people, no matter how obnoxious they may be. I did not get a reply from you, but I understand that your position is that this is the will of the people—that they got this law passed and if this is what they want, you are duty-bound to enforce their wishes. Any state employees at Lansing not wanting the job of choking people to death can resign.

You have a good point; maybe this *is* what the people of Kansas want. But I doubt it . . .

Dr. Karl wrote the following on April 20, 1965, to Joseph Jenkins and Robert Bingham, lawyers in Kansas City, who defended the two young slayers of the Clutter family, the case that Truman Capote wrote about in In Cold Blood. *Dr. Karl recalls: "The two lawyers had been severely criticized and their disbarment urged by a number of people for having defended the killers. They were, of course, appointed and ordered by the court to do so."*

I understand that you were the attorneys for the defense of the two young men who were hanged last Wednesday evening.

As a lifelong opponent of capital punishment I had hoped that you would be successful in preventing the state from making this egregious error. Unfortunately the law is still on the statute books and must be carried out if ordered, unless some flaw is found in the process. I think you found numerous flaws and I suspect that even your legal opponents knew of these flaws.

These two men did a terrible thing and received little public sympathy for their fate. However, the repudiation of capital punishment should not depend upon sympathy but upon our realization that this method of dealing with offenders is expensive, ineffective, barbaric, and immoral. That its continuation deters the effective administration of justice seems to me obvious.

Some will accuse you of having increased the expense of this execution by delaying it. But I am sure those same people would be the first to deny favoring a remitting of the opportunity for due process of law. All possible extenuations must be investigated if the ultimate destruction of an individual is to be sanctioned. You have merely demonstrated the great expensiveness to the state of retaining the capital puunishment statute. It is financially expensive as well as morally expensive.

However, I am sure that it made you unpopular with some and took courage and conviction on your part, and I respect you for this as should every citizen of this state, including those who have bitterly reproached you. The murder was dreadful; the sorrow and grief were great; the sense of helplessness, fear, and regret were widespread. But these feelings are not relieved today by the knowledge that some fellow citizens employed by our state were ordered to drag these two offenders to a post and hang them. In the days of horse thieves and cattle rustlers this may have seemed the only thing to do. Most civilized peoples have risen above that stage of civilization. I regret that my state lags.

Mr. Jenkins wrote to thank Dr. Karl, saying, "your letter came . . . like a beacon on a hostile shore. Please accept my humble thanks for this kind gesture."

Two years later, on April 11, 1967, when Illinois adopted a moratorium on capital punishment, Dr. Karl wrote approvingly to Bernard McDevitt, chairman of the Judiciary Committee of the House of Representatives of the State of Illinois:

I was glad to learn of the governor's moratorium bill on capital punishment in Illinois.

Owing to the gradual ascendancy of common sense and civilized sentiment in the body politic, this barbaric practice is almost extinct. Only one man was executed last year in all the fifty states of America, which is clear evidence of what most people think. But so long as [it] remains on the statute books as an obsolete relic of medieval law it serves to confuse juries and burden prison administrators. A collection of "death row" inmates accumulates in various prisons, which is a kind of slow torture. Killing people is not the function of the law of a civilized country even if some good reason could be contrived for it. None ever has been. No intelligent person believes that the secret execution of one or a dozen villains has the slightest effect on the behavior of other villains with the killing impulse.

And, more generally, in a letter to Harold B. Statler, executive secretary of the Kansas Council of Churches, on April 28, 1960, he declared:

We should not lower ourselves to commit a crime even against a criminal. We should raise the criminal if we can, and hold him, if we can't. But murder him? Never!

I don't believe we can murder people in the name of God, law, justice, or humanity, no matter how we construe it . . .

Nor do I agree that life imprisonment sentences should always mean life imprisonment. This assumes that human beings cannot change. I think some of them do change, and it would be wasteful for them to change and then be cruelly detained because of a rigid law formulated long before they changed. The way to detain people until they are "safe" is not through prohibitive legislation but through discriminating examination and a reform of the parole system as well as the prison system.

CHAPTER TEN

A Plea for Prevention

By all odds, prevention is the best cure for the world's afflictions, mental and physical. Psychiatrists have been slow to involve themselves in preventive programs, although "Mental Hygiene" was proclaimed as a goal over sixty years ago. Dr. Karl explains:

Mental health is now an accepted goal and even a popular cause. Psychiatrists are apt to assume—I myself always assumed—that because mental health was esoteric, because it touched on the sinister realm of mental illness, there was a slight taboo attached to the subject—a resistance to its acceptance, or even to its discussion.

I gradually came to see that the resistance was in our own minds. We thought the public ought to be interested and yet we were somewhat reluctant to be as simplistic or as didactic as we thought it necessary for their proper education.

More and more laymen resumed the responsibility for mental health education and more and more we psychiatrists neglected it. I began to wonder why that was. When I talked to the annual meeting of the National Association for Mental Health on October 31, 1953, in Cleveland I told them what was on my mind in a speech entitled "Resistances Encountered by the Mental Hygiene Movement."

A PLEA FOR PREVENTION

The speech to the NAMH annual meeting, never before published. follows:

Since you all know that I am a psychiatrist, and since you all know that we psychiatrists spend a good deal of our time examining how people feel about things, and since even psychiatrists are people and must therefore analyze their own feelings, I should like to plunge directly into my topic via the subjective route.

I didn't very much want to come to your meeting. (Looking around, I would conclude that a good many of my psychiatric colleagues felt the same way.)

I am sure that you are better off as an organization if not too many of us professionals take a hand in your activities, but you must occasionally wonder why the problems to which you are devoting yourselves so earnestly seem to get such lukewarm interest from psychiatrists. Why don't they want to come to such meetings as this and at least speed you on your way with cheers? Why do they appear so indifferent to your efforts?

Perhaps in discouraged moments you ask yourselves: "Why do we get so little help from the ones we are helping most? Are we not urging better mental hospitals? Are we not working for more research funds to extend psychiatric treatment? Are we not pleading for more outpatient facilities? Are we not proposing more psychiatric contributions to welfare work, to the courts, to the police, to the churches, to the schools, and to industry? Are we not concerned, as psychiatrists are, with the problems of the aged? With alcoholism? With epilepsy? With juvenile delinquency?

"Do psychiatrists not realize that unless we can mobilize public interest in these things that psychiatrists will be unable to carry out their own plans? You dishearten us, Dr. Menninger, when you tell us that like so many of your colleagues you didn't very much want to come to our meeting!"

Well, you can see that I have been thinking about *your feelings.* How well I have gauged them I shall have to leave to your judgment. But I feel justified in asking such questions. Taking my own reluctance as a point of examination, I tried to think constructively about the resistance encountered by the mental hygiene movement, and before long I found myself more sympathetic with you and more strongly identified with you.

I don't mean by this that I was ever unsympathetic. I think there are few psychiatrists who would come out and say that they were.

But it is true, I think, that we are not as interested in it as we should be. This may or may not be a real obstacle to the movement. It might become a very great force for good without any "benefit of clergy." But the psychological problem remains, and psychological problems intrigue me. Are we psychiatrists opposed to prevention? We psychiatrists know how great the problem is. We know how impossible it is to stamp out all the fires without some efforts at prevention. And if we, who already know these facts to which you have to educate some people, if *we* are unresponsive to the importance of what you are doing, perhaps we can derive from our own self-examination some of the psychology of the indifference of the general public to this great social problem.

Now I have somewhat misled you. I have never been as far from identification with your work as I am representing. In 1919 I persuaded the governor of Kansas to appoint a State Commission on Mental Hygiene and we organized the Kansas Mental Hygiene Society. That was thirty-four years ago. But I must add that until their spirits were revived a few years ago, it was pretty inactive, pretty ineffective all those years. At first I thought this was because it was too much a psychiatric organization. Then for a time it became a social workers' organization. And for a few years, a psychologists' organization. It is only recently that it has become truly a laymen's organization, and immediately more successful.

We psychiatrists have been spoiled, you know, by the high authority and great respect you have given us. I don't think we overestimate ourselves to begin with, but when we are called upon to give public and private opinions on every sort of topic and in all sorts of places, and are listened to so respectfully, it is easy for us to lose our sense of proportion. Every psychiatrist today is deluged with requests to do the thing that most of us do not do well; namely, make public speeches. Like this, for example! It becomes not a question of *which* speech to make, but which nine or ten speeches NOT to make. You see that I did elect to accept *this* invitation, so I am not as discouraged or as negative as I may have represented myself.

That is a part of it perhaps. I think psychiatrists have much more competence as consultants and advisers and planners than as public speakers. And it is true that, partly because of the mental hygiene movement, all psychiatrists are very, very busy. I think it is safe to say that the average psychiatrist in America, and I say the *average*, is working a ten-hour day, for at least a five and one-half day week. I personally know of several who are working a twelve and fourteen-hour day, six days a week. These are long hours gauged by modern standards, but they only testify to the importance of the very thing you are doing, and I don't think you can explain the lukewarm interest of psychiatrists in the mental hygiene movement just on these mechanical things. I think it goes deeper.

I attended an international medical meeting in London this summer where more than one hundred American psychiatrists were registered. It was on treatment methods. I went from there to the International Congress on Mental Hygiene in Vienna where less than a dozen American psychiatrists were registered, and for that matter, there were fewer psychiatrists from all countries. Subjectively speaking, the program did not seem to me to be nearly as interesting.

I have noticed it in my students, the Fellows at the Menninger School of Psychiatry. Let a speaker come who is going to talk about treatment, and our lecture hall is crowded to the doors. But let a speaker announce his topic as something about prevention and we have an embarrassingly small audience. I put this up to them recently in one of my Colloquiums. "Why is it," I said, "that we psychiatrists don't take more interest in keeping people well and preventing them from getting sick? Are we all afflicted with the *furor therapeuticus* to the extent that we cannot really become interested in reducing our work by joining forces with those who would prevent some of this sickness?"

I got some stimulating answers from my thoughtful young men and women. First of all, they admitted that what I said was true. We are not very interested in it although we know that we ought to be. "I noticed," said one of them, "that even when you were presenting the problem vividly, accurately, and with considerable feeling, I find my attention straying. I have a definite feeling of being reluctant to listen. I said to myself I ought to analyze this."

He reflected further. "Is there something about the demands of such a participation in the mental hygiene movement that conflicts with our aims, or is it with some basic personality traits in us? I think we all have to confess," he went on, "to being motivated in part by a measure of curiosity about the unique, the bizarre in human behavior and by a tendency to become more interested in unusual people than in those who do not seem to vary noticeably from the normal. Maybe it is because some of us have experienced loneliness and estrangement that we were attracted to the field in psychiatry where the very core of treatment is to be found in the development of a relationship with another person, a person who has been even less successful than we.

I think I was drawn toward psychiatry by this desire to form mean-ingful relationships and do so on a person to person basis. In pre-ventive psychiatry both of these interests (deviation and individual relationships) must be abandoned in favor of something quite different and more general. Our competence drops away from us. Frustrated though we may be in dealing with a patient, it frightens us to think of the greater difficulties, the greater hurts that would come from at-tempting to convince parent-teacher groups, businessmen, or legis-lators about these things which many of them will not admit having experienced. Effective action in this field of prevention presupposes a sense of self-confidence, a sustaining enthusiasm, and an ability to tol-erate failure which is rare in the best of us psychiatrists."

Others of my students voiced similar reflections, with variations. Said one of them, "We know how to approach patients, but we don't know how to approach legislators." Said another, "Patients want to do something about it definitely. The general public doesn't. We just go where we are more wanted." Said another, "For us these are tech-nical problems of a rather high level of sophistication. Mental hy-giene techniques consist in reducing this sophistication for popular education. Some of us can do this and some of us cannot, but none of us can find very much interest in listening to someone else do it. It isn't that we don't subscribe to the promotion of mental health be-cause we don't go to such meetings. It is that we don't have any useful and interesting function in it. What we can do, can best be done in an advisory way."

All of these comments seemed to me pertinent and weighty but as I thought about it, I reflected how difficult the work of the public health physicians had always been. I reflected how much more in-teresting fire fighting is than fire prevention. In our town the Fire Department, which has recently acquired quite a bit of new equip-ment, put on a demonstration of this equipment, and thousands of people came to see it. I wonder how many people would have come to see a demonstration of fire prevention. Now, of course, in this matter of fire just as in this matter of mental disease, the prompt treatment is considered, in itself, one of the most effective kinds of prevention. We will say some more about this presently. Right now I want to con-centrate on this psychological fact that while every one agrees that an ounce of prevention is worth a pound of cure and that a stitch in time saves nine and so forth and so on, there is something about pre-vention which interests every one less than cures or attempted cures. What is this peculiar resistance in all of us to prevention? Don't we believe what we say? Don't we believe that we can prevent anything? Is it cynicism? Or is it lack of imagination?

Professor Bernard Cohen of Harvard recently published a very scholarly study on "Prejudice Against the Introduction of Lightning Rods," of all things. He shows how much damage is done by the fires resulting from lightning every day. Somewhere in the world at this very moment there are one thousand eight hundred storms; somewhere in the world there will be forty-four thousand storms this very day. One hundred flashes of lightning occur every second somewhere! Now Benjamin Franklin showed one way to prevent a great deal of damage resulting from these lightning-set fires two hundred years ago! The beautiful cathedral of St. Mark in Venice had been injured or ruined by lightning nine times before a lightning rod was installed in 1766. Since then it has never been struck again. In spite of this, however, there was religious prejudice, there was political prejudice, there was philosophical prejudice, there was scientific prejudice, and there was popular prejudice against Benjamin Franklin's discovery. And for each of these prejudices there were arguments and opposition. When one group was won over, the other took up the opposition. Even one of the popes championed lightning rods, only to be successfully opposed by popular prejudice. Even today there are thousands of destructive fires every year which could have been prevented by the simple expedient of a lightning rod. What is this prejudice against prevention? . . .

[Even] if we did have preventive forces in operation, we couldn't prevent all crimes. Certainly not. We can't cure all cases either, but we can cure most of them, and similarly, I think we could prevent most of the crimes now being committed if we wanted to. I mean if we wanted to badly enough, enough to undertake research into the causes of crime as seriously as we undertake research into the making of atom bombs. No sensible psychiatrist would disavow the humility appropriate to our present state of ignorance, but my point is that even the little knowledge we already have about prevention isn't being used.

And you are going to say, I have no doubt, that there is a conflict of opinion as to how prevention should be effected. I can't deny that psychiatrists often appear to be disputing one another, but I would like to suggest that these disputations are not in regard to the basic facts. The progress of science depends upon developing all the possibilities and conclusions regarding specific details, but in general we psychiatrists agree very substantially, I think. . . . The fact is that thousands of prisoners are released on parole every day without anyone taking the trouble to get a psychiatric opinion of the prisoners' social competence or persistent psychopathology. The conflict of opinion, if any, is between the point of view of the law, which holds that you can determine in advance, on the basis of one particular offense, how long a person should be confined for the safety of society and write it in a book. The position of psychiatry on the other hand is that offenses of all kinds are expressions of some degree of integrative failure, and that the length of time required for the repair of that disorganization cannot be predicted on the basis of one particular act.

There is, to be sure, a great deal that we psychiatrists don't know, and there is a great deal we don't agree about.

But we do know and agree about many things which we have no opportunity to put into practice because of legal regulations and because of public resistance to prevention. Any intelligent psychiatrist or sociologist or even lay member of this organization could outline a program that would reduce crime in a given area by a substantial per cent over a period of a few years and by a much greater per cent over a period of twenty years.

Well, why not then? You know why not. No one ever seriously asked to have it done. It would cost money. It would cost a lot of money. Not as much as crime costs us, to be sure, but a lot more money than people are thinking of. You couldn't prevent having to spend a million dollars for prevention. It will take more than five cents, which is about the proportion we now spend.

So you see it comes back to what I was saying in the first place. There is some kind of a curious resistance in all of us to the idea of preventing anything and we act only when we are forced to do so. And sometimes not even then. The people in my community experienced the most destructive flood in the history of the world three years ago. It destroyed over two billion dollars' worth of property. Thus far, to my knowledge, not one tenth of one per cent of this amount has been spent in an effective plan for preventing similar damage from the next flood that is certainly coming along one of these days. We are still gambling on the chances that we will be dead or will have moved away and someone else can worry about it.

I think we ought to reflect on this curious human propensity for ducking the responsibility of prevention. We can blame some of it on ignorance; we can blame some of it on preoccupation with other interests; we can blame some of it on, shall we say, mental dullness.

If it is chiefly a matter of ignorance, a lack of knowledge of the facts, we can be more hopeful. Some of us say that when the public really wakes up to the fact that one out of every twelve babies born this year will go to a mental hospital sometime during his life, that at least one out of every sixteen Americans is suffering from a mental disorder right now, that a quarter of a million people will go to a mental hospital this year for the first time—when people wake up to the fact that 85 per cent of the patients in state hospitals could be cured instead of the present small fraction—when the people wake up to these facts, they will do something about it. They did do something about it in Kansas, and we are pretty proud of ourselves. We are proud that Topeka State Hospital, which ranked among the lowest in the nation five years ago, now ranks near the top of the list, and that it has more young psychiatrists on its staff in training than any other state hospital in the country. Our people do believe in prevention to some extent, because they have backed up the legislators, our politicians if you please, in doing something constructive about the deplorable situation, once the newspapers gave the people the facts.

Better hospitals mean better treatment, which is in itself prevention, also. We think our outpatient departments are preventive agencies. But, of course, we realize that while there are six psychiatric outpatient clinics in my town, we think there ought to be more in other parts of the state. I could tell you ways in which I don't think we are doing such a good job of prevention in Kansas. We still don't recognize our schoolteachers, especially the teachers in the primary grades, as being the most important people in the community from the standpoint of the character of the next generation. We still don't regard the superintendents of schools as the most important men in the communities. We still don't pay our teachers as much as we pay our plumbers. We still seem to consider teachers and Sunday school teachers and ministers as convenient accessories who ought to work cheap for the fun of it because we hire them.

The discoveries of Freud and their subsequent interpretation by American psychiatrists are largely responsible for making parents aware of the fact that their treatment of the child will be reflected many years later. . . .

And so, in thinking about all this, I came to the conclusion that maybe we psychiatrists share with the general public a kind of human childishness about this matter of prevention. We ought to understand it better than we do. In our theories of personality development, we consider that the child progresses gradually through stages in emotional development. At first he loves only himself. Then he becomes attached to his mother and later to his father. His brothers and sisters begin to interest him, then his playmates and teachers. As he goes through adolescence, as we call it, he begins to be interested in more people and people of the opposite sex and ultimately he selects one of these and they agree to live together forever. But the honeymoon is not maturity; it is only the beginning of a final cycle. For after a preoccupation in the mate, the capacity for love has to be extended to include the children and even this requires more of many people than they are equal to. As years go on and the children grow up, other people's children begin to be of concern to the truly maturing individual, and in a way the grandchildren, the children of our own children, are symbols for other children, for all the children in the world. And this is another sticking point in the development of true psychological maturity. There are some who cannot be good mates because they are too self-centered. There are more who cannot be good parents because they remain forever adolescents. Others cannot get beyond the stage of "God bless me and my wife, my son John and his wife, us four, no more." And when it comes to a real concern for grandchildren, for all the grandchildren in the world, and all the people in the world, perhaps this degree of maturity is only possible for a few.

It was possible for the second Isaiah, and for Amos, and for Jesus. It was possible for Lao-tse and Buddha and Confucius and Plato. It was possible for Benjamin Franklin and Abraham Lincoln and for Albert Schweitzer. And now I pay you the deeply sincere compliment that from the very nature of your program, your dedication to prevention, you demonstrate that it is possible for you.

If the gift is rare, we must expect your numbers to be few. But what you seem to think, wisely and well I believe, is that in many a common man and woman there is a capacity for this vision, this maturity, this world concern which requires only some kind of spark of enlightenment to mobilize it. There are thousands of humble schoolteachers who might find a new joy in their work and a new effectiveness if they could realize that for all the ingratitude or indifference of their students and their community, the idealism and earnestness of their present efforts will have an effect twenty years later that will certainly change the world for the better. Perhaps there are thousands of mothers who need be given the same realization, and thousands of people in all walks of life whose lack of interest in prevention stems from a lack of realization of their own potential contribution to it.

A PLEA FOR PREVENTION

This gets us back to the psychiatrists; perhaps even they need encouragement and enlightenment to develop a sense of their responsibility for prevention.

In leading these people, in encouraging them, in giving them specific facts, problems, and situations, you may be accomplishing infinitely more than one might conclude from the lack of enthusiasm engendered by particular meetings and the painful difficulties of meeting your modest budget. Perhaps it takes the greatest maturity of all to withstand discouragement.

In reflecting upon this, I began to feel ashamed of my reluctance to accept your invitation to join with you tonight in thinking about the world in broader terms than those of my daily preoccupation with the treatment of troubled people. My only apology is, in the words of St. Paul, that "God has appointed in the Church all kinds of people: first, apostles; second, prophets; third, teachers; fourth, workers of miracles, and then healers, helpers, administrators, and speakers." (He put speakers at the end of the list, quite properly.)

But, as this same very wise man continued, something is more important than any of these particular specialties and though I were to speak here tonight with the tongues of man and of angels, but had not love, I would be but a noisy gong or a clanging cymbal. And were I to demonstrate prophetic powers and understand all mysteries and all knowledge, even with great faith, but without love, I would be nothing.

To the earnest members of this organization who have not only maturity, great faith, prophetic vision, and knowledge, but over and above an abundance of that for which St. Paul was pleading, I respectfully doff my hat and pledge my allegiance and affection.

The younger people are when they are helped, the more likely that the help will do some good. Dr. Karl's heart has always gone out to children and he has felt a special obligation to help them, particularly the mentally troubled and the retarded. He traced the history of the Menninger Foundation's pioneering work with children when dedicating on October 9, 1960, a new complex of buildings housing the Foundation's Southard School.

We are about to dedicate a group of buildings to the specific purpose of helping troubled children by scientific method.

For many centuries the one recognized responsibility of society toward children was that of education. Even this was minimal and highly selective until its universal and democratic application became one of the great contributions of the American commonwealth to world history and development.

But even in America, the welfare of children, other than their home care and their education, was not on the public conscience. Provision for the exigencies of desertion and neglect, of cruelty and exploitation, of illness and abandonment seems to have been generally postponed to an indefinite future.

It it difficult to see why our forefathers, and even we ourselves, were so oblivious to the sufferings of childhood. One is impressed by this in reviewing the lifetime efforts made by the Earl of Shaftesbury to get the incredible cruelty of chimney-sweeping eliminated in England.

> The chimney-sweeper is a little slave
> Whose presence and whose horrible employ
> Are so familiar with our earliest thoughts
> That we forget to question their humanity;*

It is easier to understand the indignation of Charles Dickens and William Blake over the mistreatment of children than it is to understand why there could have been such public indifference to the things which made their outcries necessary.

Children are still cruelly treated in homes, in schools, in cities, in prisons. I have seen great cruelty being efficiently practiced on many children by enlightened and prosperous communities. Despite White House Conferences and innumerable striving organizations, children still need our special concern. For, as we all know, might makes right. We adults are in power, and we are bigger than they are. Children should be seen and not heard. They make less noise about their suffering than adults—or they do so behind closed doors. We can easily overlook it or neglect it or forget it.

It is the same with dumb animals, of course. If whales could scream, said a recent author describing the horror of butchering these magnificent animals, there would be no more of this bloody business of bursting their chests with implanted explosives or dragging them through the water with barbed harpoons. Fortunately for our peace of mind, fish, too, are voiceless, to say nothing of rabbits, doves, deer— and some children.

* John Holland, "An Appeal to the Fair Sex," *Chimney-Sweeper's Friend*, quoted in *England's Climbing-Boys* by George L. Phillips, Cambridge, 1949.

But not all children suffer unseen or unheard. Signals of their suffering come through to the sensitive ear and the sympathetic eye.

In the early part of this century it began to be recognized that children were possessed of individuality, and that neither their welfare nor their emergency difficulties could be provided for automatically and categorically. In 1915 pediatrics had become the most popular specialty in the medical schools. Psychiatry, by contrast, was certainly the least popular specialty, if, indeed, it could be called a specialty at all.

Mental illness, so we thought then, rarely affected children. They were either normal or defective. For the latter, there were special places. To be sure, there was a "precocious dementia," or *dementia praecox,* a mental illness that appeared in the very young; but this meant in the *teens.* Strange behavior in younger children was just orneriness, requiring *discipline.* Freud's suggestion of an "infantile neurosis" was preposterous!

But gradually Freud's theories gained acceptance—especially those about the child being father to the man and subject to the same psychological structures and stresses as adults. This line of thought focused the attention of the scientific world upon unnoticed, unrecognized aspects of childhood. Teachers began to be joined by psychologists and then psychiatrists in a concern for the individuality of children, their special and peculiar needs and sufferings. Psychological clinics and then child guidance clinics sprang up for a polydisciplinary attack upon particular problem cases.

It is to the application of this special interest, this special sensitiveness and skill and experience, that our new clinic-school-hospital complex is to be devoted. In it our colleagues with patience and skill and persistence will reach down their hands to little stumblers, to errant wanderers, to brave but baffled little plodders—and to older girls and boys with unhealed, broken hearts. To the uses of those doctors and teachers and case workers and care workers who shall hallow these halls and walls by their mercy and tenderness and love—to their uses we commend this building. For it is they, and not the building they will work in, which will further our common purpose. That purpose will include not only missions of mercy, in the relief of individuals, but a search for underlying principles which can be applied to vast numbers of children who will never come here or even guess that we exist.

Our new Southard School and hospital is not the beginning of something, but the continuing of something—expanding it, developing it. Like the chambered nautilus to which my father so often referred, our psychiatric work with children has outgrown several shells. The first Southard School was a two-story house at 1402 Buchanan in 1925. In 1927 we moved to 1015 Harrison Street. Six more years of development under Miss Pearson first and then Mrs. Coffman, and we moved to the Whitcomb house, the "south house" as they prefer to call it. Dr. C. F. Menninger was its first medical director, followed by Dr. Wally Reichenberg, Laura Knickerbocker, Jean Lyle, Dr. Nathan Ackerman, Dr. Leona Chidester, Dr. Earl Saxe, Dr. Anne Benjamin, and others.

In 1937 we were given the Sterling craft shop. Five years later we plunged; in spite of great apprehensiveness about the practicability of continuing children's work at all, we bought the Page House. Then came Dr. Mary Hawkins, Dr. Mary Leitch, Alberta Hillyer, John B. Geisel, and finally our present-day stalwart trio—Doctors Greenwood, Hirschberg, and Switzer—who brought this present pile into existence. Back of them was the tireless effort and generous, magnificent devotion of the members of The Menninger Foundation.

I remember some prophetic words uttered by my teacher, Ernest Southard, many years ago. We are going to learn about education, he said, from studying the child who can not learn, not the ones who can. He meant the mentally retarded child.

I remember too some prophetic words once spoken by my own wife, Jean, a director of the Southard School. It was one day—about 1935, I think—when we were all discouraged about the draining deficit and the little handful of patients. "Someday," she said, "our work with these children may turn out to be the most enduring thing we do. Let's not give up yet. People will more and more realize the importance of this neglected field. And then our little Southard School might march ahead on its own and gather a strong permanent staff and be crammed full of eager children. We will be so proud of it, and we will be glad we held on."

Well, here it is. We *are* glad we held on. We *are* proud of it. A dream has been realized. A prophecy has come true.

Of the mentally retarded child Dr. Karl said this in a talk, titled "Love Is Best of All," before the Lambs in Chicago in December, 1967:

My interest in mentally retarded children came from a great teacher, Dr. Elmer Ernest Southard, my teacher at Harvard Medical School, who was far ahead of his time in many ways. In the development of psychiatry to the problems of industry, in his efforts to bring psychological treatment out of institutions into daily life—he was a fore-runner of modern thought, fifty years ago.

Among his many interests he gave a priority to the study of mentally retarded children, and he urged me to make a place for this concern when I started my own practice in Topeka, Kansas. He said that not only was there much need for study of this group but that he believed that there was much to be learned from them by the scientist, especially about the learning process and its vicissitudes.

At the time he advocated this, it was believed that most mental retardation (or deficiency) was an unalterable state which was not subject to treatment. Since then our thinking has very gradually changed, and today such organizations as The Lambs have shown us that a great deal depends on the treatment of retarded children and young people.

One of the hopeful and inspiring facts about the treatment of these individuals is that we can all have a part in it. Understanding, love, patience, and hope, when exercised by everyone who meets these young people, open doors too long closed to them.

The program of the Lambs Pet Shop and Farm in Chicago, as instituted and carried on by Mr. Robert Terese and Mrs. Corrine Owen with magnificent faith and devotion, emphasizes work and that is good; it emphasizes work that enables the young people to meet and deal with the public and that is better; and it also gives them something to love and something to care for, something dependent upon them, and that is best of all.

Children are mentioned frequently in Reading Notes:

Children Limited is a publication which I imagine most of you haven't seen. I hadn't until [1954]. The December issue is a 16-page tabloid format newspaper. It is published by the National Association for Retarded Children, a nonprofit organization of parents and friends of the mentally handicapped. The first page tells about the National Retarded Children Week, the TV network features, and the radio programs that were given, the thousands of window posters that were used, the 500 outdoor billboards, the $2\frac{1}{2}$ million leaflets on "The Secret Child" distributed. On the front page also is an account of the convention led by these parents in Boston in October. . . .

On page 9 there is a picture of a sweet little girl presenting flowers to Kitty Kallen for her efforts on behalf of mentally retarded children. Better not look at this picture if you don't want to cry. There is an editorial on ambivalence that would do credit, if I may say so, to any psychiatric journal. Of course, the editor is talking about the mixed feelings that parents have toward any child and particularly a child who isn't quite what they had hoped for. . . .

Perhaps this paper was all the more interesting to me because of all the Christmas parties I ever attended, the one given by the local association of these parents tops the list in certain respects. As the children arrived with their parents at the Foundation's Hopkins Building, which had been beautifully decorated for the occasion, they were greeted by some of the parents who had gotten there early. They looked around at the tree and the decorations and then sat stiffly and demurely in their chairs, waiting for the movie and the eventual Santa Claus and the ingeniously contrived sleigh full of gifts. The children weren't crying—far from it—and neither were the parents. But there were a few helpers and visitors who were. There were wheelchair children and children with protruding tumors of the brain. There were overgrown babies and undersized adolescents. I really didn't look at the children so much; I looked at those brave, brave, brave parents. Some of them were young folks, some older folks; some evidently with means and some certainly without much. But all of them had a problem. Outside the rest of the world was having eggnog parties and Christmas dances and Yule logs and what not—but here in this room were those wistful little faces and clumsy little bodies, and standing behind them were those faithful parents. I started home three times but I only got a few feet each time; I had to go back.

The title of the biennial report of the Enid (Oklahoma) State School for Mentally Retarded for the period ending June 30, 1954, is WE'LL TRY! The superintendent is one Anna T. Scruggs, and her husband is the business manager. Imagine a superintendent with the spirit to entitle an official document like this!

And while reading to weep, hear how the top management of a village for the mentally defective in Pennsylvania teaches patients: According to the press, ungrateful and unappreciative mental defectives who violate rules are locked in cells 4 feet by 8 feet for periods up to six months, forbidden to speak to anyone, supplied only with cold water to wash, and given food through a slot in the cell door.

There was a good deal of bitter talk during the war about how the German citizens didn't need to play dumb regarding the atrocities of such places as Buchenwald; they knew damn well what was going on all the time! Very well, then, citizens of Pennsylvania, how now? How now?

There is a little secret goings-on in Topeka that not many people know about, although it has been visited by representatives of the Associated Press and others. It is a day playground program for the retarded children of the city and is run by a committee of the parents' association. They were fortunate in hiring a director, newly graduated from the University of Kansas. The fairgrounds let them use a building. The Coca-Cola man brings free Cokes every day—people volunteer to help, in spite of the heat. Several women's groups furnish cookies and help to serve them, various material contributions were made and all this goes to give the severely retarded children of Topeka a chance to have a place to play with other children of their own kind and with the help of the volunteers and the director, they learn to share, gain a feeling of slight accomplishment doing painting, molding clay, making wood blocks and various things designed for their level of comprehension. And so another step has been taken to contribute "to the least of these."

Did you know that through John Redjinski the State Hospital gave the playground little chairs, pull toys, doll beds, stick horses, etc., also that the social service group at the Foundation made some perfectly wonderful great big blocks and covered them with bright plastic, putting animals, letters, numbers and so on on them. (The children adore them.) Also you might like to know that several of the therapy groups here at VA are making scale models of animals and farm buildings, etc., for a large sand table to use this fall in their classrooms for the retarded children. Also there are several women patients at the Foundation (with their doctors' permission) that are giving volunteer service at the playground, some of them more than one morning a week, and that they love every minute of it!

Dr. Karl also has been concerned with helping children who are physically handicapped, and again the influence of his family and personal experiences are apparent. The following is from Reading Notes:

I had only been in practice a few years when the National Association for the Hard of Hearing asked me to make an address at their annual meeting in Chicago on the subject of the psychological effects of deafness.

I was highly flattered by the invitation, although the only quali-

fications I had for making such a contribution were the subjective experiences of having been considered partially deaf throughout my
school days and of having a father who was somewhat deaf and who
coped with it with a dignity and patience which were an example to
us all. I was impressed to find this considerable body of wistful people
concerned with this hearing problem, which I had grown up thinking
of as a family affair, and concerned with its psychological consequences.
I have no idea what I said to them in my address, but inspired, I
think, chiefly by my father's reactions and perhaps whistling to keep
up my courage, I ventured to compose a summary of my reactions to
deafness in verse in a way which now makes me somewhat uncomfortable.

"There is no silence," I began. "In the secret places of the heart,
there is always music." I called deafness a minor deprivation of the
senses which should not lead one to self-pity, resignation, depression,
or surrender. I'm not sure I agree with that idea any more; there is
certainly no music in some hearts. I think I was altogether too sanguine
and callous in the manner of youth—I do know some magnificent
triumphs over the handicap of great impairment of hearing, and I do
know of some retreats and withdrawals that I believe were unnecessary.

But this discussion of the hard of hearing passes over the problem
of complete *deafness,* congenital *absence* of hearing. What about these
people? How do they feel? What's being done for them? How do they
react psychologically to their handicap? What techniques do they
acquire for communication? What becomes of those children who have
the difficult task of understanding other people with even less equip-
ment than most of us have? Of course, we all know about lipreading
and about sign language. But just what *do* we know about them?

Well, for some time this has been the concern of a group of people
of the Institute for Psychosomatic and Psychiatric Research and
Training at the (Chicago) Michael Reese Hospital under Dr. Roy
Grinker. A team of nearly a score of workers and nine consultants
worked for several years on a study of those deaf children who became
disorganized and now [1971] from that same source comes a study by
Dr. Eugene D. Mindel and Dr. McCay Vernon on the deaf child and
his family. The title of the book is *They Grow in Silence.* I think the
authors must have originally planned to call it *They Grow Up in
Silence* and then it occurred to someone that the thing to emphasize
was *growth* and this emphasis was indicated by omitting the word
up. It is a slender, beautifully printed volume of 100-odd pages representing a five-year study. In a way, it is just the opposite of my youthful

poem many years ago. It does not minimize the handicap; indeed, it rather stresses the danger of false promises and overoptimistic expectations. Then it goes to work on a discussion of the reasons why those of us who hear view the plight of the deaf person so casually. There is some informative material about genuine hearing tests in the Audiology Clinic, and a full discussion "with compassion for parents" of the controversy of the proponents of lipreading and the proponents of sign language. They think it is a great mistake for parents to neglect any valid technique of communication which a child can learn.

I couldn't help thinking as I read this material on the report of the scientific work, appealing as it does for the need for more. It is also more eloquently expressed by such "novels" as Joanne Greenberg's *In This Sign* (1970)—a story of a deaf couple living through fifty years of debt, misunderstanding, and painful struggles. The great problem of the communication block.

Erich Segal to the contrary, one of the important ways of communicating with those one loves is to be able to say, when the occasion demands, the simple words "I'm sorry." Dr. Karl demonstrates this with an account of a touching incident, drawn from his reading.

Lawrence Kubie and Hyman Israel have contributed (in *Psychoanalytic Study of the Child,* Volume 10) a vignette which is beautiful and thought-provoking.

A five-year-old girl stood in her crib in a ward of the Neurological Institute, erect, motionless, and mute. A few weeks prior to her admission, she had suddenly become strange, refusing to answer to her name, refusing to eat, refusing to remain in bed. She would wrap herself in a dirty blanket and turn her face to the wall, wetting and soiling herself.

One of the nurses remembered that upon one occasion she thought she heard the child say in a singsong rhythm, "Say you're sorry, say you're sorry."

On this clue, a doctor took the child's hand and said to her seriously, "I *am* sorry. I am very, very sorry." Upon this she turned slowly to other doctors and said, "Say *you're* sorry." And each of them did.

Then she began to talk. A week later she was acting like other children again (although she continued to have psychotherapy for two years).

One wonders how frequently another person's life would be changed this miraculously if they could be told in the right way at the right time by some of the rest of us that we are sorry! Well, we *are,* aren't we?

On raising children, from Reading Notes:

Many modern authorities agree . . . that it is the parents who must convey whatever sexual enlightenment is to be given to children. Some, abetted by groups of alarmed parents, join the Victorian writers in distrusting the educational system's capacity to participate in any but an injurious way. They question whether as intimate a revelation as the story of a child's conception and parturition should come from a schoolteacher, and should be developed in the classroom, and not in the privacy of a family dialogue. It is possibly because of the gentle intimacy of the setting that Freud's indirect treatment of "Little Hans" resulted in such a successful cure of the boy's phobia.

Although many psychoanalysts agree that parents are the crucial teachers and demonstrators, whether planned or inadvertent, of sexual attitudes and knowledge, they also point to the limitations of this arrangement. What was especially interesting and novel about the early psychoanalytic concepts of sex education was their origin in attempts to utilize information gained from the analysis of adult patients. According to Anna Freud, however, it was quite unexpected that even the best intended and simply worded enlightenment was not readily acceptable to young children, and that they persisted in clinging to what had been recognized as their own sexual fantasies. A not inconsiderable contribution to the generation gap is the mutual uneasiness of parent and child, fed by irrational fantasies on both sides, to discuss sexual matters. For many neurotically constricted and inept parents, an objective, reality-based surrogate such as a physician or a schoolteacher may be a desirable instructor into the mysteries of life. We still have not resolved these issues.

I was shocked to read in the papers recently that a judge dismissed the case of a man who had been beating a five-year-old and a seven-year-old child. The judge said, I believe, that every man had a right to correct his own children and released him. All studies of juvenile behavior have pointed to the fact that most young criminals have been beaten and otherwise coldly or cruelly treated as little children. There is no question that we could greatly reduce crime in any area if we could reduce the cruelty on the part of parents or people who are supposed to be parents to their children.

This doesn't mean that children should not be corrected, but clubbing them and belting them and other such cruelties are not correction. They are the seeds of crime.

On the other hand, too much permissiveness may be emotionally damaging to a child. He says, "Strict enforcement, even unto the use of brutal strength, of a parent's wishes is one thing. Strict enforcement of certain rules is another. Some parents may impose structure on a child long before he can comprehend it. But others may postpone imposing any kind of structure so that the child is confused by emotions he cannot control."

He says in Reading Notes:

I wish I could organize my thoughts more constructively about the cult of permissiveness. Both Dr. Freud and Dr. [Benjamin] Spock have been blamed and credited for it. I don't think either one of them conceived of permissiveness in the way it became current. I still recall with dismay the visit of some young parents to our home years ago, accompanied by a five-year-old child who was allowed to break our phonograph records and jam the needle of the machine without one word of remonstrance from the parents. They were permissivists.

Permissiveness is really the antithesis of prohibition, but it is just as crippling. It assumes that a child—or an immature youth—who thinks he wants to do something, has the time, experience, and intelligence to consider all the consequences. Thus, irritated by the invocation of the permissive philosophy, I suffer the more from the accusation that I myself am one, advocating that all criminals be permitted to commit crimes. . . .

Today, one of the projects nearest Dr. Karl's heart is The Villages, a non-profit organization that provides homes for neglected and deserted children. He believes that helping to found and build The Villages is one of the most important things he has ever done toward preventing injustice, alleviating suffering, and preventing the flow of helpless young people into jails, prisons, and state hospitals. The first in what Dr. Karl and his associates hope will become a national, or even inter-

national, network of villages is the Eagle Ridge Village in Topeka. He
has described its goals this way:

The Villages, Inc. is a non-profit organization founded in 1964 in Topeka, Kansas, for the purpose of providing permanent homes for homeless, neglected, deserted children between the ages of eight and sixteen.

At present, there is only one Village; it is situated on 320 acres of land near Topeka where the children attend public schools and enjoy community activities. They live in cottage families of twelve with house parents. The goal is to have five cottages in all, making up five separate families as an optimum social and economic community.

The children are usually referred by state, county and private welfare agencies who provide funds for their care and maintain relations with their wards. The children are not "problems" and do not receive psychiatric treatment. They are children whom we wish to save from despair, neglect and hopelessness by taking them into our loving homes.

The unique features in this group foster home plan are: One: its preventive character of salvaging innocent youngsters before it is too late. This is far more rewarding and hopeful than waiting until they have gone down the long road of petty crime, jail and reform schools, and wasted lives.

Two: an emphasis on conservation, nature study, care and love for animals and wild life, in which we have the cooperation and direction of many outstanding scientists and teachers in the community. In this way each family learns how a destructive environment can be replaced with a constructive, loving one.

Three: the permanence and security of a true home. The homes in the Village are big families, not transient stop-gap places. They are planned to carry a child through his high school years. The child who has been shuttled through a number of detention or boarding places comes to the Village with distrust and fear, but learns to relax in security and then begins to grow.

Four: the plan to spread the concept of such small villages of no more than 50 or 60 children each to every state, county, and city in the nation, as a feasible and happy way of salvaging the hundreds of thousands of children who need this care but are at present almost unknown and unheard because they are not offenders, delinquents or criminals.

A PLEA FOR PREVENTION

Our ambition is to establish a national association and training center for such villages, all under one name and one set of guidelines and professional standards, but each being a part of its own community and public school system with its own supporters and volunteers and families.

We have two needs: First, to complete our pilot village, which means building two more cottages. We are turning away dozens of heart-breaking cases of homeless children because we have no room.

Second, we need help in spreading the concept of The Villages to the many communities that have asked for advice and help in beginning. The Villages, Inc., are therefore

A Reality, as a pilot village;

A Plan, for other villages;

A Hope, for the future.

The Reality, the Plan, and the Hope of The Villages were translated vividly into human terms by Dr. Karl in "An Ounce of Prevention," published in the magazine Success Unlimited, *December 1971.*

There are said to be 1,000,000 children in the United States who, although innocent of any crime or delinquency, are continued as wards of the juvenile court because they are unwanted, neglected, and homeless. Some have been abandoned by their parents; some have parents in prison or in hospitals for mental illness; some have violent, drunken, or fighting parents. It is these miserable ones, these children without love or faith or hope who most often grow up to be our vagrants, delinquents, and mentally ill.

I first became aware of the size of this problem a few years ago when I sat in a conference with Judge Malcolm Copeland of our juvenile court and his chief probation worker named Kent Hayes. They were describing to me a case of a boy of nine who had attempted to break into a vending machine in full view of a number of people. They paid no attention to him, but when he made an attempt to open another machine and another, someone reported him to the manager. When he was turned over to the police, he confessed eagerly and asked to be sent to the state institution for delinquent boys. Persistent questioning brought forth the facts: His father and mother had deserted a family of four children. An older brother had been "sentenced" to this boys' school for some delinquency and this younger chap had been left to care for two smaller children. The daily struggle had been too much for him. He knew his older brother was fed and cared for, and he thought he knew how to reach the same destination.

Kent Hayes, now the executive director of The Villages, Inc., in Topeka, Kansas, is a young man alive with concern for unhappy children. He cannot be content until he has done something for a helpless child of whom he learns. When he had described this little fellow, I turned to the judge and asked him if there were many of these neglected, deserted children. "In our small county there are at least 250 on our rolls—who have done no crime, except to exist."

"But there are foster homes, surely?" I asked.

"For small children, yes; not for older ones. There is no place to send them. Even for younger ones it is like a grim game of musical chairs. Many children go from one foster home to another, from home to home, and foster parents to new foster parents, or living off neighbors, relatives, and strangers. Nowhere really is home, and they are never valued for themselves. Remember Marilyn Monroe? She was passed around thus but she had great beauty and charm and survived to achieve a precarious and tragic success, but always grasping for love and care."

The judge's words disturbed one. They contrasted strikingly with political speeches about children reared too permissively. For here are millions of children "permitted" to exist—but without love, tenderness, parental guidance, or models of living. They merely exist in misery as best they can and try to survive. And what better material could exist for evolving into a criminal career? Where do the bitter, angry, violent young men of our streets come from? Where do they grow up? Where are their families? They were all once helpless, innocent babies; what set them against us? What molded them into hoods and thugs?

Population growth and urban congestion create increasing numbers of evil city neighborhoods with wretched, makeshift homes. The filth and ugliness and starkness of the crowded living quarters contribute to a pervading atmosphere of sullenness, hopelessness, fear, and hate. Many children are exposed every day of their formative years to cursing, obscenity, threats, blows, cruelty, and open defiance of law. Escape to the streets, joining one gang or another to diminish bullying and abuse from older boys, eluding the policeman and defying the weary teachers—these are the daily routine. Everywhere the grim, cold, dangerous environment remains the same; there is no safe place to go. There is no escape.

Left in this wretched life, boys sooner or later, from boredom, fear, challenge, prestige, or plain hunger, strike out at someone and get caught in the social defensive machinery. And while agencies bicker about what to do with him, where to send him, who will take him, the boy becomes more wretched, hopeless, and bitter. He becomes a "case." The "case" grinds through the juvenile court, the detention home, the industrial school, perhaps a few foster homes on trial. Later it may be the reformatory or prison for awhile—and then out again and a dreary replay.

"Why do we have so much recidivism?" the newspaper editors will ask.

"We are not being tough enough," some politicians will declare. "If I am elected, I will see that vigorous steps are taken to restore law and order."

Everyone knows that the population of jails and reformatories is largely a rotating one made up of repeaters who go in and out, in and out. Does it not seem imperative that instead of shouting for more policemen and fiercer crime pursuit we should try to break up this vicious circle? Why not do something for the children whom we know right now are going to be the criminals who will fill the jails and hospitals in another dozen years? Why are we not determined to stop the flow of *criminals* instead of wildly endeavoring to control the rate of *crime?* Why not some effective prevention instead of futile ineffective gestures toward "correction"?

(Not all neglected children come from poor neighborhoods, it is true. There are some poor little rich boys, too. And not all the children reared in evil neighborhoods and broken homes go the route described. Some have fortunate accidents of one kind or another. Some are reached and helped by the Boys' Clubs of America, the Boy Scouts, the Salvation Army, various youth agencies, fortunate foster home placements. A very small number may even receive professional help.)

And if we are serious about large scale prevention of delinquency and crime, is it not obvious and imperative that we greatly multiply our efforts to rescue these children before they are ruined? But removed to where? Assigned to whom? Who wants trouble? Who wants the responsibility? Where are the good mothers and fathers who can take on this enormous task?

This great unsolved problem has troubled me very much since I have begun to think about it. Most of my professional life has been spent in *treating* people, disturbed and distressed people, and in teaching young doctors to do so. Also I have been engaged in trying to improve prison programs for more rehabilitation and true correction.

But increasingly I see the greater importance of doing something *preventive.*

Doctors are predisposed toward treating. They enjoy their work of treating patients. It is exciting and it is rewarding. As a young doctor I treated many cases of typhoid fever, zealously, and I was proud of my labors with these sufferers. But, compare my accomplishments with that of my colleagues who studied and corrected the water and sewage systems! Vaccination isn't a very exciting procedure but it has spared millions the agony of smallpox. Such simple procedures as the abolition of the public drinking cup have prevented untold millions of premature deaths.

Some people ask, "*Is* there really such a thing as prevention? Can we prevent anything so unpredictable as crime?"

This is precisely what people used to ask many years ago about the treatment of mental illness. Almost everybody knows today that most mental illness responds to treatment, and that most cases recover. And they must learn that crime is not unpredictable and crime is in large measure preventable. We know right now who and where our 1975 criminals are.

Shouldn't the principles of prevention be applied before troubled children become angry and embittered youth? Why wait till they are sick or incorrigible?

We know it can be done. We know it *must* be done. Treatment will be too late.

Three years ago some of us began to think about a simple, practical method of prevention. We envisaged a cluster of foster homes, with perhaps a dozen of these neglected boys and girls in each, with trained and devoted houseparents. Five cottages together would comprise a village—whence the name we chose—villages of group foster homes. When we first proposed it, we were promptly offered sites in a dozen states for such establishments, but we decided to concentrate first on a pilot plant in Topeka, where we knew experienced youth workers and cottage parents. We began with one cottage named after my late brother, Will. It is the first in the Eagle Ridge Village, named after the Fraternal Order of Eagles, whose members contributed and named the William C. Menninger Memorial Cottage. A second cottage, the Helen DeVitt Jones Cottage, for girls, has been added and filled. Next came a house from the Moorman Company of Quincy, Ill., and finally, the last two cottages from the community of Topeka, largely supported by the Women's Chamber of Commerce.

While we are close enough to the larger community for participation in some of its advantages, including the public schools, the Boy Scouts, and the local churches, open and wooded country surrounds the Village. This insures a minimum of human molestation and a maximum of available natural resources. Birds, beasts, butterflies, grass, flowers, trees, soil, fresh air, and clean water have replaced alleys, factory walls, smog, garbage heaps, and billboards. This is not for an *exercise* in esthetics, but as part of a new philosophy of living which substitutes preservation and appreciation for destruction and exploitation of the environment. Nature education of an elementary sort is in progress, and a more ambitious curriculum is in the planning. And most important of all, these formerly homeless children have a permanent home, their own home and family and loving, caring parents.

Not for treatment, remember. Not for correction. And most certainly not for punishment. No "guards," no social workers, no psychiatrists. Just a home with parents and big brothers and sisters who are college students. The children all go to public schools and join in community activities. This is our model for prevention.

We believe that with these boys and girls we still have a chance to prevent the *need* of any professional treatment or "correction." Their past behavior was normal and appropriate for the environment in which they then lived. They needed—and now have—a *new environment* to react to and to remodel themselves by, new surroundings, with new styles of living and new friends. Then develops a whole new way of life. They learn what it is to be loved, and to love, to cooperate instead of only to hate and fight and steal. Orientations of caring, saving, protecting, and building evolve to replace those of fighting and destroying.

This, we believe, is crime *prevention* and youth *conservation*. To be most effective, our efforts must begin early, not after adolescence. It is too late then for new ties to develop easily. Two brothers we had at the Eagle Ridge Village illustrate this fact.

The first time Kent Hayes saw Dan at the Shawnee County Detention Home he was standing in a corner looking out a small window. This 6-foot, 130-pound fifteen-year-old possessed an appearance hard to describe. A look of sadness and fear, not the temporary look that often goes with adolescence, but a permanent look and attitude which were to remain as long as we knew him.

Dan and his ten-year-old brother Jack had been placed in the detention home six weeks earlier. They had been placed there after a teacher had gone to their home to check on their continued absences from school. He came into the three-room house and found the ten-year-old cleaning up the human waste and vomit of his father and five alcoholic friends, all of whom had passed out on the front-room floor. Dan had left home four days earlier, sleeping in a small shack he and Jack had constructed near the river. When asked why he had left his younger brother with this mess, he simply replied, "I've been cleaning up the old bastard for ten years. It's time Jack learned how." Their mother had left, never to return, when Jack was three months old.

Dan and Jack were both accepted by us in the new Eagle Ridge Village. Jack, the younger boy, immediately began to make friends and relate himself to his new parents. Dan was very quiet and withdrawn. He presented no management problems, but soon the other boys began to complain about his hostility toward the younger children. A few days later Jack told the cottage parents that Dan had threatened him with a knife. When confronted with this, Dan at first said he was just kidding, but began to cry and to say he needed help. So he was referred to a psychiatric clinic and hospital for a complete evaluation. He was there three days, then disappeared. This was nine months ago; we have not heard from him since.

On the other hand some most promising "successes" in the program have already evolved, but because this article is likely to be read by both the successful youths and their companions still in the Village, we unfortunately cannot give the exciting details of contrast between lurid past and glowing present. But I can cite you a few prospective cases—applicants for whom at present we have no room.

Mat was ten years old. He sat in the corner of a large, dimly lit room with nineteen other children and twenty beds. The supervisor sat by the open door reading a comic book.

Mat's father had left a year before and hadn't come back. Three days ago the police had come to his home and taken his mother off to jail. He was not sure why but thought it had something to do with the medicine she kept putting into her arm. When they took her she was screaming for Mat to help; he had let her down, but the police were so big, and Mat was so frightened.

A man had come to the house then and taken Mat to the detention home. He was the youngest boy there. When he cried at night the older boys hit him and told him to keep quiet.

Where will Mat go? When will his mother return? Mat doesn't know. Nor does anyone else.

Nancy's mother died a long time ago. Anyway it seems long ago to Nancy. Thirteen-year-old girls seem to need mothers. "I hear girl friends talk terrible about their mothers, sometimes, but they just don't know what it is to have none."

A few months after her mother's death Nancy noticed that her stepfather kept putting his hands on her. This was the start of something she couldn't stop and didn't know how to stop. On the night of her first date he came to her room after she had returned home and raped her.

The neighbors heard her and telephoned the police. But where now?

Several people on the outskirts of the community reported to the police that prowlers had been observed outside their homes at night. The barefoot prints on the ground nearby indicated the prowlers were all children. Nearly a week later four children were actually seen, hiding in the edge of a nearby cornfield.

It took police officers quite a while to catch the children. The oldest girl was eleven. She explained that their parents had left them two weeks earlier and they had been living on raw corn and tomatoes. They had gone closer to the houses at night in order to be near the light coming from the windows; it wasn't so scary as the dark cornfield. They didn't ask anyone for help because they didn't want to be separated; all they had left was each other.

The children were separated.

The making of a real family is a process of growing together. For this the immediate environment is especially important. Each cottage in a village has its own cottage parents who will act as surrogate father and mother. They are responsible for their ten children, responsible in many meanings of that word, and for collaborating with the other cottage parents in the village for the general administration.

They serve as *models of maturity and activity* and as sources of love and counsel. They establish and maintain the family routine and the daily schedules. They arrange and supervise the work and play and special education. A new way of life can only be taught by mature people who themselves possess the vision and the dedication; hence the proper orientation, training, and counseling of these key figures, the houseparents, is of the utmost importance. A training program for cottage parents is a corollary project of our main program.

The village in Topeka is only the first of many like it which will be scattered across the country, and is a model in which the pattern for such group homes and group villages will be developed. Training programs for foster parents who will work in other such homes and villages are being set up. A central registry for the gathering and distribution of information and the maintenance of high standards will be set up.

Above all, these homes must have the quality of permanence. The children are not on trial, and they become gradually aware that they are not going to be evicted from home without cause. They belong until they are able to go out into adult life with self-confidence and a definite plan for earning a living.

In the past few weeks, the boys have been very excited because they have been given the responsibility of a Texaco service station near the Village, under the direction of their house father. They are being assisted by a kindly manager of a nearby competitive station who says, "I used to be alarmed when these boys came into my station. Now I like them. I'll help 'em." Their teachers say the boys have taken a new interest in arithmetic. A special tutor at the cottage, Mrs. Nell Levy, has obtained a cash register for the boys to practice on in the cottage, and she says there is a great burst of enthusiastic interest in arithmetic. They are learning fiscal things, mechanical things, public service things. And they are converting the filling-station grounds into a conservation demonstration site.

We want our Villages to be characterized by a special feature of motivation, one which we believe can be inculcated and developed in them. Everyone knows, now, of the great present world danger from what we have done and are doing to our environment. These young people need us, but we need them more! We need all the help we can get to save ourselves and our planet. And we must teach this with all our hearts.

The whole world—not only a few frantic individuals—seems bent on committing suicide. We have cut down our forests, killed off our wildlife, polluted our lakes and rivers, gouged ugly holes in beautiful hillsides, wasted our precious fertile soil, and poisoned the atmosphere we all have to breathe. Some of our fellow citizens lay about them with guns and traps, bows and arrows, dynamite and poison to murder *our* wild animals (not just theirs). Others murder our rivers with needless dams, and our lakes with filth and chemicals; we befoul even the vast oceans with filth and poisons.

We read about this great threat to our world in all the magazines. This is good, for if the doom of our race and our planet is to be averted *all of us* must know the issue and join in the effort. Thousands of deterrent programs will soon be launched. But where will such leaders get their working followers? Who will volunteer? Who will understand the urgencies? Two great handicaps in the reconstructive effort are going to be the *scarcity of personnel and the slowness of the spread of the gospel.*

And it is right here that the Villages have a great and special opportunity. Since our hope lies in the involvement of the coming generation in the great task of environmental rescue, why not particularly those who have been rescued from harmful environments? The worst of all pollution and waste has been that of our youth. In the conservation villages I am describing, the pervading spirit and effort is toward the reversal of this worldwide propensity for destruction, in their own homes and in the community!

This is the central idea of our project and constitutes its uniqueness. It is a new emphasis in education. It is education for survival, which is surely the most important prevention of all.

It is as if we said to our rescued children: "You who have known dreary and dreadful surroundings can understand what it means to change the environment in which one lives. You have seen children crippled and embittered by their surroundings. Now you live in a home with people opposed to all that. They love one another, they love you, they love their beautiful world. With you they are trying to learn to live with other people and other creatures.

"One day you will leave here on your own career. When that day comes, we believe you will feel a special need to help not only other neglected children, but our dirtied, damaged earth, our raped and ravished planet. We want you to go out with a love for the beauty of the natural world and with a feeling of our love and the assurance of our help. You will go with a commitment to help save the world. It's your world, too."

And *will* they indeed go forth in this spirit? *Of course* they will, if we imbue them with it.

Will they achieve these goals? Some of them will. Certainly they will not fill the streets and the jails and the hospitals.

Does it sound quixotic? A gigantic fantasy of effecting world change with a handful of waifs? Preposterous? Impossible?

Perhaps. But something impossible must happen soon or none of us will be here. As Reinhold Niebuhr has said:

"Nothing that is worth doing can be achieved in our lifetime; therefore we must be saved by hope."

Index